ART OF THE WORLD

EUROPEAN CULTURES

THE HISTORICAL, SOCIOLOGICAL

AND RELIGIOUS BACKGROUNDS

ART OF THE STEPPES

BY

KARL JETTMAR

CROWN PUBLISHERS, INC., NEW YORK

Translated by Ann E. Keep

Frontispiece: *Tiger standing over a stag it has slain. Ordos bronze. The deeply carved surface of the body recalls the decorations on the coffin from Bashadar II kurgan. British Museum. Slightly reduced. Cf. p. 164.*

FIRST PUBLISHED IN 1964
GERMAN EDITION© 1964 BY HOLLE VERLAG G.M.B.H., BADEN-BADEN, GERMANY
ENGLISH TRANSLATION © 1967 BY HOLLE VERLAG G.M.B.H., BADEN-BADEN, GERMANY
LIBRARY OF CONGRESS CATALOGNUMBER: CARD/65-24318
PRINTED IN HOLLAND

CONTENTS

ACKNOWLEDGEMENTS

The author wishes to thank the curators of those museums and exhibitions which have permitted him to publish reproductions of works of nomadic art. He also thanks Dr U. Johansen for drawing his attention once more to the fine pieces in the possession of the Museum für Völkerkunde in Hamburg. Professor Robert Göbl of Vienna brought two particularly interesting objects to his notice and also gave him permission to publish them. Dr M. von Dewall made available to him the findings of Chinese archaeologists which are of crucial importance in judging Ordos art. It has thus been possible to keep up with the present state of research as exemplified by the latest surveys of Chinese scholars.

But the author's thanks are above all due to those scholars who in conversation have taught him a great deal about problems of animal style – particularly the Viennese authorities E. Beninger (†), who read the proofs shortly before his death, R. Bleichsteiner (†), Professor R. von Heine-Geldern, Professor and Mrs Hančar, Dr V. Griessmaier and Professor Otto Maenchen-Helfen.

My meetings with Professor R. Ghirshman were invariably highly stimulating. He pointed out mistakes which I was able to correct in the second edition. I owe a great deal to Dr F. Kussmaul, who holds similar views on the development of equestrian nomadism. He kindly gave me permission to use his map of the steppe area as a basis for the appended sketch.

Professor B. Karlgren gave the writer the first opportunity of intensive – and even financially rewarded – work in the Museum of Far Eastern Antiquities in Stockholm; he was also greatly assisted by Mrs Dagny Carter.

He had the great privilege of corresponding with E. H. Minns while the latter was still alive.

He much regrets that of Soviet experts on animal style he has met only S. V. Kiselev (†), Mrs N. L. Chlenova and S. S. Chernikov, but not S. I. Rudenko and M. P. Griaznov, from whose writings he has derived most profit.

Finally he has to thank Dr Ann E. Keep who did the translation, which was checked by the author with the patient and highly valuable help of Mr R. Crompton.

Heidelberg, April 1966   Karl Jettmar

LIST OF PLATES

LIST OF FIGURES

The drawings are by H. Prüstel, Mainz.

LIST OF MAPS

SOURCES OF ILLUSTRATIONS

The following museums and persons kindly allowed reproduction of the plates on the following pages:

The colour plates on the following pages were kindly supplied by:

I. DISCOVERY OF EARLY STEPPE ART

It is a pity that none of the great Russian historical painters depicted a scene that occurred on October 29, 1715 in St Petersburg, the newly founded capital. A son had been born to Peter the Great, Tsar of All the Russias, and the great lords of the land hurried to offer their congratulations and present gifts to the Empress Catherine. It fell to Nikita Demidov, son of a serf who had worked as a blacksmith, and who had worked up his way to become the wealthiest mine-owner of the Urals, to lay before her the most impressive gift of all: one hundred thousand roubles in coin and a collection of objects of art worked in gold. The only thing known about their origin was that they came from burial-mounds in Siberia PLATE P. 14 which had been plundered by greedy Russians for many years, to the embitterment of the superstitious natives.

In this world of baroque exuberance their golden lustre aroused general amazement; the superb workmanship of the animal figures which, in one form or another, constituted the motif of these ornaments, also won admiration. The plaques in particular, some of them as large as a man's hand, which comprised the principal group of objects in the treasure, combined an expert natural rendering of animal forms with lavish inlays of colourful stones. One theme that had a special appeal to men of the eighteenth century was that of animals in combat, represented with wild dramatic power yet possessing a controlled tension. Here a snake coiled round a boar; there an eagle with outspread wings pounced upon a shaggy yak.

Peter the Great himself set eyes upon these splendid works, and this was decisive. He was an insatiable collector with a limitless curiosity. As is generally known, he issued a strict order that all monsters and freaks born in his vast empire should be preserved in alcohol and handed over to the authorities; this provided the newly founded Academy of Sciences with the world's most repulsive and unique collection of human abnormities: a veritable chamber of horrors. So he acted in this instance too: strict instructions were forwarded to the governor of Siberia to collect for the Crown henceforth all similar finds, including any other curiosities that the ground might yield, such as the bones of animals, fish or birds. Shortly afterwards he issued an Imperial decree that was designed to establish a veritable system for the protection of antiquities, centuries before institutions of this kind came into being in other states with a less despotic form of government.

In view of the regimentation that prevailed in Peter's empire, success was assured. Two months later the first consignment already arrived from Tobol'sk, containing ten objects of the same type as those that had comprised Demidov's gift. Like the latter they were handed over to the recently founded 'cabinet of curiosities'. The governor of Siberia, Prince Gagarin, had hastened to buy up all the objects available on the market which would, no doubt, otherwise have ended in the melting-pot. In the same year he gathered a most splendid collection of fifty-five large and twenty small objects with a gross weight of nearly 53 pounds. One may well imagine that, anxious not to lose his sovereign's favour, the governor ordered burial-places to be plundered on a still more extensive scale than had been customary hitherto. He may even have launched an expedition to areas as yet unexplored. At any rate this was the last great fling of grave-robbery. At about the same time the Dutch scholar

PLATE P. 15 Nikolas Cornelius Witsen received a collection of forty pieces, all in solid gold, from friends in Russia; an earlier shipment had been seized by

PLATE I – Three wild beasts fighting for their prey. Gold plaque from the Siberian treasure. One of the oldest pieces in the Hermitage, Leningrad. Weight 517 gr. *Cf. p. 13.*

PLATE 2 – Engraving from Witsen's *Noord en Oost Tartarye* (Amsterdam, 1785), depicting objects from a collection that has since been lost. *Cf. pp. 14, 192.*

pirates. These consignments, despatched more or less illegally, were obviously the result of contacts Witsen had made during his stay in Siberia a few years earlier. Unfortunately the second collection, too, was eventually melted down by his disrespectful heirs. But at least some excellent engravings of them were made to illustrate Witsen's book.

During the late eighteenth century the stream of gold was already drying up, while the riddle of origin of these finds remained unsolved. The only clue was a rumour that coins of Roman emperors had been discovered during the search.

The significance of these finds and their 'animal style' (to introduce the term that has been in use among scholars for decades) will be more readily apparent when we consider that in the fine arts of all nomadic peoples who roamed the Asiatic steppes until not long ago ornamentation played the dominant part. Among the Kazakhs, for example, ornament is the fundamental and sole artistic motif, as Basenov recently pointed out.

The decorative patterns in the steppe lands are based upon an extremely rich combination of a few main elements, which for the most part are very abstract in character. Animals are indicated merely by a bare symbol roughly denoting the curving line of a horn or the rounded shape of a hoof. This is even the case where religious meaning is involved as well. Oral testimony alone tells us that the central panels of the famous Turkmenian carpets once represented the totem animals of the clans to

Two tigers dragging a cow off into a thicket

Legs of the cow

Tiger

Leaf (= thicket)

FIG. I – *Examples of Kirghiz narrative designs, as interpreted by Ryndin*

16

which the weavers belonged. Among the Kirghiz there are over three thousand narrative designs based upon a combination of one hundred and seventy-three 'vocables'. We can read them only with the help of the research carried out by Ryndin, whose views have not gone uncontested. It is thus characteristic that a scholar like Glück, who emphasized the 'world-wide influence of the Turks in art', based his argument upon the dissemination of an abstract decorative pattern, the geometric scroll.

It is still not clear whether this ornamentation owes its development entirely to outside stimuli. Against this extreme view it has been held that appliqué work in leather and felt, the traditional media of pastoral peoples, necessarily led to decorative styles that made use of abstract spirals and volutes. In any case it is certain that the steppe belt has again and again absorbed cultural influences from neighbouring areas. A particularly strong impact has been made by the countries of the Near East, from which influences penetrated by way of Iran and Outer Iran, in rivalry with those emanating from the age-old civilization of China. The legacy of the former peasant peoples of Central Asia, most of whom disappeared from the scene after the Bronze Age, is still felt. Thus most of what we encounter here is not original creative work, but the accumulated débris of many styles, inherited from a long and eventful history. It is no mere chance that attempts are being made to use ornamental styles for the reconstruction of these tribes' chequered past.

If one takes into consideration also the other artistic regions of Asia, it

FIG. 1

Yurt (tent) at two springs

Two dogs fighting for a bone

Spring

Dog

Lattice-work representing the tent (pars pro toto)

Bone

PLATE 3 – Young walrus. Ivory carving from the Ipiutak culture, north-western Alaska, in which influences of Scythian animal style are thought to have been detected. Museum of Natural History, New York. *Cf. below.*

PLATE ABOVE appears that only in the extreme north-east of the continent, on the shores of the Bering Strait, are animals conceived in a manner comparable to the animal style of the steppe lands. In that region the principal medium is bone. The menfolk of the tribes work bone into sculptures in the round, or cover it with engravings. Here animals and their movements are always viewed with the quick and sharp eyes of the hunter, who inherited this attitude from a long line of ancestors. And it is precisely the settled groups of hunters along the coast – the Chukchi, Koryaks and Eskimo – that have given richest evidence of their artistic talents. The work of the nomads in the interior, who were mainly occupied in reindeer-breeding, is of far inferior quality.

There also appear to be affinities with Upper Palaeolithic art in Europe. This type of art flourished among groups of hunters who owed their existence to their keen observation of animal behaviour. They too were

settled and lived in large communities, closely knit by ties of economic interest.

The difference between settled hunters and animal-breeding nomads may be explained psychologically: the nomads of the steppes, for instance, for all the love shown by the horseman to his mount, did not experience the almost sexual tension found between the lonely hunter and his prey. Nomads were constantly active; they spent no time in subterranean dug-outs, alone with their thoughts and dreams throughout the long polar night. Nomadic handicrafts were mostly left to the womenfolk and dependent craftsmen. Their aggressive vitality found expression in epic poetry.

What relevance has this for the animal style we are discussing? Is it the product of hunters, despite the fact that it originates in the steppe lands? Or does it stem from 'Hyperboreans' who, carrying in their blood the instincts of their earlier life as huntsmen, broke out of the taiga to become masters of the steppe? In support of this hypothesis it has been maintained that many pictures of cervids in early nomadic art must be interpreted as reindeer. Among those who have supported this idea are scholars of such subtlety and insight as the Russian Borovka and the Englishman Minns.

Or is the animal style due to the impact of a supremely powerful and developed civilization, so that the impression of a grandiose primitivism is totally misleading?

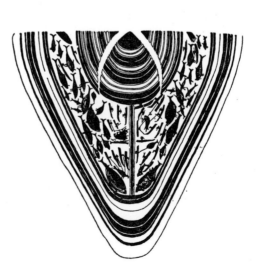

FIG. 3 – *Fishing and hunting marine animals. Realistic design on an eye-shade from the Aleutian Islands (seen from above).*

Is there after all some other spiritual source from which such works derive? This seems to be suggested by the ornamental patterns of fishermen in the Amur basin, which make use of stylized animal silhouettes consisting of spirals and curves. However, it has recently been described as merely an offshoot of steppe art. But if so, why do we not find more frequent and distinct survivals of it in the steppe lands themselves? What is it that distinguishes the 'modern' nomads from their predecessors?

Here we are touching upon problems that we must consider further at the end of this volume. First it is necessary to examine the various areas in which animal style occurs. We shall follow in the steps of the scholars who discovered it, in the course of studies extending gradually over the whole vast steppe zone, from Europe to eastern Asia. It will not be possible, of course, to devote the same degree of detailed attention to all these areas, and we shall therefore concentrate on finds made, or whose significance has come to be recognized, in recent years.

The choice of colour plates, too, is necessarily somewhat subjective. The publishers could not secure photographs in colour of objects preserved in the Hermitage in Leningrad or in the Historical Museum in Moscow. This is regrettable, since it prevents us from presenting more vividly the tremendous achievements that stand to the credit of Soviet archaeologists. The publishers have therefore been obliged to adopt a method which has already been employed in works by Talbot Rice and Ghirshman, as well as in a magnificent volume edited by Piggott. With the aid of black and white photographs, the objects in the Hermitage have been hand-coloured by the painter Heinz Prüstel of Mainz. It is to be hoped that this expedient, which in one case (that of the Leningrad hunting plaque reproduced in Ghirshman's work) resulted in all the coloured inlays obtaining a golden tint, will in future become superfluous as a result of further liberalization of East-West relations.

II. PONTIC SCYTHIA

We shall begin our survey in southern Russia, for it was here that scholars were able for the first time to assign definite dates to the heyday of the decorative system we have just described and ascribe it to a particular people – the Scythians. For this reason the term 'Scythian animal style' has often been applied to the art of regions as far distant from the Pontic area as the borderlands of China.

It was in the south of Russia, too, that scholars were first able to study the entire economic, social and political setting in which development of Scythian art developed. This uniquely favourable situation was due to the fact that the Scythians lived in close symbiosis with the Greek cities along the Black Sea coast. Most of these had been founded by Ionian colonists and performed the function of providing the ruling classes of the population in the interior with the goods that Greece generally exported, i.e. works of art and craftsmanship, but above all wine. For, after all, the Scythians were known throughout antiquity as hard drinkers who thoroughly despised the practice of diluting wine. In addition to this the colonial cities themselves produced goods on an extensive scale, and were skilled in adapting them to the taste of their barbarian customers. In return the latter supplied them with corn and timber, as well as slaves and furs from the heart of the great forests of eastern Europe. There is even said to have been a trading route leading into the far distant legendary lands of the eastern steppe.

Greek colonial cities

Rivers played a most important part in trade with the interior. The main commercial centres were therefore situated at the mouths of rivers: Tyras on the Dniester, Tanais on the Don. Olbia, the most important town, commanded the estuaries of both the Bug and the Dnieper. Other cities lay along the shores of the fertile Crimean peninsula. It has been ascertained that the densest areas of settlement were on the Kerch' and Taman' peninsulas, which face one another across the Kerch' Strait; here the earliest and most important colony was Panticapaeum.

In the neighbourhood of all these cities agriculture was carried on on an intensive scale. Along the shores of the Kerch' Strait the native population became Hellenized, and its princes soon acquired Greek names. This more complex pattern made necessary a more unified system of political organization than the cities could provide, for their mutual relations were based on moderate overlordship established by treaty. For this reason a state came into being centered upon Panticapaeum, which in the latter half of the fifth century B.C. was already governed by a native dynasty.

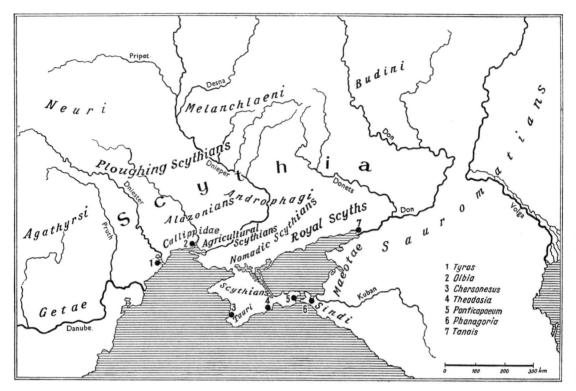

Peoples and major colonial cities in Pontic Scythia mentioned in ancient sources (after *Ocherki istorii SSSR*)

It held sway over a flourishing empire which retained its importance and its independent status until the troubled times of the second century B.C. The information which the colonists obtained about their trading partners has been handed down to us by many ancient writers, although their accounts are interspersed with a good deal of legendary material. The surviving texts were collected with admirable thoroughness in the course of the nineteenth century; on the eve of the great Russian revolution Rostovtzeff subjected them to critical examination, comparing them with the results obtained from excavations. Archaeological exploration of these cities is continuing, and new inscriptions are still being found.

Scythian tribes From these studies we learn that the term 'Scythia' was used to denote the entire area between the mouths of the Danube and Don, but that in this territory a whole series of peoples were distinguished. Among them we can discern a principal or central group of Scythians, whose personal names, in so far as they have been preserved, show that they spoke an Iranian language. They were surrounded by neighbours some of whom had adopted the Scythian way of life, while others were regarded as completely alien. Among them were the Agathyrsi, Neuri, Androphagi, Melanchlaeni and Budini. They were probably Thracians and Slavs, and possibly also Finns. Only of the Sauromatae (Sauromatians), settled in an area to the east of the Scythians, is it expressly recorded that they spoke a similar (Iranian) tongue. Among the Scythians a distinction was drawn between the peasants to the west and the nomads to the east of the Dnieper; the latter included the real ruling group, the 'royal tribe', which is said to have regarded all other Scythians as its slaves. A strange people are also to be found in the Crimea: the gloomy Tauri, who were wont to sacrifice all victims of shipwreck to their great goddess. According to Euripides, Iphigenia was her priestess, but Herodotus identifies her with the goddess herself. To the east of the Sea of Azov there lived the Sindi and Maeotae.

Time and again the nomadic Scythians evoked the astonishment of the ancient authors. They neither ploughed nor sowed; with their great herds they wandered from place to place, ever in search of new grazing-grounds. For this reason they had no permanent living quarters, but lived in covered waggons. Their food consisted of meat and milk – including mare's milk, for as early as Homer we find references to 'milkers of mares'. The men spent their days in the saddle, as though they had become permanently linked with their animals. This was the origin of the Greek notion of the centaur, half man and half horse. *Nomadism*

Scythian costume has frequently been depicted by the craftsmen of the cities on the Black Sea coast. It consisted of a soft hood covering the whole head, a short belted jerkin and long trousers. On their feet they wore soft leather boots. The stirrup had not yet been invented (although in one single scene, showing horses being broken in, we see leather slings to support the feet); the saddle was little more than a cover. For this reason the Scythians attached most of their weapons to their belt. These weapons included the gorytus (a quiver which also contained the short curved bow) and the akinakes, or short sword. In addition to this, men carried a battle-axe or a light lance. Small shields, too, are often depicted. Apparently the leaders alone possessed helmets and breast-plates. In battle the Scythians' tactics emphasized mobility. Herodotus says that nobody could escape from them nor engage them in combat unless they themselves were prepared to fight. After making a swift feint attack they would turn their horses round and flee, shooting backwards as they went. *Costume* *FIG. 4*

Before the Scythians, the Cimmerians are said to have been the masters of the Pontic steppe. Their existence is confirmed by numerous place-names in the Kerch' peninsula and legendary accounts which centre around this area. They are said to have escaped the onslaught of the more powerful Scythians by migrating southward along the eastern shores of the Black Sea; their pursuing enemies, we are told, mistook their way and, instead, followed a route that led along the Caspian Sea, thus making a **HISTORY** *Cimmerians* geographical error as large as the whole width of the Caucasus. Hence both peoples invaded Asia Minor, where the Scythians are said to have ruled for twenty-eight years.

Campaigns in Near East

The presence of these two nations in the ancient civilized lands of the south is in fact substantiated by many Oriental sources, including the Bible. But the Cimmerians by no means give the impression of having been refugees.

In the Near East at this time Urartu and Assyria had become military powers of a brutality hitherto unknown. Their objective was total domination, which the Assyrians in particular attempted to achieve by conducting wars of extermination and deporting people wholesale. On the other hand they stubbornly defended the lands of ancient civilization against invaders from the north. In doing so they had no hesitation in setting one barbarian people against another. They supplemented their own armies with northern mercenaries without, however, being able to prevent them from rebelling. The Cimmerians and Scythians were only one group among many such dangerous allies, albeit a particularly active one. In 714 B.C. the Cimmerians brought Urartu to the verge of collapse; a little later they joined it in a coalition against the Assyrians. Esarhaddon countered this threat by securing the aid of the Scythians, to whose leader Bartatua he gave his daughter's hand in marriage. Later, too, the Cimmerians continued to fight as allies of Urartu, until they were finally driven off into Asia Minor, where they were able to ally themselves with forces that had crossed the Hellespont from Thrace. The barbarians succeeded in capturing Sardes, and it was only when the Assyrians

FIG. 4 – *These genre pictures formed the decoration of an electrum vase found in Kul' Oba kurgan, near Kerch'. We see a man being treated for an aching tooth and another for a leg injury. The 4th-century Greek artisan here has depicted with rare clarity their characteristic clothing and ethnic features; the Scythians were wholly Europoid. The gorytus, too, can easily be recognized. Height approx. 5.5 cm. Cf. p. 23.*

intervened that they lost this position. The Scythians remained in the field for some time longer. They reduced the pressure on the Assyrians by scoring a decisive victory over the Medes, who were advancing from the north-east together with other Iranian tribes. This victory enabled them to carry out campaigns of plunder that took them as far afield as the borders of Egypt. Biblical texts give a vivid picture of the terror caused by the Scythian onslaught. Later they again changed sides. Joining in an alliance with the Medes, they helped to destroy the power of the Assyrians, which came to an end with the sacking and annihilation of Nineveh.

It is understandable that the first concern of the Medes, once they had consolidated their supreme power, was to rid themselves quickly of such troublesome allies. The story that the Median king Kyaxares slew the Scythian leaders during a drinking bout sounds entirely convincing. The Mamelukes in Egypt were disposed of in a similar way no more than one hundred and fifty years ago. It is also quite possible that, after suffering catastrophic reverses of this kind, the Scythian bands should have returned to southern Russia and continued their activities there.

From now on we hear no more of the Cimmerians. They disappear from the written sources and recede more and more into a mythical past. This is not the case, however, with the Scythians. In 514 B.C. a campaign was waged against them by the Achaemenid Darius I, king of the Persians, who in the meantime had replaced the kindred tribe of the Medes. In a great outflanking manoeuvre he crossed the Hellespont into Thrace and attacked the enemy from the rear. This venture nevertheless proved a failure, on account of the vast expanse of territory that had to be traversed and the strategy which the steppe peoples were to employ so successfully against their settled neighbours over the next two thousand years. The enemy forces withdrew like a phantom, and it was only with difficulty, after having pursued them in vain, that Darius was able to reach the bridge across the Ister that led to safety. Herodotus has given a powerful and poetic description of this campaign.

Campaign of Darius I

No attempt was made to repeat this advance, for henceforth the Persians concentrated their energies upon the conquest of Greece. The threat which the two peoples now faced from this common enemy may have created a favourable climate for cultural contact between them.

For some time thereafter the Scythians' position was secure. They used their power to make various attacks upon their Thracian neighbours. However, they also forged links with ruling dynasties in Thrace, as for instance with the powerful kings of the Odrysian tribe.

The Scythians continued to enjoy power and prosperity during the fourth century B.C. The profits made from the export of grain grew to be more and more important to them. New areas in the Crimea were opened up for agriculture. But they were already under pressure from Sarmatian tribes who had meanwhile crossed the Don.

King Atheas set out to give his empire firmer political organization, perhaps as a counter-measure against this threat. He waged a famous war against the Triballi in Thrace. This struggle led to the establishment of Scythian settlements in territory to the west of the Danube delta, in what is nowadays known as the Dobrudja. But at an advanced age Atheas lost his life in battle against a superior antagonist, King Philip of Macedonia.

After this catastrophe the Crimea emerged ever more clearly as the nucleus of the Scythian state. Only the area around the mouth of the Dnieper remained under direct Scythian control. The western steppe lands fell to the Getae, a Thracian tribe, while the eastern part was taken by the Sarmatians, who thenceforth held sway over the former grazing-grounds of the Royal Scythians. It is not surprising that the Scythians now attempted to gain dominion over the Greek cities at least. Their objective was to assume control of their profitable foreign trade. In this they were repeatedly successful, and even such a powerful city as Olbia temporarily fell to the Scythians. Its king, Scilurus, had coins struck showing a nomad's covered waggon and, on the reverse side, Hermes and Demeter, the guardians of trade and agriculture. Even the kingdom of the Bosporus strongly felt the effects of this policy, and as a result the cities finally turned to Mithridates for assistance. He at once seized this chance to expand his Pontic empire. His generals, by resorting to all the tricks and subterfuges of Hellenistic warfare, defeated the Scythians on land – and also at sea, for during this late period these former nomads had a fleet of their own. Manned by Greek sailors, its function was to protect the grain shipments from attacks by pirates. Shortly afterwards the Scythians found themselves supporting Mithridates in his endeavour to prevent Roman power from expanding into the Black Sea area – an attempt that was, however, doomed to failure.

Having won this victory, Rome was at first content to establish protectorates. During the reign of Emperor Nero attempts were made to undertake a more active policy, but they had to be abandoned on account of complications at home. As is evident from inscriptions, the Scythian state continued to exist as late as the second and third centuries A.D., occasionally summoning enough strength to launch attacks upon the Greek cities. Only then did it succumb to assaults by new waves of people and finally disappear from view.

RELIGION AND CUSTOMS This in brief outline is the history of the Scythians and their state, which extends over almost a thousand years. Obviously, during that time, Scythian religion and customs must have undergone considerable changes. Our main sources on these matters, it is true, date from a very early phase: Herodotus, after all, was writing in the fifth century B.C. He relates that the pantheon was headed by a goddess named Tabiti, who FIG. 5 was generally identified with Hestia, presumably because the hearth was

26

regarded as her symbol and sanctuary. There were also other female deities, such as a serpent-footed earth goddess, who was looked upon as the ancestress of the kings. Another goddess was apparently served by effeminate priests, men who had undergone a change of sex; this suggests a comparison with ancient Oriental cult practices.

Papaios was equated with Zeus, and Herakles was worshipped under his Greek name. There were neither temples nor altars. Only the god of war was seen as incarnate in an iron sword, planted upon the top of an artificial mound and worshipped with bloody sacrificial offerings. The war ritual observed by the Scythians was filled with a barbarian piety which aroused the keen interest of Herodotus (Book IV, Ch. 64–66):

War ritual

> In what concerns war, their customs are the following. The Scythian soldier drinks the blood of the first man he overthrows in battle. Whatever number he slays, he cuts off all their heads, and carries them to the king; since he is thus entitled to a share of the booty, whereto he forfeits all claim if he does not produce a head. In order to strip the skull of its covering, he makes a cut around the head above the ears, and, laying hold of the scalp, shakes the skull out; then with the rib of an ox he scrapes the scalp clean of flesh, and softening it by rubbing between the hands, uses it thenceforth as a napkin. The Scyth is proud of these scalps; and hangs them from his bridle-rein; the greater the number of such napkins that a man can show, the more highly is he esteemed among them. Many make themselves cloaks, like the sheepskins of our peasants, by sewing a quantity of these scalps together. Others flay the right arms of their dead enemies, and make of the skin, which is stripped off with the nails hanging to it, a covering for their quivers. Now the skin of a man is thick and glossy, and would in whiteness surpass almost all other hides. Many even flay the entire body of their enemy, and stretching it upon a frame carry it about with them wherever they

27

ride. Such are the Scythian customs with respect to scalps and skins. The skulls of their enemies, not indeed of all, but of those whom they most detest, they treat as follows. Having sawn off the portion below the eyebrows, and cleaned out the inside, they cover the outside with leather. When a man is poor, this is all that he does; but if he is rich, he also lines the inside with gold: in either case the skull is used as a drinking-cup. They do the same with the skulls of their own kith and kin if they have been at feud with them, and have vanquished them in the presence of the king. When strangers whom they deem of any account come to visit them, these skulls are handed round, and the host tells how that these were his relations who made war upon him, and how that he got the better of them; all this being looked upon as proof of bravery.

Once a year the governor of each district, at a set place in his own province, mingles a bowl of wine, of which all Scythians by whom foes have been slain have a right to drink; while they who have slain no enemy are not allowed to taste of the bowl, but sit aloof in disgrace. No greater shame than this can happen to them. Such as have slain a very large number of foes, have two cups instead of one and drink them both together.*

These details have always aroused the utmost interest among ethnologists, since they show affinities with the warlike customs of many other peoples. In technical language we speak of 'trophy-hunting', 'scalping' and 'skull cups'. Such phenomena show, moreover, that the Scythian mounted warrior was not yet confined within a rigid framework of feudal subjection. Like the Red Indian brave in North America, he could attain personal prestige and influence by individual deeds of heroism.

The contradiction between this and the absolute power enjoyed by Scythian kings is more apparent than real, for even modern nomadic groups with a strong love of freedom and equality of rights have an absolute ruler at the apex of their political system. Indeed, the Scythian dynasty even boasted divine origin: according to one legend, it was founded by a union between Herakles and the serpent-footed goddess. The charisma attached to royal power is reflected in the ritual performed *Royal burials* on the death of a king, which Herodotus describes in detail (Book IV, Ch. 71–72). In its sombre grandeur it has scarcely any equal in the ancient world.

The tombs of their kings are in the land of the Gerrhi, who dwell at the point where the Borysthenes is first navigable. Here, when the king dies, they dig a grave, which is square in shape, and of great size. When it is ready, they take the king's corpse, and, having

---

* *The History of Herodotus of Halicarnassus.* C. Rawlinson's translation revised and annotated by A. W. Lawrence.

opened the belly, and cleaned out the inside, fill the cavity with a preparation of chopped galingale, frankincense, parsley-seed, and anise-seed, after which they sew up the opening, enclose the body in wax, and placing it on a waggon, carry it about through all the different tribes. On this procession each tribe, when it receives the corpse, imitates the example which is first set by the Royal Scythians; every man chops off a piece of his ear, crops his hair close, and makes a cut all round his arm, lacerates his forehead and his nose, and thrusts an arrow through his left hand. Then they who have the care of the corpse carry it with them to another of the tribes which are under the Scythian rule, followed by those whom they first visited. On completing the circuit of all the tribes under their sway, they find themselves in the country of the Gerrhi, who are the most remote of all, and so they come to the tombs of the kings. There the body of the dead king is laid in the grave prepared for it, stretched upon a mattress; spears are fixed in the ground on either side of the corpse, and beams stretched across above it, and the whole covered with a roof of twigs. In the open space around the body of the king they bury one of his concubines, first killing her by strangling, and also his cup-bearer, his cook, his groom, his lacquey, his messenger, some of his horses, firstlings of all his other possessions, and some golden cups; for they use neither silver nor bronze. After this they set to work, and raise a vast mound above the grave, all of them vying with each other and seeking to make it as tall as possible.

When a year is gone by, further ceremonies take place. Fifty of the best of the late king's attendants are taken, all native Scythians – for as bought slaves are unknown in the country, the Scythian kings choose any of their subjects that they like, to wait on them – fifty of these are taken and strangled, with fifty of the finest horses. When they are dead, their bowels are taken out, and the cavity cleaned, filled full of chaff, and straightaway sewn up again. This done, a number of posts are driven into the ground, in sets of two pairs each, and on every pair half the felly of a wheel is placed archwise; then strong stakes are run lengthways through the bodies of the horses from tail to neck, and they are mounted up upon the fellies, so that the felly in front supports the shoulders of the horse, while that behind sustains the belly and quarters, the legs dangling in mid-air; each horse is furnished with a bit and bridle, which latter is stretched out in front of the horse, and fastened to a peg. The fifty strangled youths are then mounted severally on the fifty horses. To effect this, a second stake is passed through their bodies along the course of the spine to the neck; the lower end of which projects from the body, and is fixed into a socket, made in the stake that runs lengthwise down the horse. The fifty riders being thus ranged in a circle round the tomb, the Scythians ride away.*

A similarly detailed account is given by Herodotus of the burial of ordinary people, of soothsayers, and of oath-taking ceremonies. Some of these data have been unexpectedly substantiated by finds made in Central Asia, as we shall see later.

HISTORY OF DISCOVERY

FIG. 6

Litoi kurgan

The ancient sources on which we have relied hitherto are wholly silent about the existence of an independent Scythian art. This problem only appeared when the Ukraine had been reconquered by the Tsars, for this made it possible to carry out excavations in the splendid towering burial mounds that were to be found all over the region – excavations which, however, were distinguished from robberies only by the fact that they were sanctioned by the state and that the finest pieces were taken off to swell the Imperial treasures, while those of inferior quality were scattered about a number of smaller museums and collections.

The prelude to this was the opening of the Litoi kurgan in 1763. In this barrow was discovered the magnificent Melgunov treasure, so named after the general who ordered the excavation to be carried out. If interest remained keen, this was due to the large number of burial gifts which were clearly the work of Greek artists. In addition there were found curious works in metal decorated with motifs of animals – and only animals. These were at first seen as barbarian extravagances, and it was only on account of the precious metal of which they were made that they were graciously admitted to the Hermitage collections. In this way Scythian art penetrated into the archaeologist's sanctum – led by the hand by its Greek sister.

Nevertheless excavations were carried on with astonishing zeal in search of further Greek antiquities. Among those who took part were French

---

* Ibid.

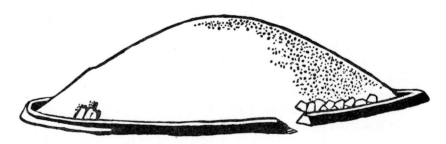

FIG. 6 – *View of Alexandropol' kurgan (height 21 m.) before the beginning of excavation work. Cf. above.*

noblemen, émigrés from the Revolution, as well as Germans. The growing interest taken in this work is attested by the foundation of local museums, at Nikolaev in 1805, Theodosia in 1811, Odessa in 1825 and Kerch' in 1826. Gradually it became clear that these barbarian relics must be attributed to the old Scythian 'master race'. From 1866 onwards attempts were made to correlate the vast finds made in burial-mounds with the description given by Herodotus of their funeral customs. Scythian trading links and military campaigns also served to explain the discovery of similar treasures in areas as far distant as Central Asia or the Balkan peninsula. When a find was even made at Vettersfelde in the March of Brandenburg, this came as a challenge to German scholarship. One of the boldest and most clear-sighted men in the field, the classical archaeologist Furtwängler, realized that the curious stylization of the animals, *Furtwängler* whereby the body of a fish, for example, was decorated with other animal forms, could not simply be explained away as a sign of degeneration. True, the goldsmiths who executed this work were of Greek origin, but they had had to adapt themselves to the taste of those who commissioned their work. But where do we find the roots of this trend, of this 'animal style' (as it came to be called, on account of the predilection shown for animal motifs)? Furtwängler pointed to the exalted austerity of Early Ionian art, which had, none the less, absorbed a wealth of Oriental designs.

With the establishment of the Archaeological Commission in St Petersburg in 1859, excavations in southern Russia were carried out ever more extensively and systematically. The greatest good fortune in discovery befell Veselovsky, a scholar who remained active until 1917; he displayed immense zeal, but was also ruthless and not always correct in his methods. Gradually there emerged a general picture of the most important groups *Chief groups of* of barrows, or 'kurgans'. A concentration of necropolises is situated on *kurgans* either bank of the Dnieper, in its lower reaches, just to the north of the Crimea, and two others south and south-east of Kiev. The group on the Dnieper is thought to belong to the heartlands of the Scythian tribes, as do also the graves in the eastern part of the Crimea. We know of others in the area of the Dniester and Bug, as well as in Volhynia. To the east of Kiev, in the area of Poltava, there is a further centre. On the Taman' peninsula finds were made of graves which showed to a marked degree the cultural influences exerted by the Greek cities. At first scholars were reluctant to face up to the disconcerting fact that burial-places also occur in areas which did not belong to Scythian territory at all; the Kuban' valley, for example, was occupied by the Sindi and Maeotae. But it was in this very region, in the kurgans of Ul', that deposits of large numbers of horses as funerary gifts were discovered. The skeletons of several hundred animals were found arranged in a regular pattern near the interment of the king.

PLATE 4 – Gold comb from Solokha kurgan. The Greek artist has here recorded ethnographical details, such as the use of imported Greek breast-plates and helmets. 4th century B.C. *Hermitage, Leningrad. Cf. p. 33.*

An idea of the wealth contained in these burial-places may be obtained from the following description of Chertomlyk kurgan in the lower Dnieper *Chertomlyk* area. Below a massive mound of earth was a shaft at the corners of which lateral chambers had been dug into the soil. Through one of these a passage led into a huge subterranean room, with concealed niches in the walls which served as hiding-places. The royal coffin formerly contained in this chamber had already been rifled. Only the huge bronze cauldrons filled with animal bones were still intact, as well as whatever had been placed in the wall-niches. Of these objects a gold phial, a sheet of gold-foil from a gorytus of Greek workmanship, showing mythological scenes, and swords whose hilts and scabbards were likewise covered with gold-plate are particularly worthy of note. In the chamber through which the passage to the main burial led were buried the ruler's queen (or concubine) and a servant bearing arms. The woman's skeleton lay upon the remains of a wooden catafalque and was strewn with small gold plaques which had once ornamented the borders of her head-cloth. The usual jewellery was also found, i.e. rings, armlets, beads and the like. Next to this stood the famous silver amphora decorated with the frieze showing Scythians breaking in horses. Close by were a silver basin and other amphorae. In the adjoining chamber lay the skeletons of the sword-bearer and a servant. They had been buried with precious weapons and jewellery in gold. Articles of clothing had apparently been hung up, but of these no more than the gold decoration had survived. Here, too, were found four splendid women's hoods adorned with open-work gold-plate and pendants, more weapons and a large number of amphorae that had probably once contained wine and oil. At the entrance to one of these chambers lay the skeleton of a servant, and in another that of a dog still on its leash.

On one side of the dromos the mound contained a separate horse burial, in the three sections of which eleven animals lay. Four of them bore gold ornaments on their harness and saddles, four of them decorations in silver, and the remaining three ornaments in bronze. The grooms, too, had been interred along with them.

In view of the great wealth contained in such royal graves – this one was PLATE P. 32 no exception – it is not surprising that the cemeteries of the common people should not have been studied systematically. These were left to excavators with limited funds at their disposal.

This unheard-of abundance led first of all to the conclusion that the entire territory under Scythian rule, extending as far as the wooded steppe zone and the foothills of the Caucasus – although it did not, by any means, constitute a state – formed a single province, and one whose development showed parallel artistic trends. The nomadic way of life, which was not tied to a fixed, well-equipped dwelling, seems to have set the pattern for the sedentary population as well, for everywhere artistic objects serve the prime purpose of personal adornment. The rich embellishment of the horses' harness fits this picture. No cultic objects of a non-personal character have been discovered; indeed, Herodotus expressly noted the absence of temples. The way in which tents and waggon-dwellings were furnished and decorated has only become clear as a result of new finds made in Central Asia, although some information can be gleaned from wall-paintings in the sepulchral chambers of the necropolises near the Greek colonial towns.

It was in accordance with nomadic usage that these works of applied art should frequently be executed by immigrant artisans from the Near East, Greece or possibly Thrace. The social position they held was not too low, as is clear from the discovery of a whole settlement of black-smiths near the Scythian royal kurgans on the Dnieper. Here there were found a number of amphorae, indicating that these artisans consumed quantities of Greek wine. Nor was its quality to be despised.

Animal motifs Of decisive significance is the fact that animals everywhere serve as the

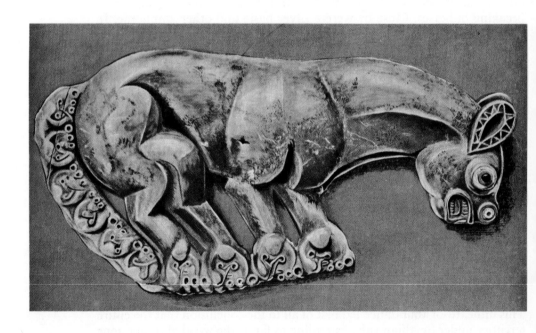

PLATE 5 – Breast-plate or shield ornament in the form of a panther, from Kelermes kurgan. Inlaid with coloured enamel and amber. An example of zoomorphic juncture, the paws and tail consisting of curled animals. Since the planes are sharply contrasted, this piece has very often been reproduced as characteristic of Scythian animal style. Beginning of 6th century B.C. *Hermitage, Leningrad. Approx. half life-size. Cf. pp. 35, 37, 189.*

FIG. 7 – *Flat strips of bone (length approx. 16 cm.) and decoration on a strap (height approx. 4 cm.) from the Zhabotin kurgans. Oldest phase of the animal style: the animals depicted belong to the native fauna, but their posture copies Syro-Hurrite and Iranian (Sialk B) models. The sign in the centre of the figure on the right is thought to be a solar symbol. Cf. p. 37.*

main motif of decoration. Not all of them are to be found among the native fauna, nor are they all domestic animals of economic importance. They constitute an odd selection. Some of the images of animals, the lion, for instance, certainly come from the Near East, and others, like the boar, are presumed to be of Greek origin.

The arrangement of the pictorial elements in relation to one another also conforms to traditional principles. First of all we find 'zoomorphic juncture', i.e. the free combination of parts of bodies taken from different animal pictures. This technique has a long history in the Near East. In the case of some of these hybrid creatures, such as the griffin with an eagle's or a lion's head, we can trace the route by which they reached the steppe lands. Inversion, too, i.e. bending the rear part of the body through an angle of 180°, is thought to have been derived from the Orient. It already occurs on Cretan seals. It is not too difficult to find southern models for the arrangement of animals in the form of a cross or a whirl. Recently scholars have even maintained that the characteristic posture of Scythian stags or ibexes, with their legs drawn under their bodies, originates in Syro-Hurrite art. This posture, in which the legs appear to be tied together, is thought to denote the offering of the animal as a sacrifice. Scenes of animals in combat, used throughout for decorative purposes, very often have as their subject a felid attacking a cervid, and correspond to traditions common in the south. The idea of curving the animal's body to form a circle, thus creating the so-called curled animal, presumably derives from eastern Asia.

PLATE P. 34

Looking over this list, it may well seem difficult to understand how some works executed at this time in the Pontic area nevertheless bear the indelible stamp of genuine individuality. Objects of this kind do not give the impression of being modelled; the forms are rendered by inclined planes marked off by curves where they intersect. The number of motifs

FIG. 8 – *Bronze pole-top (standard?) from the kurgan near Ul', Kuban' area. Approx. 500 B.C. The austere form of the early period is still preserved here, as can clearly be seen. In spite of this, a late dating is justified by the highly abstract treatment, the small bird's head growing out of the ibex's neck, and the apotrophaic eye. Hermitage, Leningrad. Height approx. 28 cm. Cf. p. 37.*

is skilfully limited, and these in turn are reduced to bare essentials. Apparently the idea is to evoke tension, the potential ability to move rather than movement itself. The animals' bodies remind us of springs; their joints are accentuated; everything expressive of greed and power is emphasized – the jaws of the felid, the tusks of the boar, the antlers of the stag.

This group of works constitutes the specific Scythian contribution and is the work of native artisans. Hence attempts have been made to explain some of the peculiar characteristics as due to the employment of a traditional technique. A contrast of inclined planes is often created where wood, or especially bone, is the medium. This technique of cutting in *'Schrägschnitt'* elegant curves is called 'Schrägschnitt' – as opposed to simple notching by taking straight chips out with a knife. Work of this kind is known as 'Kerbschnitt'. Some of the unnatural postures, too, could be explained by the peculiarities of the material. After all, the artist was seeking to fit the animal's body into the confined area of a bone plaque. It seems as though the characteristic features of an earlier type of craftsmanship live on, even when they are translated into an alien medium such as gold or bronze.

In the assessing of other characteristics, attempts have been made to trace their spiritual roots back to the primeval past. It is assumed that each animal feature was regarded as a symbol charged with magic power and irradiating beneficent influence. These units endowed with power and influence are thought to have been collected and combined in order to ensure the welfare and protection of the warriors. With some primitive peoples we do indeed find over-accentuation of certain parts of the body,

FIG. 9 – *Belt-clasp from Zhurovka, Dnieper area. 5th-century bronze casting. Possibly following a Greek model, the two heads are joined together by the jaws. A trend towards flatter treatment is noticeable, which becomes even more marked toward the end of the 5th century. Hermitage, Leningrad. Cf. below.*

such as the joints. Excessive emphasis is designed to increase the magic effect.

This principle seems to have been transferred to the objects produced by Greek artisans. They, too, use animal motifs steeped in tradition – some of them derived from the more advanced civilizations – in a new way so as to appeal to a people gradually emerging from a world governed by a magical outlook on life.

This thesis seemed adequate to explain the historical development which the animal style underwent in southern Russia. *Development of animal style*

The early phase is assigned to the late seventh century B.C. and is best represented by the Zhabotin kurgans. In this phase we not only find animal images imbued with magic power, but also other symbols of blessing. Little Greek influence can be detected, whereas that of the Near East has indeed left traces. The stage of full development is reached with the early sixth-century kurgans (Kelermes, Litoi, and a little later Kostromskaia). The influence of the Near East now makes itself manifest in the presence of works inlaid with coloured stones. Nevertheless it is only now that the symbolic value of animal form is most keenly appreciated; and this explains why a few splendidly stylized animal bodies – a cervid, birds of prey, one small beast of prey, the ibex and the Oriental griffin – form the entire repertoire. FIG. 7 PLATE P. 34 FIG. 12

In the late sixth and fifth centuries B.C. the harmony and unity of this art are no longer maintained. The very fact that Greek artists were employed introduced alien elements which did not always blend with local traditions. In one case we may note either slight signs of degeneration, in another a reversion to the earliest stylistic trends. Possibly the artists are seeking other means of attaining a magic effect, and therefore introduce scenes of animals locked in combat. Inversion is also used more frequently. Of the numerous famous kurgans representing this stage, Zhurovka, Ul' and Elthegen, and the 'Golden Kurgan' near Simferopol' should be mentioned. FIGS. 8, 9

During the fourth century B.C. animal scenes lose more and more of FIGS. 10, 11

FIG. 10 – *Animal heads arranged in the shape of a whorl. Ornamental plaque used for horse's harness. Silver, from Krasnokutsk kurgan. 4th century B.C. Cf. p. 37.*

their plasticity. Either we are left with simple lines, as had already been the case in the earliest times, or else a lavish scroll-work composition comes into existence. This stage is represented, for example, by Chertomlyk, Solokha and the main find at Kul' Oba.

The last phase of Scythian art is characterized on one hand by extreme stylization and on the other by an almost ungainly realism. This may also be attributed to influences from Middle Asia*, probably transmitted by the victorious advancing Sarmatians.

Study of chronology In working out this chronological scheme – for it is no more than a scheme – scholars of many different nationalities have collaborated. The Englishman Minns produced in his monumental work *Scythians and Greeks* the first comprehensive account, which is still of great value today. The Russian scholar Rostovtzeff published a brilliant survey and the Latvian Ginters wrote the first monograph an a Scythian weapon, the sword. An important part was played by German scholars. In the 1920s and 1930s the field was dominated by a generation of men who had an absolutely open mind towards the problems which the eastern part of the continent posed. Only now is it becoming clear that many of Ebert's views were correct. In 1938 Schefold undertook the most substantial attempt to provide a chronology, upon which we have mainly been relying in this chapter. Schefold invariably based his datings on funerary gifts of Greek origin. His approach has since frequently been criticized, on the grounds that objects deposited simultaneously need not have been produced at the same time; but in practice no very serious errors are involved here.

---

* See page 170.

FIG. 11 – *Bronze belt-plate or frontlet of horse's harness from Kuban' area. 4th century B.C. An extreme example of the forms of the late period, the object is flat and the ornamentation consists largely of scrolls. Hermitage, Leningrad. Cf. p. 37.*

Meanwhile scholars' interest in animal style had repercussions in widely different fields. In the West they were rather limited; only 'art nouveau' with its basically ornamental tendency found a source of confirmation and inspiration in Scythian art. In Russia, however, the links were much stronger. During the early years of the Soviet régime some radical visionaries identified themselves with the Scythians. They saw in them the great antagonists of Europe and the Greeks, and discovered in them their own boundless 'maximalism', their own vaunted spirit of utter relentlessness. An intellectual movement appeared known as 'Scythianism', after a well-known poem by Alexander Blok containing the lines:

'Scythianism'

'You're millions, we are hosts – and hosts – and hosts!
Engage with us and prove our seed!
We're Scythians and Asians too, from coasts
That breed squint eyes, bespeaking greed!'*

Little attention was paid to the fact that the Scythians, as depicted by the Greeks, looked completely Europoid, rather like Russian peasants. Only the great physician Hippocrates describes them as definitely Mongoloid in appearance, with flat features and without beards. But finds have not corroborated his statement.

In contrast to this wave of enthusiasm the contribution made by Soviet scholars between the two World Wars seems scant and mediocre. The most important work was probably done by Rau, a Volga German, who perfected and systematized the dating of arrow-heads, and by Borovka, whose artistic analysis showed a high degree of empathetic insight. The life work of both men ended abruptly. Rau was driven to despair by the prevailing misery of those years and committed suicide; Borovka perished in one of the purges.

Soviet scholarship

Those of their colleagues who remained more faithful to the party line spent much of their energy obediently attacking the theories of Rostovtzeff. This greatest of Russian experts in this field was already suspect as an émigré; and his main thesis, that the Scythians had appeared from the east as nomadic conquerors, already possessing the animal style in fully developed form, and had superimposed their culture upon the matriarchal peasant communities of southern Russia, seemed the epitome of bourgeois arrogance. N. Ia. Marr, son of an Irish seaman and a Caucasian woman, who was at that time regarded as a pioneer of proletarian scholarship, had a different explanation to offer. As a philologist, Marr believed it to be demonstrable that large groups of peoples never migrate *en bloc*. If, despite this, a new linguistic group suddenly appears in a particular area, this is explained by Marr as a modification of the language structure corresponding to a new stage attained in the evolution

---

* Translated by Sir C. Kisch, *Alexander Blok: Prophet of Revolution* (London, 1962), p. 152.

of the social system. In the late 1920s this stimulating, but undoubtedly exaggerated, thesis was elevated by the Soviets into a generally valid guiding principle for historical studies. Soviet archaeology was accordingly set the task of proving that the Scythians were indigenous to southern Russia. This had a paralysing effect upon independent investigations. In any case, as a result of the economic stringencies of the time, little money was available for excavation, and books had to be printed on very poor paper, with almost worthless illustrations.

Not until after the Second World War did Soviet scholars succeed in regaining the lead. It was now realized that the mania for proving autochthonous origin had also had its merits. In the service of this illusion, the study of ceramics and utensils was greatly intensified. Even poor graves were carefully examined and classified.

Recent excavations Settlements attracted particularly close attention. Thus it was established that, contrary to the account given by Herodotus, settlements surrounded by earthworks also existed in the main area of the Pontic Scythians, where they dwelt at least during the winter. One of these strongholds, the vast Kamenskoe Gorodishche, covering an area of 12 square kilometres, was probably used as a residence by the great Scythian kings. It is situated close to the royal kurgans.

The new kind of information acquired made it possible to distinguish in southern Russia, on the basis of variations in funeral rites and ceramics, several complexes which apparently belonged to different tribes. Attempts are now being made to correlate them with the names of the tribes given by Herodotus. Once more it was shown that the animal style extended beyond the limits of the area inhabited by the Scythian-speaking population. It must also have been adopted by tribes of Slavonic or Thracian origin.

For the bulk of the populations in the steppe and 'forest steppe' it is possible to prove that they developed from local Bronze Age cultures. No massive invasion took place even of the steppes around the lower Dnieper, where Herodotus located the core of the Royal Scyths. It has, however, been possible to establish that an ethnic drift which extended over several centuries took place westwards from the Volga area. Thus Cimmerians and Scythians must have been neighbours for a lengthy period of time. They may have been two tribal confederations that formed within one and the same people.

For a long time attempts to trace local forerunners of the animal style did not lead to any positive results. Despite all the efforts made by Soviet scholars little of importance has been added to the sparse data already accumulated by Ebert. In the Pontic area images of animals remain a rarity during the Bronze Age. Then, towards the end of the seventh century B.C., we suddenly encounter the animal style of the Zhabotin phase – in a fascinating combination with new forms of weapons and harnesses. The range of weapons has already been described: gorytus, akinakes, battle-axe and short spear. The sudden transition to this 'Scythian triad' in the seventh century B.C. takes place at a time when Cimmerians and Scythians had long been waging war in the Near East. Thus they must have formed clearly defined complexes in their homeland as well.

PLATE 6 – Ornamental gold disc, perhaps part of a horse's harness. Greek workmanship, with Oriental motifs. Vettersfelde. 6th century B.C. *Museum für Vor- und Frühgeschichte, Berlin. Length 17 cm. Cf. p. 44.*

One may well ask what was the cause of this sudden change in equipment and in art. According to the present state of research there are three possible explanations.

1. While in the Near East, bands of Scythians became familiar not only with better equipment but also with new types of ornament. As they were already employing Ionian craftsmen in their homeland, this did not lead to a straightforward borrowing, but to a new synthesis in which Greek taste was the dominating factor. This was so effective that it rapidly made headway and spread far and wide.

This theory was already formulated in broad outline by Ebert, who never accepted the concept of immigration. After the Second World War it was again put forward by Grakov.

2. The animal style may have existed earlier in the Near East or Iran in fairly developed form. The transfer to the north may be due to bands of mercenaries streaming back home by way of the Caucasus: they may simply have seized artisans and taken them along with them. They were then gradually superseded by Ionian craftsmen.

This second theory has been given an impetus during the last few years, since objects executed in animal style have been discovered in Persian Kurdistan, at first as part of a large hoard. There is no doubt that these objects are linked to those of southern Russia. In any case they date from a remarkably early period. Thus archaeologists began to wonder whether animal style art as a whole might not be an offshoot of a development that occurred in the Near East.

This concept has its main supporter in Sulimirski. He believes that a band of Scythians, after crossing the Caucasus, settled in Azerbaidjan and there adopted a completely Transcaucasian cultural pattern. After achieving outstanding military successes, they were

FIG. 12 – *Animal figures on gold plate surrounding shaft of iron axe from Kelermes kurgan. This is an Oriental, possibly Urartian work which was carried*

finally compelled to withdraw by the Medes. Thereupon these Scythians subjugated all their fellow-tribesmen who had stayed behind in southern Russia. They then rose to the status of a royal tribe. Their expanding power, he believes, is reflected in the dissemination of the animal style which they brought with them.

3. The third possibility is the hypothesis that the animal style came into existence somewhere in Central Asia or southern Siberia. There may have been contact with the Pontic area from the very beginning, the seventh or eighth century B.C. (There is no need to postulate a massive migration of peoples.) Thus stimuli from the east were received which finally produced the Pontic animal style. This theory could be supported by reference to the earliest cauldrons cast in bronze found in southern Russia. They are almost certainly of Siberian origin, deriving ultimately from a Chinese prototype.

The younger Soviet scholars, belonging to a generation no longer influenced by Marr, are more and more inclined to accept such a solution. There remains, however, the question as to the degree of originality we are to ascribe to such an artistic centre in the heart of Asia. Did it receive its main stimulus from the east, the south or, indeed, from the north, as suggested long ago by such eminent scholars as Minns or Borovka?

A further complication arises from the possibility that the animal style reached southern Russia not only directly but also by a longer route through Iran and the Caucasus, and that it was transmitted by the bands of mercenaries of different origin who met in the camps and on the battlefields of the Near East. (This idea was advanced by the author some years ago.)

These problems cannot be solved at the present stage in the argument. We cannot even discuss them without first casting a glance at the other regions of the steppe. We shall therefore reserve treatment of them for the final chapter.

off to the Kuban' area. It has a rich repertoire of motifs, only some of which are found later in Scythian art. Hermitage, Leningrad. Cf. p. 37.

III. SCYTHIAN FINDS IN CENTRAL EUROPE

Vettersfelde hoard
PLATES PP. 41, 45, 46

At Vettersfelde in Brandenburg there was discovered in 1882 the complete equipment of a Scythian chieftain. Several large pieces were made of gold. They were lavishly decorated in animal style, although this was plainly the work of a Greek artist, commissioned by a barbarian ruler. Furtwängler (whom we have already mentioned in connection with the work he did on this hoard, which also included a number of lesser treasures) conjectured that it had been hidden by a band of Scythians who had retreated into the depths of central Europe before the attacking armies of Darius.

Later on it came to be doubted whether a retreat took place on such an enormous scale (scholars were probably thinking in terms of the wars against Napoleon or Charles XII). It was thought more likely that these pieces had belonged to the leader of some band intent on plunder. There were indeed some clues that pointed to such a hypothesis. It was known for a fact that Scythians made raids as far afield as the borders of Egypt. Since it was also held that in southern Russia the Scythians ruled as nomadic overlords over unwarlike peasants, the question arose whether this process might not have been repeated in central Europe, the only difference being that there is no indication of this in western literary sources. Had they settled and founded a kingdom in this area as well?

Such an eventuality became all the more significant when it was increasingly observed that pertinent finds were concentrated in particular areas. Weapons and jewellery of the Scythian type grew noticeably more frequent in central Hungary, and again in Transylvania and central

FIGS. 13, 14

Bulgaria. They belong to groups of finds, all dating from the same relatively early period, judged by southern Russian standards. Again and again attempts at dating these point to the sixth and fifth centuries B.C. Some

FIG. 13 – *Gold stag from Zöldhalompuszta. Presumably the decoration on a shield. 5th century B.C. Hungarian Historical Museum, Budapest. Overall width 23 cm. Cf. above.*

of them might even go back to the seventh century. Besides some pieces which may have been imports, there are many bold modifications of Pontic types, evidently influenced by inherited taste.

Fettich has reproduced the finest pieces and analysed them in exemplary fashion. He contests the view that the appearance of Scythians in this region was just an episode, and maintains that they must have settled there on an extensive scale. Finally, however, the alien ruling class was absorbed by the mass of the population – a fate that had previously befallen eastern nomads in the lands of the Hungarian plain. Other scholars, too, reckoned that the historical consequences of the nomadic advance must have been considerable; in particular, the so-called Lusatian culture is said to have suffered greatly from Scythian raids. *Fettich's theory*

This conception has been criticized by Soviet archaeologists. As in all other instances, they have tried to gain acceptance for a less militant and 'migrationistic' interpretation. To this end it has been pointed out that the main Scythian area, which must undoubtedly be located in the steppes along the banks of the Dnieper, was surrounded by tribes which, although dependent on the Scythians culturally, were by no means subject to them. The Scythians' way of life and their art evidently proved most attractive, for they served as a model even for the Anan'ino culture, in the depths of the forest steppes of central Russia, although this was an *Soviet view*

PLATE 7 – Golden fish, thought to be a shield ornament or the frontlet from a horse's harness. Vettersfelde. 6th century B.C. *Museum für Vor- und Frühgeschichte, Berlin. Length 41 cm. Cf. p. 44.*

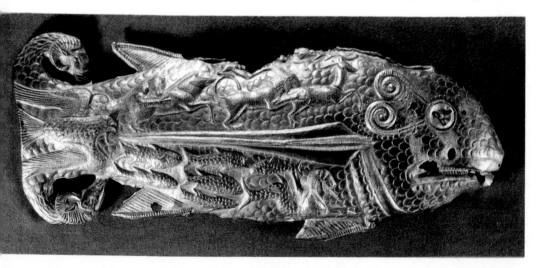

active culture ready and able to defend itself. Are we not then dealing here with a similar irradiation of civilizing influences, in this case of Scythian influences into central Europe? One point that suggests this interpretation is that these influences often seem to stem from the forest steppe zone, e.g. from Podolia and the middle Dnieper, where there were no Scythian inhabitants but at the most a Scythianized native population. An explanation may thus be found in trade links and cultural borrowings of every kind, but not in the establishment of a vast empire.

For even Soviet authors do not exclude the possibility that Scythians occasionally appeared in person in areas under their influence to indulge in vigorous bouts of plundering, and no doubt the natives – most of whom were Thracian tribes – were fully able to fight for their lives. Some objects may thus have become the property of local warriors who regarded them as trophies. Contacts of this kind were interrupted only when Celtic influences became predominant. In Bulgaria alone have princely tombs been found from the fourth and third centuries B.C., in which the ritual

PLATE 8 – Gold sheathing covering the upper part of the *akinakes* scabbard found at Vettersfelde. Greek workmanship. 6th century B.C. *Museum für Vor- und Frühgeschichte, Berlin. Length 19 cm. Cf. p. 44.*

FIG. 14 – *Bronze matrix. Massive casting. Found at Garchinovo, north-eastern Bulgaria. 6th century B.C. Formerly in the Shumen Museum. Overall length 35 cm. Cf. p. 44.*

and funerary gifts are reminiscent of those in the royal kurgans of the lower Dnieper. This can be explained by the close relationship, strengthened by intermarriage, that existed between Scythian and Thracian notables. Even when they fought one another, these men adhered to the same code. Competition was fierce; and this may have had some bearing on the fact that in Thrace, too, it came to be regarded as a mark of social standing to engage craftsmen of Greek origin, or at least with Greek training. The famous Panagiurishte treasure must be seen in this context. Mrs Mantsevich even believes that the silver vessels found at the Kul' Oba kurgan were not produced on the Bosporus but in Thrace, with its abundant resources of metal. But actual migration occurred only on a limited scale. Reference has already been made to the settlers' territories in the Dobrudja. Here, in 'Little Scythia', the national stock was preserved long after the steppe had fallen into the hands of the Sarmatians.

In sum, we may say that in the present phase of research attempts are being made to show that the role played by the Scythians in the history of central and eastern Europe should not be exaggerated. These attempts have, indeed, probably gone rather too far.

IV. SCYTHIAN ELEMENTS IN THE CAUCASUS

The plains to the north of the Caucasus range, the drainage basins of the Kuban' and Terek, naturally belong to the domain of the Scythian animal style, although the nomads or peasants who lived here had languages of their own and may have retained earlier 'Cimmerian' traditions. But the tribes in the high valleys on either side of the main Caucasian range led an existence governed by completely different rules and determined by more ancient traditions. Small communities lived here isolated from one another by high ridges that were difficult to cross. They were able to preserve their independence against enemies from outside by retiring into their mountain fastnesses when attacked. On the other hand, they were relatively close to the great centres of civilization in the Near East. Merchants and bands of warriors crossing the passes acted as a constant stimulus to further progress.

Local cultures   This state of affairs may explain why during the Bronze Age metal objects and jewellery often took on exaggerated fanciful forms. Local cultures

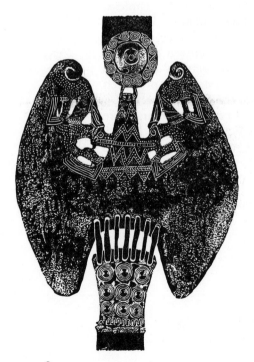

FIG. 15 – *Reconstruction of metal buckle of a belt from Isti-su necropolis, north-eastern Caucasus. This piece consists of a round boss, the loop, decorated with S-spirals, and the hook, which is broadened out on either side to form kidney-shaped flaps. Their upper parts are turned into the torsos of fantastic animals. Connected to this piece by rings is the bronze sheathing which once covered the end of the leather belt. Although this composite work already belongs to the 'Scythian' period (6th–5th century B.C.), the basic tendency of the northern Caucasian Bronze Age towards exaggeration and fantasy continued to make itself felt. It is evidently based upon the Oriental scheme of 'a deity between animals'. Width of central part 19 cm.*

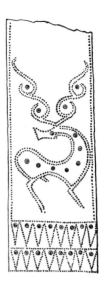

FIG. 16 – *Animal figure on a belt from Dusheti, northern Caucasus. Whitish metal. This late piece (dating from the Scythian period) also shows that the autochthonous art of the northern Caucasus followed stylistic norms different from those of the Scythians. Hermitage, Leningrad. Width approx. 8 cm. Cf. below.*

FIG. 16

came into being, in which axes, belt-buckles and pins were so fashioned as to become symbols of rank; they were lavishly decorated and had luxuriant, at times downright grotesque, outlines. Here extensive use was made of animal and human figures, as well as fertility symbols. Their religious significance can only be guessed at.

Caucasian bronze-casters, who had rich ore deposits to work from, sold their wares far and wide. It was presumably they who evolved the forms of snaffle that were in use in the area between the Bug and Don during the eighth and seventh centuries B.C. This, however, brings us to the critical period before the animal style proper had begun to spread, and we have to consider whether Caucasian animal sculptures formed a convenient starting-point for this artistic trend. Stags abound in the Caucasus, and have been frequently represented there since the middle Bronze Age. Did the Scythians perhaps derive their predilection for these and other motifs from this source?

If, however, we look at the matter more closely, we find that there can be no such simple solution. We see that the Caucasian animal silhouettes are formed of convex curves. The small sculptures are often converted into a kind of hollow bulb, pierced by so many openings that the body consists almost entirely of a fine network of metal strips. In contrast to this, objects belonging to the same craft traditions are rather rare in southern Russia: for example, the so-called standards or pole-tops. For the bulk of the material there is no clearly demonstrable relationship of this kind. On the other hand, southern Russia was a ready market for Caucasian products. Bronze vessels of Caucasian type with animal-shaped handles were apparently popular over a wide area. On the other hand, graves are found in the Caucasus containing Scythian weapons and Scythian

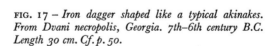

FIG. 17 – *Iron dagger shaped like a typical akinakes. From Dvani necropolis, Georgia. 7th–6th century B.C. Length 30 cm. Cf. p. 50.*

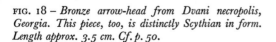

FIG. 18 – *Bronze arrow-head from Dvani necropolis, Georgia. This piece, too, is distinctly Scythian in form. Length approx. 3.5 cm. Cf. p. 50.*

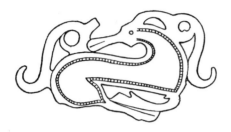

FIG. 19 – *Belt-clasp from the so-called well-graves at Koban. (The term 'well-graves' is used for burials in a deep well-like shaft.) With its elegantly curving lines this piece recalls that shown in Fig. 16, but it also has typical Scythian characteristics: the head turned to the rear and the legs drawn under the body. This shows that a process of fusion occurred. Length 11 cm.*

jewellery. It seems as though in many tribes there were outstanding warriors who modelled themselves upon their powerful neighbours. Finds of a steppe character are concentrated along the routes over the passes FIGS. 17, 18 (the cemeteries of Dvani and Samtavro in the central area, and Mingechaur in Azerbaidjan). Two of these routes run across the central range, and two by-pass it to the east and west.

It is not difficult to find an explanation for this pattern of discoveries. As we know, the Scythians were setting the fashion in the whole of the Pontic steppes and beyond. Bands of Cimmerians, followed by Scythians, crossed the Caucasus to intervene in the affairs of the Near East. They must have had strategic bases on the way – in which their name lived on for centuries afterwards. The fact that even today in Georgian the word for 'hero' is derived from the name of the Cimmerians, may give an indication of the role played by these adventurers from the north. Contact was most intensive during the early Scythian period. Later local principalities established themselves in which Achaemenid and Hellenistic influences prevailed.

In the northern part of the central range a process of fusion took place. Here motifs from the steppe were evidently taken over by the bronze foundries, developed further and adapted to native taste.

About the beginning of our era the Caucasus comes under the domination of a new alien element. This time it is the Sarmatians who advance into the mountains, even far beyond Ossetian territory, where their (Iranian) language has survived up to the present day. But they bring with them a type of art which cannot be discussed here, as it lies beyond the scope of this volume, although it also carries on some ancient, indeed very ancient, traditions.

Cimmerian and Scythian bands

FIG. 20 – *Caucasian dagger. The handle and blade are connected in the same way as we observe in the akinakes, but the open-work design and the pommel point to a native tradition going back to the 'Cimmerian' Bronze Age. Museum für Vor- u. Frühgeschichte, Berlin.*

V. ANAN'INO CULTURE IN EASTERN RUSSIA

The way of life and the art of the horsemen in the steppe lands exerted influences which penetrated into north-eastern Europe and Siberia. They were transmitted by a people whose cultural and ethnic centre lay to the north and north-east of Kazan', on the rivers Vetluga, Viatka, Kama and Belaia. Attempts have been made to identify this people with some of the tribal names mentioned by Herodotus.

Excavations were carried out in this area at a very early date, in the mid-nineteenth century. The necropolis of Anan'ino gave a picture of a strongly independent warlike culture. No more than ten years after its excavation it was dated with a fair degree of accuracy. Research continued without interruption, because the families of merchants and wealthy business men living in this area displayed an interest in its remote history. Nearby Kazan' was an important centre of scholarship. Thus it was soon noted that cultural links existed between Anan'ino and the south. True, its walled settlements with their earthworks were at first attributed to a different phase. They were remarkable for the fact that unusually large amounts of bones were found there.

At the end of the nineteenth and the beginning of the twentieth centuries the most brilliant Russian archaeologists worked on material that had been accumulated here. Finally, the Finnish scholar Tallgren produced a comprehensive study of almost uncanny perfection. He knew the entire literature, had studied finds in state-owned and private collections, and had personal experience of relevant excavation work. On this basis he assigned to the 'Anan'ino culture' a dating which by and large has *Dating* remained unchallenged: seventh–third centuries B.C. Of course he was not yet aware of the exact limits of this group of finds. Nor could he solve a number of problems concerning the economy, social organization and religious beliefs of this people. Their racial composition also remained FIG. 21 uncertain. These were the problems that over the next few decades were mastered by Soviet scholars, who always felt a certain resentment at Tallgren's superiority. It was not difficult for Schmidt, Smirnov, Efimenko and Zbrueva to question his authority in this field, since they were able to base their theories on a vast number of more recent and informative excavations, carried out by well-planned and closely-supervised expeditions. Efimenko showed originality and independence of mind in evaluating his material. The results obtained by the other three scholars harmonized with one another so well that we now have a full picture, relatively free from uncertainties.

FIG. 21 – *Large gravestone from the necropolis at Anan'ino, showing a warrior. The necklet is clearly recognizable. The dagger and bow-case are affixed to the belt in the Scythian manner. The outline to the left of the dagger is probably meant to indicate the pick. The lack of a beard is explained by the presence of a Mongoloid element among the Anan'ino people. Cf. p. 51.*

The settlements of the Anan'ino people were situated along the courses of rivers. They were so small, measuring 60 × 150 metres in area at the most, that they cannot have been inhabited by more than a few dozen persons. In most cases they were surrounded by earthworks and a moat; in other cases they are thought to have been enclosed by palisades. The people gained their livelihood by cattle-breeding and husbandry, as well as by hunting and fishing.

Trade played a tremendously important role. Their bronzes, which were virtually mass-produced for export, evidently found a ready market in the depths of the forests of eastern Europe. Socketed celts cast on the banks of the river Kama found their way to Finland and Scandinavia. They were even exported to western Siberia. The first iron objects were apparently distributed through the same trading network. One can imagine that they were bartered for furs, which the inhabitants of the Pontic steppes were glad to obtain. No doubt other products as well, such as amber, were exchanged over just as great distances. The Anan'ino people kept slaves and thus may also have engaged in the slave trade.

The maintenance of such a communication network suggests that there existed an advanced military technology and a superior form of organization, which naturally led to social stratification. This conclusion is corroborated by detailed study of the Anan'ino cemeteries. These were situated on the banks of rivers, which apparently played a most important part in their conception of the life hereafter. The skeletons were in most cases in an extended position and were buried along with carefully graded funerary gifts. Chieftains were given lavish bronze jewellery as well as picks decorated with figures, evidently as a symbol of rank. Apart from them, clearly distinguished, was the large group of free-born warriors. The differences in military equipment may be indicative not only of varying degrees of wealth but also of age. Other men's graves contain no funerary gifts whatsoever – evidence of the slavery already mentioned. Women's graves are differentiated in a similar manner. The curious funerary gifts found with some female skeletons can only be explained as cultic objects, indicating that women officiated as priests or shamans.

In men's graves a number of additional skulls were found. These may

FIG. 22 – *The practice of carrying Scythian bow-cases is authenticated not only by the gravestone shown above but also by a bronze miniature.*

indicate that human sacrifices formed part of the death rites, but they may also have been trophies for, as we know, the Scythians, who set the fashion in so many respects, also took the heads of their victims.

In addition there is the fact that the weapons of the Anan'ino people also display many Scythian features. They had the typical bow-case and the short sword, the akinakes. Thus it is not surprising that the animal style occurs here again.

Conditions here are of course completely different from those obtaining in the south. We have good reason to assume that as early as the second millennium B.C., i.e. during the Bronze Age, the wood-carvers of the north were eager to render animals in an artistically simplified and yet realistic manner. The best specimens have been found in the peat-bogs of the nearby Ural mountains. Here splendid pieces have been preserved sunk into the morass as sacrificial offerings. Among them is a wooden trough in the shape of an elk, thought to have been used to catch the blood of animals slaughtered during the ritual. Wooden spoons have also been discovered, in the form of geese and ducks, which are likewise believed to be cultic objects. The artistic perfection of these carvings is in strange contrast to the crudity of the human figures, which are taken to be statues of deities.

FIG. 24

In the period of transition to the Anan'ino culture, curiously enough,

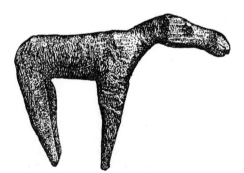

FIG. 25

FIG. 25 – *Ornamental plaque with embossed work, after a Caucasian model. Lugovsk necropolis. Cf. below.*

FIG. 26 – *Bronze button from Anan'ino with characteristic design used by mounted warriors in the period preceding the animal style phase.*

there occur pieces imported from the Caucasus. They may have been brought here by bands of warriors returning, laden with booty, by boat (by the Volga – Caspian route) after having taken part in military operations in the south. The Anan'ino people certainly give the picture one would expect to obtain when investigating such 'Vikings' of the early Iron Age.

An evaluation of this background could easily lead to the thesis that the 'Scythian' animal style actually developed here, in the wooded steppe zone, and that it is rooted in the carving tradition of the north fertilized by influences from the advanced cultures of the south.

Influence of steppe

But Tallgren's sound analysis has knocked the bottom out of these hypotheses once and for all. Some of the animal style objects in the Anan'ino culture were simply imported from the south, either through trade or as booty. Others were produced locally, and were based upon designs borrowed from the inhabitants of the steppe lands. Certain trends repeatedly met with resistance on the part of those who adhered to local taste, and especially to local religious concepts. Griffins and 'curled animals' were very popular, whereas scenes showing animals in combat were wholly rejected. Instead local animals, such as the bear and elk, came to play a leading role. The fact that they now came to be used as decoration on combs, spinning-whorls and knives was apparently due to southern influence, as use of the animal style in the practice of magic gradually gave way to its employment from sheer delight in decoration. The treatment, however, continued to be realistic. This has rightly been regarded as a survival of the native tradition of craftsmanship.

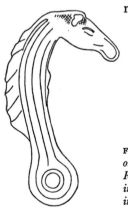

FIG. 27a, b – *Hook in the shape of a horse's head and ornamental bronze plaque in the shape of a bird of prey. Realistic and highly stylized pieces appear side by side in Anan'ino art. There is a corresponding piece to 27b in eastern Kazakhstan. Anan'ino and Zuevsk necropolises.*

As time went on, archaeologists learned to distinguish even the various routes linking this area with the steppe lands. It became clear that the Anan'ino people were in contact with Sarmatian tribes as well as with the Scythians. This certainly does not imply any ethnic kinship.

The wide trading system in the forest region, however, was presumably based upon old linguistic affinities, linked with the consolidation of the Finno-Ugric group of languages. Linguistic connection, moreover, may have contributed to the establishing of a trade-route leading eastwards through the wooded steppe zone. And it is from the forest regions of the east that those Mongoloid immigrants may have come, from whom the Anan'ino people inherited their high cheek-bones and flat noses – features which Soviet anthropologists have observed in the skulls found in the graves.

All over the wooded steppe zone at this time entrenchments were springing up that served as refuge camps. The impression given is one of the northerners forming a common front in self-defence against nomadic invaders.

FIG. 28 – *Battle-axe from Elabuga with particularly lavish decoration in animal style, which probably had some religious significance. Certainly the symbol of rank of a chieftain.*

VI. EXPANSION OF THE SARMATIANS

Herodotus mentions the 'Sauromatae' as eastern neighbours of the Scythians. They live in the regions beyond the Don, or – according to the view of the ancients – already in Asia, and appear among those who joined in alliance against the invading armies of Darius.

Amazon legend Legend has it that they sprang from a union between the young unmarried Scythian men and Amazons (Herodotus IV, 110–117). These female warriors had previously been defeated by Greek heroes, who had carried them off in their ships. But they had freed themselves, thrown their guards into the sea, and had finally landed on the shores of the Maeotis. Here they seized some horses and thenceforth lived by pillage, until our young warriors succeeded in winning the hearts of these coy beauties, and a new people came into being. But the Sauromatian women are said to have ridden to battle and to the hunt on horseback, as their maternal ancestors had done of old. Only after killing an enemy were they allowed to marry, so that some of them were obliged to remain single. The Sauromatian idiom is said to be akin to that of the Scythians, and to have been debased only by the influence of the Amazons.

In all this there is no doubt a grain of truth. The Sauromatae, in later sources referred to as Sarmatae, were an Iranian people like the Scythians. This may be clearly inferred from the names mentioned in the ancient sources, and is finally corroborated by the fact that the Ossetes (Ossetians) in the Caucasus, late descendants of this people, still speak a language belonging to the same group.

Conquest of the steppe We have already seen that the Sarmatians moved westward at the end of the fifth and beginning of the fourth centuries B.C., and that this movement occurred on an extensive scale in the third and second centuries. As a result a large part of the Pontic steppe was laid waste, and finally the Scythians could maintain their position only at the mouth of the Dnieper, in the Crimea and in Little Scythia. At the same time one can discern a tendency for the advancing bands to split up and form different tribal federations: the Iazyges were the westernmost spearhead, followed by the Rhoxolani. The Aorsi and Siraci swung round to the south-west, so that they finally penetrated into the Caucasus at various points. In the central area, however, the most powerful group was that of the Alans. During the great migrations some of the latter reached Spain and North Africa, while the remainder held out for several centuries in southern Russia. The Ossetes in particular are derived from this group. Many peoples took over the heritage of the Scythians. Parts of the Pontic

PLATE 9 – Phalera (ornamental plaque for horse's harness) from the Black Sea coast. Silver sheathed with gold plate. Approx. 2nd century B.C. *Cabinet des Médailles, Paris. Cf. p. 64.*

area were first occupied by Thracians, and later by Celtic and Germanic tribes. But the Sarmatians, who had borrowed some things from their neighbours, such as the use of the fibula in their costume, remained the dominant element until the formation of the Gothic empire. On this account they frequently came into conflict with the Romans. The Roman empire had to protect the frontier along the Danube against a Sarmatian – Germanic coalition, and at the same time to preserve the independence of the last Greek colonial cities by military strongpoints. Even in the Caucasus the 'front' had to be held, which explains why we find ample data about these constant and omnipresent enemies in the works of Roman and Greek historians, although they do not tell us very much about their conditions of life. Their economy no doubt continued to be

Social conditions   based in the main on nomadic pastoralism. As a unit of social organization, the tribe seems to have survived all the vicissitudes of history. It is possible to see how chieftains with armed followers consolidated their power and came to form a class of notables. The astonishing expansion that took place is often attributed to the possession of superior weapons: with their long sword and long spear, and with their bodies encased in armour, the Sarmatian horsemen were able to adopt shock-tactics. The affinity with the charge of the Parthian cavalry is obvious and is borne out by ancient representations, as for example in the reliefs on Trajan's Column.

Archaeological discoveries   For some time there was a tendency to ascribe to the Sarmatians all late Scythian kurgans. This was a mistake, however, and Tolstoi and Kondakov were the first to correct it. Sarmatian cemeteries in their original area east of the Don were discovered only at a remarkably late stage, after 1900.

FIG. 29 – *Small stone altar-table decorated in animal style. From Liubimovka. Width 28 cm. Cf. p. 60.*

PLATE 10 – Flask decorated in animal style from Khokhlach kurgan (so-called Novocherkassk treasure). 1st century B.C. *Original in the Hermitage, Leningrad. Photograph of an electrotype in the Victoria and Albert Museum, London. Height 9 cm. Cf. p. 63.*

The Russian scholar Gorodtsov, who was no genius but a man of wide knowledge and enormous diligence, laid the foundations that made possible Rostovtzeff's subsequent great achievements. During the late 1920s in particular, careful and well-planned excavations were carried out in cemeteries of the Volga area, with the result that on the eve of the Second World War the material from six hundred graves of this phase, situated between the Don and Volga, was ready for analysis and evaluation. Since the War field-work has continued at a vastly increased pace. The Stalingrad and Volga – Don expeditions were especially concerned with the areas due to be inundated as a result of the construction of artificial reservoirs.

In this case, too, the vast accumulation of material was used to launch a frontal attack on the position of Rostovtzeff. The latter had maintained that the Sauromatae and Sarmatae were two different peoples. The

Sauromatae he regarded as a peasant people with a matriarchal system, and the Sarmatae as a wave of Iranian nomads, who rolled in from the east and formed a dominant stratum over the Sauromatae, thus inheriting the slightly altered name. We have already mentioned the reasons why Soviet scholars reject Rostovtzeff's thesis; they go back to the ideological prejudices of the 1930s. This does not, however, detract from the fact that their views are justified by the material. Soviet scholars have succeeded in proving that an ethnic and cultural continuity existed in the Volga area and at the southern tip of the Urals from the late Bronze Age onwards. No traces of massive immigration have been found; the Sauromatae and Sarmatae must thus have been one and the same people, who came into being on the basis of the so-called timber grave and Andronovo cultures of the Bronze Age.

Nor can we say that 'matriarchal' tendencies were limited to the Sauromatian period, for in later centuries women's graves were still being equipped with weapons. In the central kurgans of some burial-grounds richly equipped women's graves were found.

FIG. 29   That the office of priest could also fall to the fair sex seems likely in view of the presence among the funerary gifts of small 'portable altars' made of stone (in the Ural region).

Rau's chronology   Much care and ingenuity have been spent in efforts to classify the funerary inventory chronologically. Paul Rau established a scheme which has remained basically valid up to the present day. What he referred to as the 'Blumenfel'd stage' (named after a Volga German village) is nowadays called the 'Sauromatian stage' and is ascribed to the period between the sixth and fourth centuries B.C. It is followed by the 'early Sarmatian' (fourth–second century B.C.), the 'middle Sarmatian' (first century B.C. – second century A.D.), and finally the 'late Sarmatian' (second–fourth century A.D.).

Through the Sauromatian area there ran a clearly-marked border. The tribes on the lower Volga were opposed to those settled south of the

FIG. 30 – *Arrow-head from Zhigo-levsk kurgans. Cf. p. 61.*

FIG. 31 – *Sword of the Sauromatian phase, lavishly decorated in animal style, from Novaia Bogdanovka. Length 42 cm. Cf. p. 61.*

Urals. In both areas, however, use of cavalry arms and harness began simultaneously; we see immediately the full equipment that was also characteristic of southern Russia. Some types are indigenous to the FIG. 30 steppes, such as arrow-heads in the shape of a small socketed spearhead, while others originated in the Near East. The adoption of the new armoury must have taken place all of a sudden at the end of the seventh or beginning of the sixth century B.C. But the connection with the Scythians must have petered out very quickly. For example, they started to use swords that were longer than those in the Pontic steppe. FIG. 31

In the 'early Sarmatian' stage the Prokhorovka culture, in the steppes south of the Urals, is one of the most vigorous centres. This area was exposed to Central Asian influences, which were presumably transmitted by groups of immigrants. The appearance of new burial rites may be linked with this. The skulls, in any case, now display greater racial variety.

Perhaps as a reaction to these centrifugal tendencies in the 'middle Sarmatian' stage, we find a surprising uniformity in arms and equipment. The pommels of the long iron swords become annular or sickle-shaped. Settlements are almost entirely non-existent – thus indicating a nomadic way of life.

In the 'late Sarmatian' phase funerary rites, too, take on a uniform character. Almost all the skulls are deformed, on account of the practice of binding up the head in early childhood. Archaeologists were struck by the fact that it was difficult to put on the helmets worn in those days. Importance is attached to the use of the complex bow, the ends of which are reinforced by oblong bone plates. This type of bow was evidently introduced by immigrants from the east. The fact of their arrival is demonstrated by craniological studies. As well as the purely Europoid type found in earlier graves – the Sarmatians were blond, as writers of antiquity relate – we now find Mongoloids with more flattened features. Once the course of events in the original Sarmatian area had been clarified, it was much easier to understand the prehistory of their colonial territories. Soviet scholars are, however, by no means content with the results hitherto obtained.

Until a few years ago there were in the entire Pontic area only two *Sarmatian graves* hundred graves that were clearly Sarmatian in character. Sometimes one finds graves typical of one area whence these people had come: for example, rectangular shafts in which the skeletons lie diagonally in an extended position. Social differentiation is more marked than was the case in their homeland. The shapes of their vessels maintain earlier Pontic traditions, which points clearly to the fact that the basic population continued to live on, in some places at least, under Sarmatian rule. More thorough examination has been given to Sarmatian expansion in the area of the Danube delta and in the basin of the Kuban'. In these

FIG. 32 – *Decorated boar's tusk, part of horse's harness. From a kurgan near the village of Blumenfel'd (Samara). The peculiar features of the Sauromatian phase are clearly apparent here. Length approx. 16 cm. Cf. p. 63.*

regions the Sarmatians went over to agriculture, built fortified villages, and displayed intense activity in the field of arts and crafts, so that they were able to supply their goods to tribes in the hinterland.

There are now signs of a Sarmatian advance to the south-east, into the depths of Central Asia. But this was not nearly so far-reaching and decisive in its consequences as was assumed by some scholars, who spoke of a 'Sarmatian phase' in the life of all peoples throughout the steppes.

Since Minns and Rostovtzeff wrote their classic works, it has become customary to contrast the Scythian variant of animal style, which is monochrome and has a strong taste for the 'Schrägschnitt'*, with a later Sarmatian phase. The latter is less concentrated in its artistic character, but makes up for this by introducing a polychrome effect, using champlevé and cloisonné. Enamel and coloured stones are combined with precious metal. Frequently we find objects in open-work, and occasionally the character is totally ornamental. In other instances we encounter realistic, but rather clumsy reliefs produced by modelling, not by carving. The sure touch in the treatment of proportion disappears.

Rostovtzeff's theory In a captivating and imaginative aperçu Rostovtzeff interpreted this later animal style and gave it its place in the general line of development. He proceeds from the fact that already in an earlier phase inlaid work in variegated colours appeared in southern Russia – at Kelermes in the early sixth century B.C. Polychrome work, he concludes, is thus a basic part of animal style, a feature adopted from Assyria or Persia. In southern Russia, of course, this element very soon gave way to Greek taste. But in the innermost parts of Asia it survived, as may be seen from the magnificent pieces in the Oxus treasure.

This animal style, with its strongly-marked Iranian features, was preserved in Central Asia, and later reached its peak at the time of Christ, as is evidenced by the gold plates in the 'treasure of Peter the Great'; it was brought to southern Russia by the Sarmatians. At this time Greek taste had already become unsure of itself and no longer offered any resistance. The political decline of the Scythians had deprived the workshops of their most faithful customers. Early Parthian influences made themselves felt. In this way polychrome work finally emerged victorious. It was combined with Hellenistic ornamental designs to produce interesting hybrid forms and retained its vigour right up to the age of the great migrations.

---

* A type of carving whereby the knife is so held as to produce curved shavings, in contrast to the normal straight cut ('Kerbschnitt').

Soviet archaeologists have no conception of similar brilliance to set against this hypothesis. They were scarcely interested in purely aesthetic developments; and a few years ago it was expressly noted that no new views on such matters had been advanced. Yet the new chronological system of the Soviet archaeologists has had certain consequences that cannot be passed over in silence. New light has also been thrown upon these matters by the excavations carried out in the Altai, about which more will be said later.

First of all it has become evident that during the Sauromatian stage the animal style is associated with the same typically Scythian types of weapon and harness as elsewhere. Here too, they form a triad. The FIGS. 32, 33 complex must have asserted itself very quickly, as early as the beginning of the sixth century B.C., at first among mounted warriors, who probably also brought its basic elements home with them from some campaign. Women's jewellery at first adheres to other principles, according to Grakov. No traces whatsoever of Greek influences are to be found here. (Nor for that matter is there any indication of polychrome work.) In the Urals one may note closer links with southern Siberian forms, whereas in the Volga area the tendency is rather to follow western lines.

In the centuries that followed this artistic creativity among the broad mass of warriors seems to have evaporated. Weapons take on an ever FIG. 34 more clearly-marked and stereotyped character suited to their purpose. Sheaths covered with gold plate (Prokhorovka, Buerova Mogila) are decorated with abstract designs.

Toward the end of the 'middle Sarmatian' period the animal style reappears, but in an entirely different context. It occurs in lavishly-equipped graves of men and women, and is concentrated in particular pieces of jewellery, such as necklaces, made of precious metal. Illustrative of these is the jewellery worked in gold from the Khokhlach kurgan, the so-called 'Novocherkassk treasure'. This contains, as well as a small flask PLATE P. 59 and several cases, some magnificent diadems, one of which is embellished with Hellenistic cameos; it is crowned by stags exactly in the ancient Scythian manner, arranged between quite untypical trees.

This late animal style is combined with polychrome work. But it is only one tendency among many others. Small plaques sewn on to clothing

FIG. 33 – *The monumental simplicity of the proto-Scythian animal style is still more evident in this bone spoon from Biche-Oba, near Orenburg. Greek influence is entirely lacking here. Length 12 cm. Cf. above.*

63

are now purely geometrical in form. Some objects exhibit that rather ponderous realism that must serve to express so much static dignity in Sassanid art.

Rostovtzeff has no doubt over-emphasized the importance of the animal style in this complex pattern of artistic tendencies. This was why he was also so ready to regard as genuine the gilded silver belt, studded with brightly-coloured stones, allegedly found at Maikop. The griffin ferociously seizing its prey, which drew from him enthusiastic praise, and the realistic dying horse are, however, not the work of a craftsman from the second century B.C., but were executed by an extremely skilful and astute jeweller from Odessa, who made use of the illustrations of Siberian gold plates in the magnificent work by Tolstoi and Kondakov, which he copied. At that time, in 1910 or thereabouts, the models concocted here were still being assigned to Hellenistic times. The goldsmith therefore worked in Hellenistic features, and these in turn were eagerly used by scholars as corroborative evidence for the dating they had established. Incidentally, the lead plates published by Salmony in the *ESA* came from the same doubtful source. Today we know that the artist even made use of elements of the 'style nouveau' in his creations.

In spite of this we need not dismiss as erroneous the thesis that the combination of animal style and polychrome work originated in the east. As we shall see, a combination of this kind did indeed exist continuously in Central Asia and southern Siberia. But the finest works of this kind – and these include some of the 'Siberian gold plaques' – date from an earlier phase. Only in a few remote areas was the tradition kept alive for long enough to exert an influence on the Sarmatians, and then only after it had already undergone considerable modification.

FIG. 34 – *Belt-hook from Mastiugino. This piece, from the 4th century B.C., already belongs to the period of transition leading to the early Sarmatian era. The animal style forms are modified and not particularly expressive. Cf. p. 63.*

VII. MINUSINSK BRONZES

For many years after the Cossack Ermak had broken the spell and crossed the Urals, the Russians pushed on through the forest steppes, reaching the Pacific coast within a remarkably short period of time. From this zone it was possible to exercise control over the limitless forest areas, in the depths of which natives hunted fur-bearing animals – not so much of their own accord, but in order to pay the poll tax imposed upon them. In this sparsely wooded belt, too, the Russian peasant found the best soil in Siberia and a familiar climate.

The steppe itself remained for the time being in the hands of powerful independent nomadic peoples. In the east they gradually became subordinate to the Manchu dynasty. The latter preserved them in their ancient ways, with deliberate cunning, in order to maintain a recruitment area for savage warlike barbarians who would be constantly at their disposal. In the west, however, they kept their independence well into the nineteenth century; it was only then that the Tsar decided to extend his empire to the south, partly for commercial reasons and partly, no doubt, to bring the wealth of India within his reach.

Only a small part of the steppe cut off from the rest came under Tsarist *Geographical setting* administration at an early date. This was the basin of Minusinsk – the picturesque undulating land on either side of the middle Enisei. This area is surrounded by mountain ridges covered by *taiga*, the wild trackless virgin forest of Siberia. In the south and south-east rise the peaks of the Saian range; to the west access is blocked by the Kuznetsk Alatau; only along the northern spurs of this range is there an easy route into the wooded steppe zone to the west. In the north-east, behind a barrier pierced by the Enisei, lies another island of steppe country, the smaller basin of Krasnoiarsk and Kansk.

It is here that our narrative moves to Asian soil, since this is where big excavations and intense studies began to be made – for reasons that will readily be understood.

One of the earliest linguists, Castrén, called Minusinsk a 'gigantic *Merhart's description* cemetery'. In his reminiscences of Siberia, Gero von Merhart has left us a graphic description that deserves to be quoted here:

> 'If it could be stated how many kurgans there are on each square kilometre of barren steppe, this would certainly give some idea of its appearance. But no mortal soul has as yet counted the kurgans of the Minusinsk district; and should the miraculous day ever come when an inventory can be compiled of the archaeological monuments

FIG. 35 – *Rows of stones marking burial-grounds of various dates. Abakan steppe. Cf. below.*

FIG. 35

there, it would still not tell us anything of the countless graves destroyed by peasants who have since settled in the area. Mere statistics cannot do justice to such a marvel as the grave-strewn steppe along the Enisei. Let us instead climb one of these mountains, with the mighty river rushing past the rocks below, and edelweiss shining forth from among the sparse steppe grass on its slopes; from the top we have an uninterrupted view across to the bare summit of the Borus, the next high mountain in the Saian, and beyond to the rampart of the Kuznetsk Alatau darkening in the distance and to the low undulations of the steppe to the north; let us cast our eyes over the slopes and hollows and valleys, the hills and plains that lie around and below us in strange tranquillity, motionless yet so very beautiful. Here, at our feet, we can see the first cemetery in a lonely dip high on the mountain-side we have climbed: mound after mound, in an irregular mass, each encompassed by weathered stones, with slabs – thin, but broad and tall, often of grotesque shape, depending upon the way they chanced to break; some have fallen to the ground, others are cracked and crumbling, but most of them still stand boldly, massed together in this valley of death like a petrified herd of mysterious dark red animals. We seek to bring some order into this confusion, and to count them: there are more than one hundred mounds in a single narrow space, none of them less than ten square metres in extent, and many several times as big. And down there, at the foot of the mountain, we glimpse another, and a second, and yet a third field of barrows, a short distance apart; further away, on the river-bank, is a Russian village, and then more kurgans, scattered far and wide across the plain.'

No less fantastic than the physical character of this landscape is the history of its exploration. The prelude – as was the case everywhere else in Siberia – took the form of plundering raids on the graves. This was one of the side-effects of Russian colonization, which was developed to an astonishing degree of perfection in the course of generations. The *bugrovshchiki*, as these grave-robbers were called, handed down from father to son their skill in a craft that they regarded as wholly respectable. They knew from the pattern of the stone fences on the surface, and from the size of the mounds, which of them contained rich hoards of gold. They calculated exactly in which direction the shaft had to be dug in order to strike the treasure. No wonder that at that time there was a regular market price for plundered Siberian gold.

In addition to this the ground between the graves, once brought under the plough, yielded a vast number of bronzes. Daggers, knives, axes, buttons and pendants were among the objects which peasant ploughmen brought home from the fields. They were commonly ascribed to the 'Chud', a legendary people of the past.

The second source, namely chance finds, did not even dry up after the graves containing gold had been exhausted. Over the years this source yielded the lion's share of the forty thousand known Minusinsk bronzes. This plunder would probably also have found its way into the melting-pot without further ado had not scholars in the meantime evinced interest in this wondrous land. This was thought to be the homeland of the Bronze Age culture of the Ural-Altaic family of peoples before they split up – the original centre from which they spread out over northern Eurasia. For this reason curators of museums throughout the world endeavoured to secure specimens from this abundant source of bronzes. Washington, London, Oxford, Paris, Berlin, Vienna, Budapest, Oslo, Helsinki and Stockholm all paid their roubles and obtained their share. Several years ago a fairly large store was rediscovered among the possessions of the Ethnographical Museum in Hamburg. In spite of this there was enough left over for Russian collections, particularly for those in the local museums at Minusinsk, Krasnoiarsk, Tomsk and Irkutsk.

But before being dispersed in this way these bronzes went through the hands of many small buyers and agents, who carried on a lucrative trade in them. One example may suffice. From 1879 onwards Ivan Petrovich Tovostin, a copper-smith, worked at a small village in the neighbourhood, and later in the town of Minusinsk itself. The local people – Russians as well as Tartars – frequently gave him bronze objects which they wanted to be melted down and made into samovars or small ornaments. After some time he began to buy such objects, at first on behalf of Kuznetsov, a gold-prospector (who incidentally also wrote works on archaeology). Two years later he set up on his own and undertook regular journeys to make such purchases, on which he distributed printed leaflets

Tovostin's collection

offering sensational prices. These ranged from 10 to 15 kopeks apiece. He then sold his purchases to tourists, officials and army officers, charging as much as 20 roubles for a fine specimen. Nowadays one would say that he went into the souvenir business in a big way. Then it was becoming fashionable for travellers to this remote and isolated area of steppe to bring back as a memento a dagger or a magnificent knife: they were so well-suited, when all was said and done, to serve as letter-openers on one's writing-desk. Customers were found abroad as well. The Historical Museum in Kiev alone allowed itself to be saddled with eight hundred pieces – of little value, as Tovostin remarked later. He himself eventually became infected with collector's mania. He put the unique specimens on one side and, on his retirement at a ripe old age, sold his private collection to Helsinki, where Tallgren worked on it and published it in a highly important edition, thus immortalizing Tovostin's name.

Adrianov
Parallel to these collecting activities, the results of which were incidentally also published and utilized in Russia, a very few excavations were pursued for the advancement of scholarship. The most interesting of these were carried out by Alexander Adrianov from 1887 onwards. He was still a novice in the field, as he himself writes, when, spade in one hand and an archaeological textbook in the other, he came across mummified bodies whose faces were covered with plaster masks. Decades later he was sentenced to be deported for revolutionary activity, and – apparently thanks to the understanding shown by the Tsarist judicial authorities – returned to the Minusinsk area, where he resumed his excavations. In 1918, despite his revolutionary past, he joined Kolchak's army – and was shot as a counter-revolutionary in Tomsk two years later.

Merhart
Gero von Merhart, the Austrian prehistorian who subsequently became a professor in Germany, was for good or ill fated to spend some time in this area during the First World War. To begin with, he was kept in a prisoner-of-war camp; later, when conditions eased somewhat following the overthrow of the Tsarist régime, he was given a job at the Krasnoiarsk Museum, a privilege which, with iron-willed determination, he utilized to the full, despite gnawing pangs of hunger and the lack of any kind of assistance. Indeed, he volunteered to have his release from captivity postponed for half a year. The book which he wrote, based upon his studies and excavations, bears witness to his desperate struggle to master his subject. In spite of this, neither Merhart nor Tallgren, that greatest of Finnish scholars, achieved success in systematizing the vast material chronologi-

Teploukhov's chronology
cally. This task was completed only by the Russian archaeologist Teploukhov, who applied an almost ridiculously simple criterion. He worked out a typological sequence for the characteristic surface features of the graves – stone fences and mounds. Extending from the early Copper Age until long after the birth of Christ, this system gave the key to the whole of Siberian prehistory.

But Teploukhov's work was cruelly interrupted: he disappeared in one of the great purges of the Stalin era and even today is still awaiting posthumous rehabilitation. Strangely enough, the best interpreter of his work in the West, a young American named Gaul, likewise met a tragic death, the manner of which accords well with this eventful chapter in the history of archaeological discovery. During the Second World War he was chosen on account of his linguistic talents to be parachuted into Czechoslovakia as a liaison officer, where he was taken prisoner and shot. It was not until Kiselev appeared on the scene that scholarship was again *Kiselev* carried out along normal peaceful lines. After extensive excavation work – also in the Altai and the Saian mountains – he was able in 1949 to produce a comprehensive study of the prehistory of southern Siberia. In this work he presented an unparalleled amount of material, as well as a chronology based not, as hitherto, upon the surface features of the graves, but primarily upon ceramics and metal objects. Unfortunately this study was written at a time when Soviet archaeology was obsessed with the ideas of N. Ia. Marr, and is therefore not free from schematism.

Most of the work published later – for example, the investigations carried out on the skulls found – has provided no more than a few interesting details. A book of greater consequence is that by Kyzlasov, devoted to the period about the birth of Christ. Quite recently several authors, among them Chlenova, have produced further penetrating critical studies. From these it is clear that the dating given by Kiselev is not final. Of great value is the research carried out by the anthropologist Alekseev, in which he corrects the somewhat too schematic earlier findings of Debets.

After Kiselev's work we may take it as proven that representations of animals played a part in the Minusinsk region earlier (i.e., already at the time of the Karasuk culture) than they did in any other part of the steppe **KARASUK** area.

There can be no doubt that agriculture was carried on at the time in question. This is indicated by the extensive irrigation works which may be assigned to this period. Despite this no settlements have been found. Thus our principal source of information is the burial-grounds. The dead *Burial-grounds* lie in very flat stone cists, which have naturally been plundered, sometimes beneath a small mound of earth, but in any case surrounded by a fence of stone slabs forming neat rectangular shapes, each slab being stood on end. They were buried in a stretched position and laid flat on their backs; alongside the skeletons were found bronze ornaments and small plaques sewn on to the clothing. Evidence of funerary gifts in the form of food is provided by bones of animals, and by vessels with rounded bases; presumably the knives found there were eating implements. FIG. 37

It is quite obvious that the typological inventory must have been greater than the funerary ritual suggests. The only question is the extent to which it is permissible to supplement this from the wealth of stray finds. Kiselev resolutely includes all the forms that cannot be ascribed to periods with a 'more elaborate' funerary ritual, especially if they form a link between the earlier Bronze Age and the Iron Age. There thus emerges a more or less complete picture of the weapons used, which includes picks, daggers and relatively simple arrow-heads. The most important implement was the socketed celt.

This roundabout reasoning was also used to postulate that the Karasuk people produced small animal sculptures. A further argument was that knives of exactly the same design as those found in the graves sometimes have an animal-head terminal. Only after this hypothesis had been put forward was it corroborated by a fortunate find.

The occurrence of animal motifs in ornamentation, in one at least of the late Bronze Age steppe cultures, is naturally of the greatest importance *Origin of animal* for the solution of the problems that concern us. Perhaps we are here at *style?* the very root of the animal style? The first question is to which chronological phase these small sculptures belong.

FIGS. 36–38 – *Although found in widely separated areas of Eurasia, these knives belong to the same typological group and the same chronological horizon (albeit a broad one). Cf. p. 71.*

FIG. 36 – *Large knife with handle in shape of animal's head, from An-yang.*

FIG. 37 – *Knife with handle in shape of animal's head, from a grave near Abakan. Karasuk culture, Minusinsk area. Cf. p. 69.*

FIG. 38 – *Bronze knife from Seima, central Russia. Two standing horses surmount the handle. Overall length approx. 40 cm. Cf. p. 162.*

Kiselev did not rest content with his initial statements; he took his hypothesis a stage further. By comparing almost the entire metal inventory he came to the conclusion that Karasuk was dependent upon a metallurgical centre of the first order which had come into being in northern China about the middle of the second millennium B.C. It is known to us from excavations carried out at An-yang, the later of the two capitals of the Shang dynasty (approx. fourteenth–eleventh century B.C.). Kiselev found plentiful evidence of connecting links between these two widely separated areas: the Ordos bronzes – chance finds on the northern border of China, which we shall consider later – as well as isolated bronzes in Mongolia. Since the anthropologist Debets had just declared that the skull material of the Karasuk period was Sinid and not Europoid, as had been the case in the preceding phase, Kiselev boldly assumed that migrants came from the Ordos area to Minusinsk, carrying with them a higher metallurgical tradition derived from the Shang culture. The Shang, when burying their kings, were accustomed to sacrifice a large number of prisoners-of-war captured in adjacent areas, so that the reasons for this migration are not far to seek. Moreover, the representatives of the Karasuk culture are said to have already been semi-nomads, in whose economy sheep-rearing played an important part. This would explain not only their great mobility but also the frequent use of the ram's head as an artistic motif.

Links with China

This hypothesis was already anticipated by Kühn. The Sinologist Karlgren likewise saw the consequences that would follow from it, i.e. the possibility that the entire animal style might be derived from China. The author of this volume has contributed to the spreading of this idea. Unfortunately it was a little over-simplified.

In the meantime we have discovered that most of the Karasuk types are of local origin. The so-called angulated knives, for example, are derived from the Glazkovo copper daggers (Angara – Baikal area). In the latter case, the blade was inserted into a bone handle at an obtuse angle. Such daggers belong to the first half of the second millennium. In China they occur much later, apparently introduced by borrowing.

Local types

But above all the ethnic composition of the Minusinsk population during the Karasuk period proved to be a hopelessly complex matter. We find an archaic Europoid type, well known to us from the early second millennium, but seemingly absent from the immediately preceding period. Possibly the angulated knife formed part of the equipment of these people. But the prevailing type were relatively elegant brachycephals, with a faint resemblance to Mongoloid stock. They correspond most closely to the modern Pamir-Ferghana type, which may be found among the Tadzhiks or Uzbeks of the present day. Alekseev regards this as an indication that we have to reckon with immigration from Central Asia, perhaps from the Tarim basin, but not from the Ordos region. In that area, according to

FIGS. 36–38

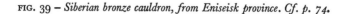
FIG. 39 – *Siberian bronze cauldron, from Eniseisk province. Cf. p. 74.*

Alekseev, during the period under discussion we must rather expect to find broad-faced Mongoloids, ancestors of the present-day Mongols or Turks.

But this again is taking things too far. We have to bear in mind that at this time peoples of Europoid type were appearing even in the Chinese borderlands. Enough remains of the supposed link between Ordos and Minusinsk to make it necessary for us to reckon with at least one ethnic component from the south-east. That such contact took place is substantiated by the stray finds that are occasionally made in central and northern Mongolia.

Kiselev, who at first rashly ascribed the Karasuk culture to the period 1300–800 B.C., accepted dates that were far too early for An-yang (sixteenth–fifteenth century B.C.) and did not take sufficient account of the relevant Chinese material. Later on the view came to prevail that borrowing took place not only during the Shang but also during the early Chou period. Now attempts are being made to subdivide Karasuk into several cultural areas and into different chronological phases. The first one may even antedate An-yang and be dependent on the unknown centre that brought metallurgy to China.

TAGAR The following culture – which Kiselev named 'Tagar' after an important site of that name – is closely related to Karasuk, e.g. in the funerary ritual, which continues to develop in an unbroken line. It seems strange, however, that at this time, the beginning of the Tagar period, a radical change should take place in the prevailing anthropological type. We find large-faced people of Europoid stock, as was the case during the Copper and early Bronze Ages. The explanation has been advanced that an ancient group of people who had been driven out or confined to the forest steppes in the south and east at the beginning of the Karasuk phase now returned from their refuges and won supremacy, fighting side by side with immigrants from central Kazakhstan, who infiltrated the area from the later part of the Karasuk period onwards. But it may be that this ancient population remained in the country throughout and merely changed over to a different form of funerary ritual of which we are unaware, such as, for example, exposure above ground. Only after replacing the upper class that temporarily held sway over them could they adopt the costly funerary rites the latter had practised. It is interesting, incidentally, that the mounds of earth were definitely thrown up

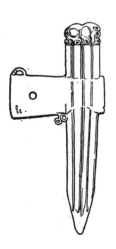

FIG. 40 – *Bronze battle-pick of ancient form, with standing animal on the neck. State Historical Museum, Moscow. Length approx. 20 cm.*

PLATE 11 – Miniature knife and scabbard. Apparently from Tagar II. *Museum für Völkerkunde, Hamburg. Approx. life-size. Cf. p. 76.*

after the stone fences had been erected. Obviously burial took place in several stages, each of which was connected with certain festivals. We shall come back to this point when we deal with Altai art.

Men were interred together with their personal jewellery and weapons. Thus we now find daggers and knives, picks, arrow-heads and yoke-shaped bronze staffs which were presumably used to reinforce bows. It is interesting to note that even women were buried not only with their jewellery, but occasionally also with weapons.

The graves did not contain parts of horses' harness, although among the stray finds we do encounter a number of snaffles which prove that here, too, we are dealing with mounted warriors. Food was prepared in huge cauldrons of cast bronze, as was the case in the Pontic area; the archetypes of these, incidentally, were derived from China, as may be deduced from the shape of the handles.

FIG. 39

Directly reminiscent of the Scythians are the pole-tops found in some men's graves, evidently those of honoured warriors. They are invariably decorated with animal sculptures. Animal motifs also occur on other objects.

Teploukhov, who worked only on the results of his own excavations, placed all these images of animals in the second and third phases of the Minusinsk kurgan culture; i.e., he assigned them to the second half of the first millennium B.C. Accordingly it was of course not difficult to ascertain their origin: they may have been adopted by all kind of roundabout ways, and for this reason in a correspondingly modified form, from the Pontic area. Kiselev, however, who was here working in a field which he had made peculiarly his own, tried to disprove this and suggested a different classification of the material.

Kiselev's classification: first phase

According to Kiselev, the variety of forms during the first phase is not very great. On the knives, which lack the well-defined articulation of the Karasuk period, the pommels have been modelled into animal heads. Sometimes they are shaped in the form of standing animals: little bears or boars, with the snouts pointing sharply downwards and the legs joined together in pairs so as to form a double arc. It is mainly on pole-tops that we find figures – at first rather ungainly – of ibexes and boars with exaggerated large muscles. The fourth main motif is that of a beast of prey, curled up in such a way as to form a complete circle. From the very beginning, the form of these objects is schematic: not only the eyes and nostrils, but also the paws are rendered as rings. This is a peculiar feature that is also found in other representations of animals. Relatively frequent are birds' heads. These sometimes appear reduced almost to a spiral-shaped curl, but sometimes consist of several elements, including a beak simplified to a volute. These representations give rise directly to those of bird-griffins.

Kiselev points out that we have here two groups of motifs of different origin. The first one – pommel in the shape of an animal head or standing animal (ibex, bear or boar) – may be derived without much difficulty from local prototypes. The second group (curled animals, heads of birds of prey, ring-shaped paws) are lacking in the Karasuk inventory. But on the other hand they appear in the earliest Scythian kurgans of southern Russia. Since Karasuk elements, such as the standing animal, in their turn occur in the Pontic area a little later, Kiselev infers from this that we have to reckon with two creative centres of the animal style: one in southern Russia and one in Siberia, which had already cross-fertilized one another at an early stage. The basis for this connection between them was that they were both in the phase of transition to nomadic cattle-breeding. Kiselev was writing at a time when Soviet scholars, under the spell of Marr, were always looking for (and finding) local roots; and therefore he simply ignored the fact that in the Pontic area there is no preliminary stage of animal style analogous to that of the Karasuk culture. As we now see, a much more plausible explanation would be that a centre hitherto unknown transmitted constituent elements of what later became the animal style on the one hand to southern Russia, where the preconditions for it did not as yet exist, and on the other to southern Siberia, where indigenous tendencies in this direction had already appeared. Perhaps the short sword, the typical weapon in both areas, may also originate in the same region?

But the idea that Siberian motifs were borrowed by southern Russia has nothing to contradict it. This route is authenticated for the pick, for the cauldron cast in bronze, and presumably also for various kinds of knife.

Influence on southern Russia

The links with Anan'ino are, however, much closer still. This may partly be explained by the existence of an ancient trade-route that ran along the edge of the forest belt, but particularly by the common interest in self-defence which the inhabitants of the forest region shared vis-à-vis the nomadic tribes of the south. They formed to some extent a defensive front – as is shown, for example, by the erection of earthworks. Those of the Minusinsk area are devoid of any deposits caused by constant human habitation, and were probably used only in time of war.

The social structure of the tribes on the northern periphery of the steppes probably changed only very gradually. Thus during the first phase of Tagar culture we do not find royal graves such as were constructed by the contemporary Scythians; the placing of weapons in women's graves may also be explained as a survival of the Bronze Age. Economic and political units were apparently still joined by consanguinity. Signs found on some bronzes are interpreted as marks of ownership. Occasionally a hoard contained several symbols of this kind. It is believed that these were stocks kept by bronze-casters who were already working for a wider market.

Second phase The next stage, which apparently lasted from the end of the fifth to the beginning of the second century B.C., brings not only pronounced social differences but also significant innovations in ritual. On the other hand, some typological series continue without interruption.

The dead are now buried collectively, in huge mounds. Their wooden chambers remained permanently accessible. Burials were carried out in them continually, apparently after the bodies had previously been exposed. Only in this way can one explain why bones were deposited after they had already been sorted – all the skulls, for example, being placed in one heap. Several skulls were found in which the facial features were modelled over in clay, producing impressive portrait masks. Instead

PLATE P. 73 of real weapons and implements, the deceased were now given miniature ones in bronze; at first these still retained the original proportions, but later this was no longer considered important.

PLATE 12 – Bronze stag with legs drawn under its body. Type I according to Chlenova's classification. First appears in the 5th cent. B.C. (Tagar II). Perhaps influenced by some Central Asian tradition, the same one that influenced early 6th-century Pontic representations. *Museum für Völkerkunde, Hamburg. Approx. life-size. Cf. p. 77.*

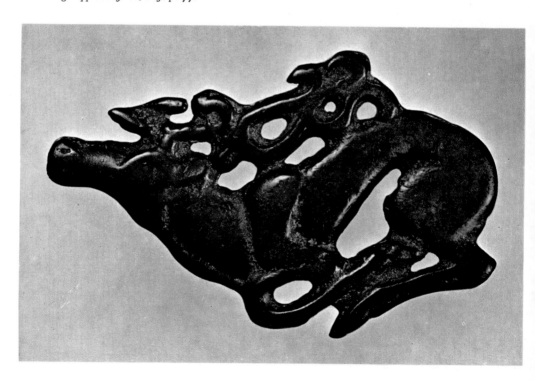

Once the chamber was filled – frequently with over one hundred dead – the interior wooden structure was set alight, turning the entire kurgan into what was in effect a charcoal-kiln. Owing to the narrow shaft, insufficient air penetrated, so that the wood which was only charred was preserved. The masks, too, escaped destruction due to this kind of accidental firing.

Grave-robbers who came across ossuaries of this kind may have helped to spread the legend related by Merhart:

'A long, long time ago, it came to pass that trees began to grow, such as nobody had ever seen before – birch-trees with white trunks. But a prophecy began to spread among the people that a white Tsar would appear whose power would be irresistible. So they decided to kill themselves rather than be overcome, built wooden houses deep into the ground, heaped up massive mounds over them, and when the time had come, hid in the graves they had erected for themselves. They set fire to the supporting beams, and the massive weight of the soil caving in on their heads parted them for ever from the sun, for only as free men did they wish to behold it.'

Only a few of these huge mounds, some of which reached a height of ten metres, were graves of individuals – obviously princes who had risen out of the mass of the people and were now able to utilize the labour of large bodies of men. In the subterranean corridors leading to the chambers there were found skeletons almost completely devoid of funerary gifts, probably those of slaves buried with their masters.

In the middle phase of the Tagar culture, too, the picture can be filled out with the aid of numerous stray finds. They belong to the same types as the miniatures, except that most of them are of iron.

The ornamentation shows that the motifs of the Karasuk period still live on, but they lose some of their realism and expressiveness. This is clearly evident from the figures of ibexes that form handles on the rim of medallion-shaped mirrors. The legacy of the Karasuk period, moreover, includes the yoke-shaped copper staffs already mentioned, now with animal-head terminals.

Alongside these, there also appear further motifs which were widespread in the 'Scythian' area, such as the stag with its legs doubled under its PLATE P. 76 body, curiously enough drawn with details such as one finds in southern Russia only at an earlier date, the beginning of the sixth century B.C. Heads of beasts of prey show the powerful exaggeration of feature so frequent in the Volga area.

Only once has a grave of this type yielded fragments of a square plaque which served as a belt-clasp. This scrap of evidence leads Kiselev to the assumption, which is nevertheless probably correct, that a large number of Siberian gold plaques developed in this very phase. We shall have to deal with this problem later, but only after we have become acquainted with all their demonstrable cultural affinities. The analogous representations noted among chance finds are not very impressive, possibly because the finest pieces were executed in precious metal and for this reason were melted down. However this may be, these plaques feature the usual scenes of animals in combat.

Kiselev does not discuss one group of knives which is decorated not with animal figures but with spiral scrolls. It must nevertheless be ascribed to the middle phase, on account of its shape, and also of the material used, namely bronze. With individual pieces it is very difficult to decide whether the decoration was abstractly conceived or whether plants served as a model. In some cases it could even be based upon a highly stylized animal body.

Strzygowski believed that this was a strongly individual development of spiral ornamentation, and accordingly referred to it as the 'geometric scroll'. Tallgren, by contrast, claimed to be able to recognize as its ultimate model the vine-scroll which had been adopted from Greek art by way of Central Asia. A tendency to use similar motifs, he maintains, may be noted in Europe during the fourth century B.C., where it had a most important effect upon Celtic art. This parallel naturally implied a certain readiness on Tallgren's part to assign the same dating to the geometrical scroll of the nomads.

All these peculiar characteristics of the second phase did not prevent Kiselev from regarding it as a direct continuation of the first, which developed locally.

Chlenova's theory Recently such radical doubts have been cast on this view that even the use of the same label appears questionable. Chlenova writes that we must reckon with immigrants into the Minusinsk basin from Central Asia at the beginning of the fifth century, who not only brought with them new weapons but also introduced certain motifs, especially that of the crouching stag – their tribal symbol. (One could supplement this by also mentioning ornamentation in the form of spirals and volutes.) Perhaps these were Saka (Sacae, Dacians) who withdrew to the north after the campaign of Darius I. In their Central Asiatic homeland (it may correspond to modern south-east Kazakhstan) they had until then preserved motifs already obsolete in the Pontic area.

This is not only a fascinating hypothesis, but one that must be taken seriously. We shall see later what help it gives us in understanding the way in which the graves were constructed.

Furthermore, this would be a splendid vindication of Teploukhov, for the 'genuine' animal style would after all appear late in the Minusinsk area and would have had curious immature forerunners.

Third phase The following period, which apparently extends from the beginning of the second century B.C. into the first century B.C., is described as the end of the Tagar culture, and is a transitional phase. It is only sparsely

PLATE 13 – Fragment of a belt-plate showing an animal grazing, and an ornamental piece whose purpose is unknown. Both objects exhibit affinities with late Ordos bronzes and belong to the latter phase of Tagar culture. *Museum für Völkerkunde, Hamburg. Life-size. Cf. Plate on p. 159.*

79

represented in the Minusinsk area proper. Its main centre is in the north, in the region around Krasnoiarsk. About this time it began to be the custom to cremate the dead *before* they were placed in the chambers of gigantic kurgans. The use of masks developed in a consistent fashion. Social differences may also be identified now in the collective graves, and iron is employed even in the production of miniatures. Animal forms are rare and can hardly be regarded as very characteristic.

TASHTYK Meanwhile in the south there follows the Tashtyk culture, which lasts into the sixth century A.D. Some scholars, especially Kyzlasov, hold the view that this, too, resulted from an invasion by a steppe people, coming from the south-east. This influx, however, has left scarcely any trace in the skull material that is now being studied, obviously because the immigrants almost without exception cremated their dead. They settled in an area east of the Enisei, where they were responsible for the 'yurt-shaped collective kurgans' found there, that is, kurgans resembling tents with rounded tops.

The original population, on the other hand, concentrated in the area west of the Enisei, where the exterior shape of their kurgans also remained unchanged, i.e. as a truncated pyramid.

Similarly, the flat graves in which individual burials had been made at the same time, evidently belonged to the autochthonous element of the population. Here, as the finds at Oglakhty show, the ancient ritual bore

FIG. 41 the strangest fruit. The dead were mummified, given masks, and finally buried together with a doll, almost as large as a man, which, if we may go by modern parallels, may have been carried about for some time by the widow to mitigate her grief. It was still the practice to include among the funerary gifts miniatures of weapons and objects in daily use.

Influence of Hsiung-nu It is no doubt correct to assume that this new invasion by steppe peoples was brought about by the foundation of the empire of the Hsiung-nu, a people whose archaeological monuments we have yet to consider. The Minusinsk region was also under the sway of this people when it was at the peak of its power. This was the time when the Hsiung-nu were waging a bitter struggle against China, which was frequently compelled to pay them large sums in tribute. A Chinese general, who had been taken prisoner, was installed as governor on the banks of the Enisei.

It is therefore not surprising that silks of Chinese origin should also have occurred in the Minusinsk region. Fragments of ceremonial sunshades show that new symbols of rank came into use as well.

As is evident from the gradual assimilation in burial rites, the immigrants
Tashtyk art fused with the ancient population to form a new ethnic unit. In their art the representation of animals continued to play a considerable role for a long time to come, and they even retained individual motifs such as the griffin's head or the standing boar.

But it is this very group of images that is devoid of any trace of realism.

Most of the figures are silhouettes without any claim to aesthetic value. Even more significant is the change in the function they fulfil. Kyzlasov sensibly interprets them as amulets. In this way an explanation can be found for the griffin's head made of an astragalus, or the crossed horses' heads which occur very frequently. A most curious small bronze bird, namely a goose with movable lower jaw, has been interpreted as an implement used in magical practices. However this may be, it is certain that representations of animals were no longer used here for ornamental purposes: they had a new and more concrete meaning.

On the other hand, Tashtyk culture produced realistic monumental sculpture. Death masks of the late period were elongated to the level of the chest, and so formed whole busts. Full-length human figures must also have been made, but of them only those parts have survived which were worked in wood, i.e. the head and hands.

But in particular there were well-proportioned statues of animals, such as horses and reindeer. They were obviously placed in the grave to serve as mounts for the dead warrior. It is extremely tempting to assume a connection with the (funerary) sculptures that formed part of the regular funerary equipment of the gentry in China during the Han period.

Religion presumably played a role in the case of the stone statues of recumbent rams. Of these we again have copies in the form of small bronzes. Other casts executed in a similar way feature recumbent does. But this interesting art probably cannot be classified under the heading of the animal style. It seems that it finally comes to perform magical functions, and artistic perfection is no longer sought after.

FIG. 41 – *Death masks of the early Tashtyk period. The one on the left, from Uibat, shows plainly the Mongoloid features of the invaders from Central Asia. Also clearly visible are traces of paint which may represent tattooing. Cf. p. 80.*

Geographical setting South-west of the steppe lands of Minusinsk, in the heart of Central Asia, lie the Altai mountains. The highest peak, Belukha, rises majestically to the height of 4503 metres. The parts of this region that belong to China and to the Mongolian People's Republic are virtually unexplored by archaeologists. But the Soviet part has over the past decades yielded finds which today form the pride of the Hermitage collection, and are the most important modern source of information on the cultural pattern of the early nomads. Why this key position should have fallen to a mountainous area, rather than to any part of the steppe, becomes more readily comprehensible when we recall what is known from history about the economic opportunities offered by the environment.

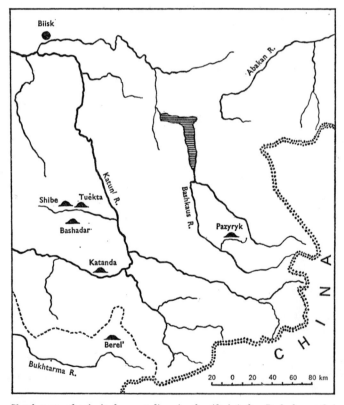

Sketch-map of principal necropolises in the Altai (after Rudenko, 1960)

It is certain that man has hunted the extremely rich stock of game in this region from time immemorial: we encounter sites dating from as early a period as the late Palaeolithic. Agriculture, which developed here from the early second millennium B.C. onwards, remained limited to the open areas north of the mountains. Even today there is much greater scope for cattle-raising. The high meadows in the heart of the mountains may be used as alpine pastures by the settled agriculturalists of the foothills, or alternatively agriculture may be dispensed with and a kind of 'vertical nomadism' may develop, such as is practised today by the Kirghiz of the Tian'-shan'.

The important point is that cattle-raisers could go to their mountain pastures only in summer. If, despite this fact, burials took place here – and it is in this very zone that we find the richest graves – they must have thought that this was actually their spiritual homeland, or at least their ultimate place of refuge. Indeed, we know that in the case of the Turks and Mongols the sanctuaries of their clans were situated in the mountains, on high pasture land, where they were able to re-unite and recover their strength after suffering reverses – as, for example, attacks by more powerful neighbours.

Proceeding now to the history of discovery and research in this area, we may first of all note that the *bugrovshchiki*, the professional grave-robbers of the early Russian colonial period, apparently did not attain their ends here. Although members of the Imperial Siberian expeditions, most of whom were Germans, discovered many archaeological monuments in this region, the bulk of the gold finds obviously come from the adjoining steppe areas to the west or from the Minusinsk district. HISTORY OF DISCOVERY

This was not only due to the inaccessibility of the Altai. This apparent freedom from pillaging, though gratifying in itself, has a sad explanation which has only recently been discovered: the largest and richest kurgans were already plundered in antiquity.

Presumably this was because there existed in the Altai a 'pluralistic' society, to use the modern sociological term. Under the rule of 'vertical nomads', agriculturalists evidently lived at the foot of the mountains and hunters (or even reindeer-breeders) higher up. No considerations of reverence or piety prevented these subjugated groups from plundering as many graves as possible whenever their nomadic masters were temporarily weakened or absent.

Thus even the splendid collection made by Florov, an engineer who was in charge of all mining in the Altai between 1793 and 1830, consists almost exclusively of objects in wood, bone and bronze. By a roundabout route these pieces found their way into the national collections, the finest ones being housed in the Hermitage. *Florov's collection*

FIG. 42

Excavations for purposes of scholarly research were carried out in 1856 under the young Wilhelm Radloff, who was employed as a teacher in *Radloff's excavations*

FIG. 42 – *Head of a tiger, in wood. Part of a horse's harness. Florov Collection, Hermitage, Leningrad. Diameter 7.5 cm. Cf. p. 83.*

Barnaul. This scholar, who came from Berlin and in the course of several decades became the Nestor of Russian Turcology, opened two huge kurgans in the high valleys of the southern Altai. Beneath the mounds he came upon shafts which had no doubt once contained rich graves but had long since been rifled. As in the Scythian graves of southern Russia, the dead had been provided with horses as funerary gifts, some of them in harness. Curiously enough, a number of objects survived, although they were made of perishable material. In the Katanda kurgan the skeletons were still lying on wooden biers placed right in the middle of the burial-chambers, which were built of tree-trunks. The articles of clothing may even today be admired in the Moscow Historical Museum. One odd feature was that they lay rolled up in a bundle concealed on top of a massive beam of the timber-work supporting the roof. Evidently a grave-robber had been prevented from coming back to collect the loot which he had hidden here.

Radloff was naturally not aware of the full significance of his finds. He did not know how they were to be classified culturally or historically (they contained interesting objects in animal style); nor did he understand the role played by the frozen ground in preserving normally perishable materials. As a consequence his discoveries were not followed by systematic excavations.

During the following decades almost all that was done was to collect surface finds, which found their way into local museums, and to inspect the numerous sites where open-cast mining had been carried on by prehistoric man. Only occasionally would some amateur or other take up his spade.

Adrianov Shortly before the First World War Adrianov, who is familiar to us from his work in the Minusinsk district, after making a number of reconnaissance journeys, extended his field of exploration to the southern valleys of the High Altai. He unearthed for the most part smallish graves that had been carefully stripped. Quite unexpectedly he then came across a stone circle in the middle of which was buried a small treasure of bronzes and gold plates with scenes depicted in the animal style. It seems possible that in this case, too, a robber had hidden part of his booty but never collected it.

In the Soviet period the picture quickly changed. Hardly had the civil war and the shootings ceased than the State Ethnographical Museum in Leningrad organized an 'Altai Expedition', which began its work in 1924. *Altai Expedition* It was led by S. I. Rudenko, who had already won his spurs in excavations in Sarmatian territory as well as in studies of Bashkir folk-lore. He distinguished himself by his devotion to the task and his talent for organization.

His most able collaborator was M. P. Griaznov, who may have been his superior in originality and circumspection. The almost inevitable consequence was that tensions arose between them, the effects of which have apparently continued to make themselves felt up to the present day, although each of these scholars can meanwhile look back upon a life's work commanding the greatest respect. Quite recently Rudenko reviewed Griaznov's preface to a volume of plates with a refreshing candour undimmed by the wisdom of advancing years, to which Griaznov reacted with youthful verve. The datings suggested by these two scholars constantly diverge, which is a little confusing for the student, but of course highly stimulating from a general point of view.

The two champions apparently suffered a common fate: they both fell victim to the purges of the Stalin era. In 1936 Griaznov was reported by Tallgren to have been among those who had been dismissed, and according to entirely unauthenticated reports Rudenko is said to have survived a number of deportations solely on account of his knowledge of surveying, which proved useful not only in archaeological excavations but also in the digging operations carried out by prisoners in the labour camps.

This situation may have some connection with the fact that the work of the 'Altai Expedition' was brought to a conclusion in 1929, although it could already look back upon tremendous successes and had every prospect of following them up with others. Two kurgans were opened in which the funeral chambers had been preserved by frost. First-class results were obtained in particular from kurgan I at Pazyryk which contained well-preserved frozen bodies of horses, which the Soviet authorities exhibited with pride at the Paris World Fair in 1936.

At that time, however, the initiative had passed to other scholars apparently less compromised by their bourgeois past. Most of them (Sergeev,

Markov, Kuznetsov, Chernikov) worked on smaller kurgans and remains of settlements in the foothills, on account of the very scanty means available to them – and also because this was necessary in order to explain the general background behind the gigantic kurgans which were apparently erected for princes.

Altai-Saian Expedition Only the Altai and Saian Expedition under Kiselev, who to some extent followed in the footsteps of Rudenko, still had the chance to investigate more extensive sites – without however ever coming across the desired 'lens of permafrost'. (This term designates the lens-shaped section of ground below the stone covering of the mound, which is permanently frozen due to the reflection of the sun's rays by the stone covering and to the penetration of icy water in springtime. Thus a deeply frozen zone is formed which excavators first had to thaw out in order to extract the objects hidden in the grave.) They did, on the other hand, find an undisturbed women's grave which the plunderers had missed.

Shortly before the Second World War the Hermitage and the Archaeological Institute of the Academy of Sciences joined forces in a campaign with which the leading scholar Sosnovsky was associated. In 1939 Griaznov made a reappearance with an extremely successful dig.

Recent excavations After the Second World War really generous funds were made available, evidently for the first time. Curiously enough, the supervision of these excavations was entrusted neither to Kiselev who, it is true, was writing a general study of southern Siberian archaeology, nor to Griaznov, whose survey of the Altai was destroyed in 1941 as a result of the war, but instead to Rudenko, who had emerged from obscurity and was given the unique chance of continuing work on the Pazyryk group. Kurgan II at Pazyryk put everything hitherto discovered in the shade, and was surpassed only by kurgan V of the same group. Rudenko repeatedly published interesting accounts of the progress of his work – for example, of the finds made in kurgan II during a single summer. During this short span of time it was only possible to melt down part of the lens of permafrost; the rest was still awaiting treatment with hot water. Strangely enough, it was this interim report that met with the greatest popularity – this, and not the completed study, was translated into German.

After concluding his excavations at Pazyryk, Rudenko, spurred on by his success, and despite occasional critical remarks by his colleagues, turned to similar chains of kurgans where the conditions of preservation were similar. Once again he was aided by good fortune in making his discoveries at Tuëkta and Bashadar. At last modern techniques of investigation could be employed: absolute or relative datings could be established on the basis of the radiocarbon method and dendrochronology (the study of tree-rings).

If Griaznov fell behind in terms of outward success at this time, he compensated for this by putting forward hypotheses that were accepted by almost everyone except Rudenko, and by excavations in the approaches to the Altai region, which yielded material of no more than average quality but did establish a sound stratigraphy.

The investigations that have been carried out for some time by Chernikov in the area west of the Altai will be dealt with elsewhere. This scholar has so far studied in detail only the material belonging to the Andronovo culture. Moreover, during the last few years older, half-forgotten excavations, such as those of Sergeev, have been analysed and published. As there is so little agreement about the dating and general evaluation of the most important Altai antiquities, it seems advisable to approach these unsolved problems with the utmost caution. We shall therefore discuss first of all the wooded steppe on the banks of the Ob', the foothills north of the Altai. This is the domain of Griaznov. Basing himself upon his own excavations and others made earlier, which he more or less saved from oblivion, Griaznov subsumed the finds dating from the period between the seventh century B.C. and the first centuries A.D. under the heading 'Bol'shaia Rechka culture'. It is the first culture in the area that contains specimens of the animal style. The population which created this culture was certainly not nomadic. There are permanent settlements, and on these sites Griaznov was able to make important stratigraphic observations. The economy was based on agriculture and cattle-raising, supplemented by fishing and hunting. In contrast to the preceding phase, the graves also yielded Mongoloid skulls; this fact is explained by immigration from adjoining forest lands.

BOL'SHAIA RECHKA

The first phase of the Bol'shaia Rechka culture already contains signs of extensive use of the horse. There are horse cheek-pieces, the shape of which suggests far-reaching links with areas as far afield as eastern Europe. Iron was not yet known in the region; the bronzes recall in their form those of the Minusinsk basin. It is interesting that some of these types show affinities with Ordos bronzes. There definitely existed very close contact with the inhabitants of the adjoining steppe areas.

First phase

FIG. 43

FIGS. 44, 45

Griaznov explains the unusually poor quality of the finds belonging to the second, or Biisk, phase (fifth–third century B.C.) as a negative consequence of this very contact. The settled inhabitants of the wooded steppe, he believes, were repeatedly attacked and robbed by their nomadic neighbours. There are indeed settlements of the period bearing traces of destruction by force. Half-buried in the condyl of one human skeleton was a bronze arrow-head of the type used by the steppe warriors. The workshop of a bronze-caster contained fragments of numerous clay moulds. For the first time the animal style decoration appears on a few objects.

Second phase

FIG. 47

Only in the last, or Berezovsk, phase (second century B.C.–first century A.D.) did the use of iron finally become predominant. A slight economic recovery is noticeable. Griaznov explains this as due to the fact that the

Third phase

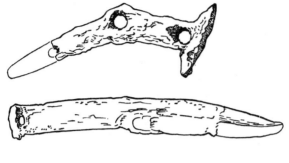

FIG. 43 – *Bronze psalion, western in form. From Griaznov's excavations near the village of Bol'shaia Rechka on the Ob'. Cf. p. 87.*

FIG. 44 – *Bronze knife, from the same site as the psalion in Fig. 43. Cf. p. 87.*

FIG. 45 – *Bronze object, probably part of the decoration of a belt. The shape is reminiscent of that of Ordos bronzes. From Bol'shaia Rechka. Cf. p. 87.*

sedentary population was at that time held to tribute by the nomads. The huge subterranean dwellings, which also served as stables, are superseded by houses above ground.

To turn now to the High Altai, we find here too in the initial phase a quantity of material limited enough to be clearly surveyed. It is evaluated by specialists with a fair degree of unanimity. The graves in which the dead are buried together with a horse in harness, but which do not as yet contain any iron, are classified as belonging to the Maiemir phase, which, like the first phase of the Bol'shaia Rechka culture, is assigned to the seventh–sixth century B.C. But in contrast to the sites in the foothills, this phase already contains objects which can without any doubt be regarded as belonging to the animal style. Since only a small part of the original funerary inventory escaped the grave-robbers, we must be content with several 'curled-up animals' (these gold plates once covered wood-carvings),

Maiemir phase

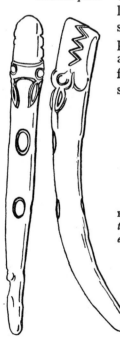

FIG. 46 – *Psalion of a later type (containing only two apertures for cheek-straps). From Griaznov's excavations on the Ob' (Biisk phase).*

FIG. 47 – *Condyl of a human bone with a Scythian-type arrow-head sticking in it, interpreted by Griaznov as evidence of the struggle between the wooded steppe people and the nomads of the south. Cf. p. 87.*

FIG. 48 – *Bronze knife from the Bukhtarma river (Altai area). The pommel shows the head and front paws of a bear (?). From the kurgans near Solonechnaia Belka excavated by Adrianov. Half life-size. Cf. below.*

a bronze knife with an animal-head terminal, and a plaque in the shape of a bird's head (to be sewn on to clothing). Therefore any stray find that can provide additional information is welcome. A round bronze mirror with a raised rim certainly belongs to this phase; the reverse shows six magnificently stylized stags. A cast bronze helmet is also worthy of note. It belongs to a type which occurs most frequently in the Kuban' area but has affinities with areas as far distant as northern China. The absence of permanent settlements dating from the same time has, of course, been taken as evidence of a nomadic way of life.

A little later, immediately after the introduction of iron, we find the earliest kurgans to have been conserved by frost. The earlier group (which may correspond roughly to the Biisk phase in the foothills of the Altai) is represented by eight huge tumuli, which have been thoroughly studied, surrounded by a fair number of medium-sized and small ones. It is impossible to give a comprehensive account of this abundance of material. But in order to avoid destroying the spell that overcame the excavators, and which even today grips visitors to the Hermitage, by premature analysis and by the dry schematization that is necessarily inherent in any survey, we shall now describe at least one kurgan in all the bewildering richness of its contents.

Kurgan II at Pazyryk belongs to a necropolis which contains five huge kurgans and a number of smaller ones arranged in two parallel rows. It is situated in the eastern Altai, at a height of approximately 1500 metres

FIG. 48
FIG. 49

FIG. 50

PAZYRYK

Pazyryk II

FIG. 49 – *Ornamental button in the shape of a bird's head. Bronze covered with gold-foil. From the so-called Maiemir steppe treasure (Altai) excavated by Adrianov. Approx. half life-size. Cf. above.*

FIG. 50 – *Reverse of a bronze mirror of archaic form. Stray find from the Altai. Hermitage, Leningrad. Approx. half life-size. Cf. above.*

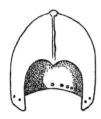

FIG. 51 – *Cast bronze helmet of early Scythian type from the Altai. Probably fashioned after a model in a different material (leather). Similar bell-shaped helmets were also worn in China. Stray find. Hermitage, Leningrad.*

in what was formerly the bed of a glacier. As already mentioned, it was opened by Rudenko in the summer of 1947 and 1948.

The mound, 36 metres in diameter and almost 4 metres high, is covered by a layer of stones. A crater-like recess in the centre bears witness to the activity of grave-robbers. A row of stones extends in a straight line to the east. Under each kurgan a central shaft was sunk which contained the actual grave. The mound under the outer layer and the uppermost part of the shaft were filled with a mixture of clay and stones. In this were found wooden shovels and wedges – tools used when the kurgan was being built; also a massive wooden disc-wheel, 30 centimetres in diameter, which may have been used for transporting the coffin.

The shaft measured 7.1 by 7.8 metres in cross-section and 4 metres in depth. At the bottom was a layer of stones, on which earth had been spread, and on top of this a platform of beams. On this stood the funerary

FIG. 52   chamber, in the form of two log huts telescoped into one another. The internal measurements of this chamber were as follows: length 3.65 metres, width 4.90 metres, height 1.50 metres. The ceilings of the inner as of the outer chamber were lined with birch-bark and brushwood; between the walls along three sides was a space two or three times the breadth of a man's hand. The weight of nine layers of beams was taken by a supporting frame consisting of poles 35 centimetres in diameter, three facing north and three south, connected by joists. By the north wall of the pit space was left for the horses that were placed in the grave as funerary gifts; these were also covered by the three topmost layers.

The inevitable grave-robbers were of course not impressed by this effort to ensure protection; they hacked their way through all the layers of beams straight down into the chamber.

Horse burial   The horses were likewise buried in the frozen ground; but since they lay less deep and to one side, their corpses may have thawed several times; for this reason they had largely decomposed and had been crushed by the layers of beams. It could, however, be ascertained that all seven animals, which were placed in a row one behind the other, lying on their left or right side, with their heads facing east, had been killed by a blow on the forehead with a pick of rhombic cross-section. The hair of their coat, in so far as it had been preserved, showed that they were all dark in colour, with their manes clipped and their tails plaited or twisted with great skill.

FIGS. 53-56   Four horses had beautifully carved wooden cheek-pieces terminating in animal heads – felid, goose, sheep and ibex – covered with tin- and gold-foil. One horse had only simple horn *psalia*, but on the other hand it

90

possessed a fine frontlet made of deer-horn. It features two heraldically arranged geese in the jaw of a beast of prey with horns and long ears. Each half is a complete composition in itself: the half-head of the beast looks as though it is in profile. This specimen has traces of yellow and red paint. Button-shaped discs of deer-horn are embellished with stylized PLATE P. 93 lotus blossoms and are likewise painted red and yellow; they were apparently placed at the intersections of straps in this set of harness.

Small wooden plaques with carved felids, likewise covered with gold-leaf, also formed part of this harness, in which the cheek-pieces (=*psalia*) terminate in heads of beasts of prey.

Two horses wore mask-like headgear of felt and leather which is un- FIG. 57 fortunately very poorly preserved. One of these apparently represented an ibex being attacked by a bird.

The saddles consisted of felt saddle-cloths and leather cushions, and were stiffened by wooden frames. Appliqué felt designs in many colours, probably worked especially for the funerary procession, made a splendid show on the saddle-cloths. We see a griffin, an elk or a scene of animals locked in combat, as for instance a leopard attacking an elk. Even the saddle-bows have leather coverings glued on, and are decorated with tin- and gold-foil. Only once do we find the saddle fitted with breast- and tail-straps. At the rear leather straps were attached, weighted down with wooden balls into which tufts of hair were inserted.

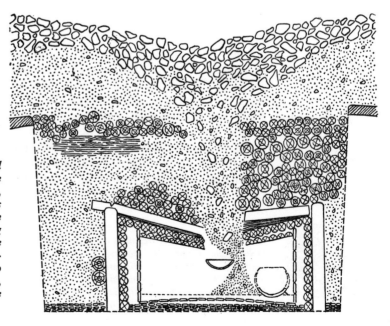

FIG. 52 – *Cross-section of mound and chamber of kurgan II, Pazyryk. We can clearly see the covering of stones, the material used for filling, the layers of beams, and the construction of the chamber. The grave-robbers who dug their way in also moved the lid of the sarcophagus to its later position. Afterwards rubble slid in. Water also trickled through, filling the chamber, and froze – so helping to conserve the non-durable material. Cf. p. 90.*

Next to the horses were placed small shields of parallel staves, exactly similar to those depicted by Greek artists from the Pontic cities when portraying Scythian equipment. One fur bag contained cheese. The

FIG. 58

particularly fine carving on a badly damaged whip-handle features a horse in flight attacked by a felid, whose body is coiled around the handle in a spiral form.

Funerary chamber

In the funerary chamber the floor was covered by a transparent layer of ice about 12 centimetres thick. It had begun to form from condensation of moisture before the grave was plundered; in the meantime delicate substances, such as foodstuffs, which had been added as funerary gifts, had decomposed. The rest of the chamber was completely filled with yellow muddy water which had poured in afterwards through the shaft made by the robbers; and this had frozen so suddenly that it stopped for all time the process of decomposition. Thus even the robbers contributed something positive to the preservation of these remains.

The floors of the chamber, and the walls up to the height of 65 centimetres, were covered with black felt. The decorative trimming of white

FIG. 59

felt, above which was a frieze of gaily-coloured lotus-blossoms, evidently appealed to the robbers all too greatly, for they stripped it off except for a few remains. The same fate befell the ornamental borders of narrow rugs.

Along the south wall stood the sarcophagus, and along the east wall eating utensils and musical instruments; opposite were the incense-burners with all their accessories; while on the north side, outside the chamber, the horses were deposited.

FIG. 60

Four small tables with oval bowl-shaped plates were used to hold meat dishes. The robbers used the plates, and when they had finally done with

FIG. 61

them destroyed them. The small legs of the tables had been inserted only loosely and in most cases remained stuck in the lowest layer of ice. One small table had legs turned on a lathe; two others were supported by

FIGS. 53–56 – *Psalia or fragments of psalia from kurgan II, Pazyryk, belonging to the four particularly splendid harnesses. The designs combine realism with bold stylization. Wood covered with metal foil. Cf. p. 90.*

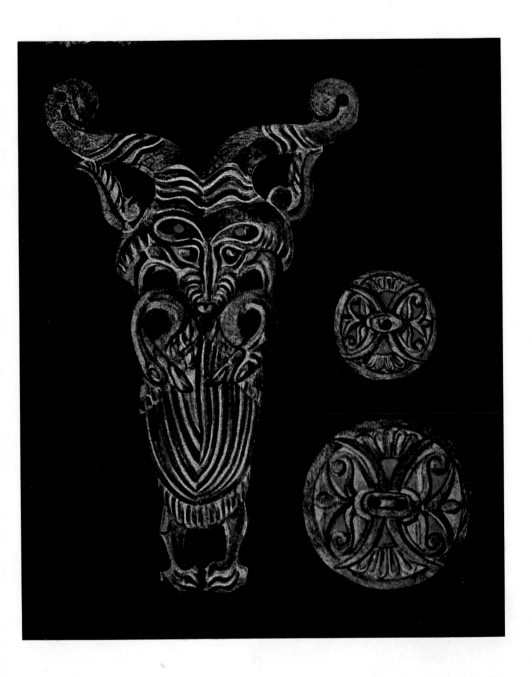

PLATE 14 – Frontlet and buttons of horse's harness. Horn, carved and painted. From kurgan II, Pazyryk. *Hermitage, Leningrad. Slightly reduced in size. Cf. p. 91.*

FIG. 57 – *Presumably only those horses which had a privileged place in the funerary procession wore a special headgear, made especially for this solemn occasion from such materials as leather, felt and metal foil. Cf. p. 91.*

FIG. 58 – *Terminal of whip-handle. Representations of horses are rare, and this one is of unusual expressive power. Cf. p. 92.*

FIG. 64

FIG. 63

FIG. 62

rampant lions of the greatest elegance. Once again we note that they were covered with tin- and gold-foil, and that parts were also painted. Immediately next to them were clay vessels and two vases of the same size and shape, half a metre in height, such as are widely disseminated in the smaller kurgans of the Pazyryk period. The curved body of one of them was embellished with appliqué leather covered with tin, featuring a frieze of striding cocks; the other had fragments of lotus silhouettes.

The same set includes wooden vessels, carved with a knife of which the blade was bent to one side. One of these looks like a scoop, with a rounded base and a rim bulging slightly outwards. The handle, bent downwards to form an obtuse angle, has a piece of horn at the end terminating in a horse's foot. The other wooden vessel has only a short vertical projection to serve as a handle. Each of these vessels with a rounded base has a circular stand of thick black felt, covered with thin felt in black or red and sewn up with woollen thread. There was even a fragment of carpet with such circles of felt worked into its surface, but in one of them there

FIG. 59 – *Decorative border with gaily-coloured trimmings in appliqué felt. The motifs are clearly Near Eastern in origin. Cf. p. 92.*

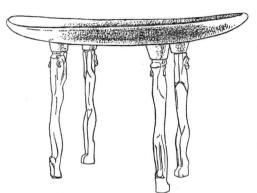

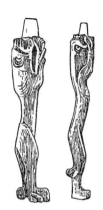

FIG. 60 – *In almost all the kurgans tables of this kind, with bowl-shaped tops, were found. They can be taken apart by pulling out the legs and thus easily transported – an indication of the nomadic life led by the Altai people. Diameter of the tops approx. 60–80 cm.; height approx. 30–35 cm. Cf. p. 92.*

FIG. 61 – *The legs of such tables, fashioned in the shape of lion figures, are also based upon Near Eastern models; they bear witness to unusual skill on the part of the carver. Cf. p. 92.*

stood, of all things, a vessel with a flat bottom. An iron knife with a flat handle decorated with gold, which was found right next to these objects, probably also formed part of the tableware; not far away lay its wooden sheath.

Rudenko assumes that the musical instruments were used in ritual, but they may have been used to play music during the meal. One of these instruments was a small drum consisting of plates of horn, in the gently curving form of an hour-glass. Over the seams are stuck gold laminae, decorated with braided ornamentation. Close by were two resonators, carved out of massive blocks of the same tree-trunk. This may have been a double instrument, a kind of lyre. The purpose of a hammer made of deer-horn remains a puzzle, since it would have been far too heavy for a drumstick.

Along the south wall stood the sarcophagus, a massive hollowed-out tree-trunk more than four metres in length. On the shorter sides it is furnished with large loops which may have been used to transport it

Sarcophagus

FIG. 62 – *Hand-carved wooden vessel resting upon a ring of felt. Cf. p. 94.*
FIG. 63 – *Wooden scoop with bone handle in shape of an animal's leg. Cf. p. 94.*
FIG. 64 – *This type of vase is characteristic of the Altai during the Pazyryk period. It probably originates from Middle Asia. Cf. p. 94.*

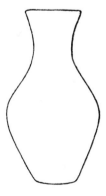

95

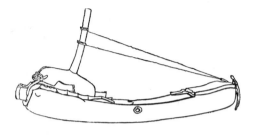

FIG. 65 – *Stringed instrument made of wood, reconstructed from surviving fragments. Length approx. 80 cm. Cf. p. 95.*

FIG. 66 (below) – *Textile design from kurgan II, Pazyryk, showing the geometric and abstract decorative systems which continued to be used in addition to the animal style.*

FIG. 67

FIG. 68

FIG. 69

or to lower it into the chamber. The front, sheathed in birch-bark, was decorated with appliqué leather showing two reindeer striding along one behind the other. The hollowed-out part was lined with a double layer of black felt; the floor was covered with a carpet.

The plunderers had torn off the lid and thrown it against the west wall of the chamber. Since the corpses of the deceased were frozen solid, the robbers were compelled to smash in the front before they could drag out the two bodies – those of a man and a woman, as we shall hear later on. In spite of this the sarcophagus still contained various other articles, possibly including some that did not actually belong there.

A wooden 'cushion' covered with leather probably served as a head-rest for one of the dead.

A leather bag with carrying-straps, stiffened at the top by a stick terminating in two lion's heads, evidently formed part of the woman's belongings, which explains the very personal contents. When it had been thawed out, a flat leather case was first revealed, consisting of a fairly large piece of leather, with a smaller one sewn on to it on three sides. The border and the sewn-on part are decorated with appliqué trimmings, a rich composition of lotus ornaments. The central panel is taken up by an S-shaped spiral. The 'inversion' so popular in the animal style is here translated to the vegetable world. Similar decoration is featured on a small leather flask. The next piece to appear was an attractive little leather container, hemispherical in shape, with a round leather disc as base. The opening at the top was closed by a convex lid. A wavy design of flames embellished the base and a pattern of trefoils the lid, on to which gold laminae were sewn. The contents comprised coriander, which in antiquity served not only as a spice but also as a remedy and for purposes of magic. It was evidently imported from the south.

Naturally, the funerary furnishings also included a mirror, which was Greek in shape. It consisted of two silver plates clamped together, of which the one in front was fitted with a handle of ox-horn. Between the bulge in the centre and that at the rim of the rear plate, worked in high relief, a network of very fine lines was incised.

96

FIG. 67 – *Leather silhouettes of reindeer, used to decorate the sarcophagus. Overall length approx. 80 cm. Cf. p. 96.*

In the case of an iron fork with diverging prongs all attempts at interpretation have so far failed, since the object can hardly have served as an eating utensil. A small pouch of hide, evidently worn around the neck on a leather strap, contained black hair which apparently belonged neither to the man nor to the woman, as well as finger-nail parings. It obviously served as an amulet.

Other articles at the bottom of the sarcophagus may have dropped out of a bag – such as, for example, the fragment of a comb made of horn. A broken ear-ring was also discovered, the companion-piece to which was later found in a fold of skin on the woman's neck. Both of these had obviously been decorated with stones of variegated colour. Beads of bone and cornelian were also found in the sarcophagus, on the floor of the chamber, and even in the passage made by the grave-robbers.

FIG. 70

Under the head-rest was a diadem. Along and on top of a narrow strip of wool covered with leather strutted a whole procession of cocks. The animals were carved in especially thick leather. From the band dangled

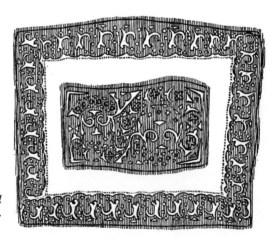

FIG. 68 – *Leather container in the shape of a 'wall bag': the piece affixed to the centre is open at the top. Cf. p. 96.*

PLATE 15 – Stag. Carved wood; antlers of leather, originally covered with metal foil. The purpose of the figure is unknown, but it may have been part of a diadem. *Hermitage, Leningrad. Height (incl. antlers) 14 cm. Cf. p. 99.*

FIG. 69 – *Reverse of a mirror with a handle; it is of the western type. It was taken as evidence for the view, now discarded, that the Pazyryk group belongs to a later Sarmatian phase. Cf. p. 96.*

FIG. 70 – *The design of this ear-ring shows affinities with similar pieces found in Peter the Great's treasure. Cf. pp. 97, 187.*

small strips of sable-skin, formerly trimmed with ornamentation. In addition to this, under the head-rest there were also some carved wooden figures, all of them covered with tin- or gold-foil. Again the wings, horns or ears were of leather. A small stag with boldly sweeping antlers is standing on a small chamfered ball; it has a peg beneath it, and must therefore have been fixed on to some surface. To judge by the leather fragments, six similar figures of stags seem to have existed. Close by lay two more griffins with short wings and huge crests, as well as the small gold-covered head of a horned lion-griffin. Rudenko assumes that all these animals formed part of a diadem, but the last piece actually formed part of a necklace.

PLATE P. 98

FIG. 72

Another curious sculpture of undetermined purpose was also found in the sarcophagus: the head of a griffin carrying in its open jaws the head of a stag. The flat sides of the sculpture are carved in relief, each side featuring a griffin holding a goose in its claws. The heads of these griffin figures, which project from the surface, were carved separately and then inserted by means of a peg. The ears and crest are cut out of thick leather; the entire work was formerly covered with gold-leaf.

FIG. 71

We meet an identical composition again outside the sarcophagus, although executed in a completely different way. A leather strap suggests that this wooden sculpture was affixed to some object. Here the stags' antlers terminate in birds' heads. Undoubtedly the curious combined motif (stag's head in a griffin's jaws) had some religious or heraldic significance.

The dead themselves were found on the floor, on the lower layer of ice: a man and a woman, whose bodies had been mutilated by the robbers,

The dead and their clothing

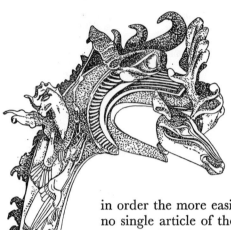

FIG. 71 – *Griffin's head in a mythical composition. This may be a standard. Height approx. 30 cm. Cf. pp. 99, 232.*

in order the more easily to remove their costly jewellery. In the process no single article of their clothing remained intact. The largest piece to have survived is from a long mantle made of squirrel-skin, with the fur on the inside. It has extremely long sleeves, so narrow that it would have been impossible to put one's arms through. It was evidently worn slung over the shoulders like the *kandys* of the Medes and Persians. On the outside it is covered with parallel seams, sewn with strong sinew, which give it both great stiffness and a design of strong individual character. Appliqué work in leather is affixed in prominent places; it represents cock's combs with small pieces of copper covered with gold inserted into them. The edges are trimmed with horse's skin.

An apron which apparently belonged to the same garment is made from identical material by the same technique. The trimming consists of pelts of otters and sables. On the other hand, we have a strip of fur decorated with leather in variegated colours and rhomb-shaped gold plates in openwork, the purpose of which remains unclear. A man's shirt of extraordinary length and width is also recorded by Rudenko; the sleeves converge to a narrow opening at the wrists. Fragments of at least three different belts were identified. They were made of fairly thin leather, but

FIG. 72 – *Reconstruction of a neck circlet. The animal figures in front are of wood covered with metal foil. This is a particularly fine specimen which can be compared only to some circlets from the Siberian gold treasure in Leningrad. Cf. p. 99.*

FIG. 73 – *Sleeve of a ceremonial cloak decorated with different materials including metal. Animal style motifs appear side by side with abstract ornamentation. Cf. p. 100.*

FIG. 74 – *Belt, elaborately decorated with sewing and metal foil. Particularly fine example of the geometric scroll employed in the Altai in an early phase. Cf. below.*

the stitching with threads of sinew was so close that they looked as though they were made of cloth. Tin-foil was used to reinforce them. The first one lacked any kind of decoration. The second one had gold-covered leather straps sewn on, which formed an elegant geometric scroll such as one finds on some Minusinsk bronzes. Compared with this, the ornamentation of the third belt gave the impression of lacking dynamism: it was adorned with appliqué work in the shape of horizontal rhombs, between which tin- and gold-plate were inserted. At the point where the straps lead off were affixed rectangular ornamental plates, cast in silver, depicting an ibex with its head turned to the rear being attacked by a lion. The animation given to the beast's body by the designs of dots and

FIG. 74

FIG. 75

FIG. 75 – *Small silver plates of this kind reinforce the belt at the spot where the straps for carrying weapons were attached. The Achaemenid legacy is clearly apparent here. Cf. above.*

FIG. 76 – *Decorative scheme on footwear (the instep is here seen from above at an oblique angle). Animal motifs are here combined with excessively lavish curvilinear ornamentation. Cf. p. 102.*

FIG. 77 – *Small ornamental plaque: two eagle-griffins contrasted with one another in heraldic fashion. Motifs have here clearly been borrowed from the Near East. Width approx. 9 cm. Cf. p. 103.*

arcs as well as by the chevron ornament that runs across the lion's neck reminded Rudenko of Assyrian reliefs.

The woman had two pairs of boots fashioned with great skill from the most varied kinds of material. Even the soles were ornamented. In one case the design is curvilinear, reminiscent of plant forms. The second pair is even more complicated. The leather soles, which in this case too were flat and unheeled, were surrounded by a double border worked in wool. Three rhombs were embroidered on the sole, the largest one beneath the ball of the foot, a smaller one beneath the heel, and a very small one in the middle. The two larger ones were further sub-divided in a network pattern. In the centre of each panel was a crystal of pyrites; there was a total of 42 such crystals on each sole. (Pyrites must have been obtained as a by-product of mining operations.) It is evident that such magnificent soles only showed to perfection when the wearer sat with her feet crossed. The uppers were embellished with embroidery and appliqué leather, worked into artistic ornamental scrolls. Across the instep ran a

FIG. 76   border trimmed with small golden aquatic birds. Still more lavish was the

FIG. 78 – *(Left) Mummified head of a woman. (Right) Mummified head of a man. In the Pazyryk period the mass of the Altai population was Europoid and belonged*

decoration of the legs, which were slit at the back, and gave the greatest prominence to the lotus motif. In addition, small glass beads were used as trimming.

Each pair of boots had socks made of felt – one in one piece, and the other with the sole let in. The seam at the back ran a little to one side of the heel, obviously to prevent rubbing.

Scattered all over the chamber were various small ornamental plaques; unfortunately it has not been established where they were affixed. Among them there stand out those in embossed copper-plate covered with gold. On one of these we see two bucks with crests, facing each other in heraldic style, and in another two eagle-griffins in the same posture. A small FIG. 77 figure of a horse, used as a pendant, was cast in bronze and then worked with a chisel. A fine realistic carving of an elk, on the other hand, was executed in leather. Next to the wall of the sarcophagus there was also found a strip of thick leather adorned with a 'procession of cocks'. Small plaques representing griffins in postures reminiscent of Assyrian art were presumably intended as ornaments for clothing. Other fragments featured bodies of animals arranged in heraldic style.

Let us now turn to the dead bodies themselves, which were preserved FIG. 78 amazingly well by mummification and freezing.

The woman was approximately forty years old, tall and strong, with delicate hands and feet, undoubtedly Europoid in type. The hair has been shaved off, possibly in connection with trepanation. The pigtail of soft wavy black hair, found elsewhere in the chamber, contained in a case, was probably hers. Apart from a fistula in one tooth there was no sign of the effects of illness, nor any trace of a violent death – although possibly women may have been poisoned before being buried with their menfolk, as was the case in the ancient East.

Radical, however, were the operations that had been performed on the *Mummification* body in connection with mummification. The scalp was folded back on

to the type represented by the lady. The man resembles a Tungus of the present day; it is assumed that he was an invader who rose to very high rank. Cf. above.

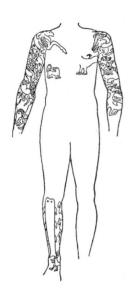

FIG. 79 – *Arrangement of tattooing on a man's body. Evidently only those parts of the body left free of clothing were treated in this way. Cf. p. 105.*

FIG. 80 – *The tattooing on the right shoulder and right arm has been particularly well preserved. The design displays amazing freedom and sureness of touch. Cf. p. 105.*

to the right parietal bone, the skull then chiselled open (the process is known as trepanation), the brain removed, and the cavity filled with some vegetable substance. The section of bone removed was then neatly inserted again and the scalp sewn up with horse-hair. A similar process was carried out on the abdomen: an incision was made from the xiphoid to the symphisis, the entrails removed and replaced by vegetable material. Thereupon it was carefully sewn up again.

Curiously enough, similar incisions ran from the buttocks to the upper part of the thigh. Here the muscular material was removed and the cavity filled with some other substance. This hardly gives the impression of having been done for purposes of mummification. Since Herodotus (IV, 26) says of the Issedones in Central Asia – a tribe perhaps identical with the Altai population and certainly its neighbour – that they devoured their dead ancestors as part of the funeral repast, it may be suspected that this is a case of endocannibalism – a communion rite carried out during the burial ceremony.

Injuries on the skull seem to have been caused by the grave-robbers having struck them with their axes. The head, hands and feet were chopped off, and even the fingers severed from the hand.

The man was about sixty years of age at the time of his death, very powerfully built, and with his broad cheek-bones typically Mongoloid in appearance. Unfortunately this mummy has not been preserved so well – quite apart from the injuries caused by the grave-robbers. But obviously he had already suffered misfortune during his lifetime. In the right parietal bone were two oval-shaped holes, and one on the left,

FIG. 82 – *Fantastic animal, displaying particular elegance of line. It also shows the characteristic inversion. Cf. below.*

FIG. 81 – *Detail of the tattoo in Fig. 80.*

evidently caused by a pick. It is not possible to tell whether these blows were mortal wounds inflicted in battle or the *coup de grâce* to put him out of his misery. As they were dealt from different directions, the first interpretation seems more likely. In any case, the old man was certainly killed on the battlefield.

After this he was scalped. An incision was made from one ear to the other and the scalp pulled off. After the body had been recovered from the enemy, the mutilation had to be covered up before burial. A false scalp was laid over the bare flesh, and this was then sewn on tightly with horse-hair.

For the rest the body was treated in a similar way to that of the woman. The skull was trepanned and the abdomen opened up to replace the viscera, which would otherwise soon have decomposed. On the thighs, it is true, there is no sign of the muscles having been removed, but there are small incisions. Perhaps these were used to saturate the body with a preserving fluid. The false beard, which was tied on to the dead warrior's shaven chin, is striking. It consisted of horse-hair and hung down from a strap like a fringe; it had been blackened so thoroughly that lumps of colouring-matter still clung to it.

Most curious of all, however, were the tattooed designs that covered the extremities, as well as parts of the chest and back. They must have been executed (using soot as material) when the man was still much younger, and in any case considerably slimmer. Unfortunately few large areas of skin are well enough preserved for the pattern to be clearly recognizable. Those parts that have been preserved best – the arms and the lower

Tattooing

FIGS. 79–82

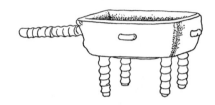

FIGS. 83–84 – *Metal vessels used for inhaling narcotics. Overall width approx. 30 cm. Cf. below.*

right leg – feature magnificent and fanciful examples of animal style. The man who worked this tattooing must have been an artist of unusual ability. He joined one composition boldly on to the next, and had a marked preference for inversion.

By the western wall of the chamber another mirror was found, as well as several figures in wood and leather and various small beads. It was made of bronze and was contained in a case of leopard-skin, decked out with small beads.

Inhaling apparatus By far the most important discovery, however, was a bronze cauldron with a narrow base and, on the sides, two handles covered with birch-bark. The vessel had a layer of black felt at the bottom and was filled to the rim with large stones, between which were seeds of a kind of wild hemp, some of them charred. As hemp contains a strong narcotic, this FIG. 83 bronze cauldron no doubt served to produce intoxicating vapours. Over it was a curious stand, consisting of six poles. From one of these a leather flask was suspended, decorated with appliqué trimmings in animal style, and in this there were more hemp seeds (*Cannabis sativa L.*, more precisely *C. ruderalis Janisch* – apparently a wild variety). Together with this cauldron and stand went a leather blanket decorated along the edge and in the central panel with winged lion-griffins pouncing upon elks; unfortunately it was badly damaged. We are dealing here with genuine inhaling apparatus.

In the corner, near where the sarcophagus stood, fragments of leather were found which bore traces of a lacquer coating, small ornamental copper plates in the form of animals facing each other in heraldic style, part of a necklet with carved griffins' heads, and a patch of leather (an amulet?) that had stitching at the corners.

FIG. 84 A small stone table with four legs, evidently used for burning sacrificial offerings, corresponds to the 'portable altars' of the Sarmatian area. In addition to this there were found various shreds of clothing and of a narrow leather belt studded with metal.

In another corner was another stand consisting of six poles covered with

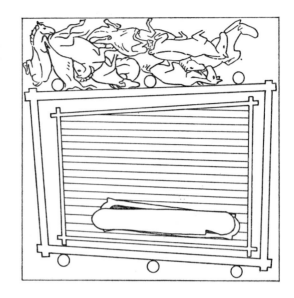

FIG. 85 – *Kurgan I, Pazyryk: view down the shaft, showing the chambers, placed inside one another, with their supporting structure, next to which are the heaped-up bodies of the horses. The sarcophagus is already open. Cf. below.*

FIG. 86 – *Decoration of horse's harness in the form of a palmette. Kurgan I, Pazyryk. Slightly reduced. Cf. p. 110.*

birch-bark, and under this a pan, square in shape, supported on four legs; it was likewise filled with stones and hemp seeds. On one of the sides it had a handle and on the other three loops by means of which it could be hung up.

It need hardly be added that these finds justified the hopes which had been cherished by scholars and collectors ever since the animal style first came to their notice; it had always been supposed that works of craftsmanship in perishable material had existed but had been irretrievably lost – yet here they were.

Kurgan I at Pazyryk, which, as already mentioned, was excavated by Griaznov and Rudenko almost twenty years earlier, has a mound even larger in diameter and on exactly the same plan. It seems to have been stripped even more thoroughly – if indeed that were possible. Thus a corpse was not found here: it was probably brought to the surface by the robbers to be examined more closely. In general it appears that they sifted their booty on the spot. In the mass of earth that afterwards slipped into the shaft they had made, all manner of fragments were found, which had apparently been cast aside as valueless. The broken-off handle of a socketed celt seems, however, to have been one of their tools and not to have belonged to those who built the kurgan.

The sarcophagus, made from a tree-trunk, was found in the chamber and is in a fair state of preservation. It was adorned with appliqué work in leather which features cocks, facing one another as though reflected in a mirror. A fragment of the hangings on the wall bears a frieze of lions' heads. To the general astonishment of the excavators, the horses offered

Pazyryk I

FIG. 85

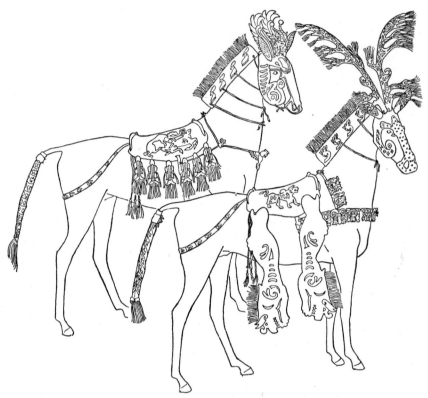

FIG. 87 – *The two animals leading the funerary procession were decorated particularly lavishly. Their saddles bore easily damaged felt appliqué worked especially for the funerary rite. The headgear is fashioned in such a way that some scholars thought the horse had been disguised as a reindeer. For this reason the headgear was also referred to as a mask, and the inference was drawn that the Altai people had once engaged in reindeer-breeding. An interpretation of this kind is no longer tenable in view of the numerous combinations of motifs on such headgear now known. Reconstruction by Griaznov. Cf. below.*

as funerary gifts proved to be untouched, although the robbers had exact knowledge of their whereabouts. They were hacking a hole in the retaining wall of the chamber when they suddenly gave up the attempt.

Horse burial Although the carcasses of the horses are deformed, owing to the pressure of the masses of earth and stone on top of them, they are nevertheless in

FIG. 87 quite a good state of preservation. There are ten geldings, which were evidently treated with elaborate care and had a long tradition of breeding behind them, although it is by no means certain that they were of foreign, southern origin, as was for a long time maintained. The frequently cited

PLATE 16 – Scenes showing animals locked in combat, in appliqué felt, used as decoration on saddle-cloths. Reconstruction. From kurgan I, Pazyryk. The designs show ibexes being attacked by a lion-griffin *(top)* and an eagle-griffin. In the upper piece the influence of the Near East is particularly noticeable. *After Suntseva. Cf. p. 110.*

108

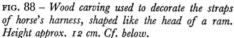

FIG. 88 – *Wood carving used to decorate the straps of horse's harness, shaped like the head of a ram. Height approx. 12 cm. Cf. below.*

FIG. 89 – *Psalion in the shape of a stag. Half life-size. Cf. below.*

FIGS. 88–89

FIG. 86

FIG. 90

PLATE P. 109

story that when the contents of their stomachs were examined, it was discovered that they had been fed on corn, has also turned out to be a legend. All ten harnesses are intact; they are of the type already familiar from kurgan II at Pazyryk. Besides these we have saddles, all of which have low bows. The decoration on them, for the most part carvings covered with gold-foil, comprises some superb works in animal style. Certain of these harnesses (the fifth and seventh) also feature a large number of abstract forms, interpreted as highly stylized plant motifs. The use of human masks as hanging ornaments is unusual. The saddles were decorated, in all probability solely for the burial ceremonies, with many-coloured appliqué work in felt. Some of these designs depict animals locked in combat, and are distinctly reminiscent of Near Eastern models. Here, too, we again encounter the cock, which is rarely depicted elsewhere in the Altai. The two finest horses have sheaths to hold their manes, and also the 'masks' with which we are already familiar, although these, it is true, are of different construction. Scholars were greatly puzzled by the fact that all the horses had incisions on their ears, such as one still finds used nowadays in Central Asia as marks of ownership. These vary from one animal to another – a point which was at first

FIG. 90 – *Wood carvings decorating a horse's harness, in the shape of human heads. Whereas the piece on the left corresponds to a western model, that on the right may represent a member of the local population. Slightly reduced. Cf. above.*

FIG. 91 – *Hood with a crenellated crown on the top. This design was no doubt introduced from the Near East, possibly from Anatolia. Cf. below.*

explained by the assumption that they had been seized as booty on different occasions.

In the material used to fill in the shaft of the grave there was discovered a yoke used for harnessing oxen and the remains of a cart. Apparently the builders were in the habit of throwing into the pit broken or superfluous implements.

Kurgan III at Pazyryk has approximately the same external measurements as kurgan II; the interior was fitted out according to the same principles, but was badly damaged despite an extensive lens of permafrost. In this case, too, the material used for filling contained the remains of a cart. The tree-trunk sarcophagus was empty, as the robbers had dragged out the body of the dead warrior. He wore a hood with a kind of crenellated crown. That the hashish rite was performed here is authenticated by the finding of fragments of a stand with six poles. Twenty-four arrowshafts were also discovered, painted with curious spiral and volute designs; the arrow-heads belonging to them are missing.

This man was honoured with a funerary gift of fourteen horses, five of which still had old-fashioned bronze bridle-bits. Of their harnesses enough has been preserved to enable one to recognize the same mixture of animal

Pazyryk III

FIG. 91

FIG. 92

Horse burial

FIG. 92 – *Painted ornaments used to decorate arrow-shafts. Cf. above.*

FIG. 93 – *Ornamental bone plaque used for a saddle-bow, showing elks' heads. Width 14 cm. Cf. p. 112.*

III

FIG. 94 – *Figure of a wolf, with characteristic inversion of its hind parts, used to decorate a horse's harness. From kurgan IV, Pazyryk. Width approx. 8 cm. Cf. below.*

style and schematized plant motifs. Fragments of 'horse masks', as well as peculiar shields composed of staves, fit into this familiar picture. It is, however, unusual that a felt jerkin should have been found with the horses. From an artistic point of view the most interesting pieces are FIG. 93 kidney-shaped wooden plaques with reliefs featuring heads of elks on a painted red ground, surrounded by bold sweeping curves, yet exhibiting a magnificent treatment of proportion.

Chinese influence is attested by the find of a piece of patterned silk as well as by the occurrence of lacquer.

Pazyryk IV Kurgan IV at Pazyryk yielded, at a normal depth beneath a much smaller mound, a chamber of the usual size. It had been crushed by the weight of rocks piled on top. In it stood two tree-trunk sarcophagi, one of which contained the skeleton of a man and the other that of a woman. Remains of the contents were scattered about the chamber: fragments of small tables, wooden head-rests, and small poles from two sets of inhaling FIG. 94 apparatus. This kurgan, too, had fourteen horses. They wore iron bits which were decorated, *inter alia*, with beautifully carved wooden psalia. Some of the decoration on the straps of the harness has survived as well, and so has a whip.

FIG. 95 – *Attempted reconstruction of a felt wall-carpet. Two fantastic animals are depicted locked in combat. The treatment of line differs from that usual in the Altai. Chinese and Middle Asian models are recognizable. The medallions on the sphinx's body may perhaps be explained as the result of Thraco-Cimmerian influence. Cf. p. 114.*

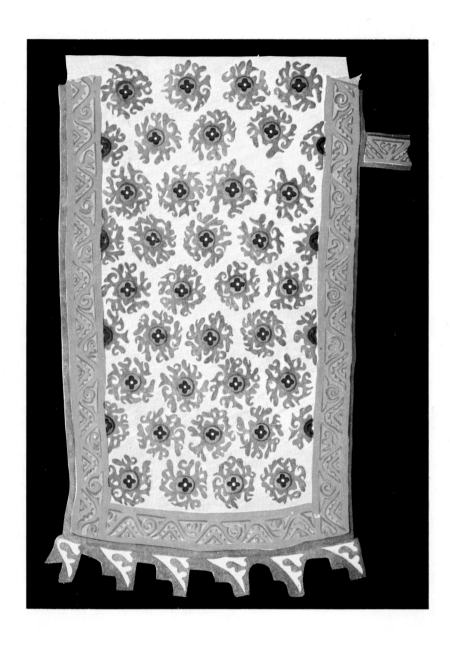

PLATE 17 – Ornament on caparison, from kurgan V, Pazyryk. Appliqué felt designs. *Hermitage, Leningrad. Cf. p. 116.*

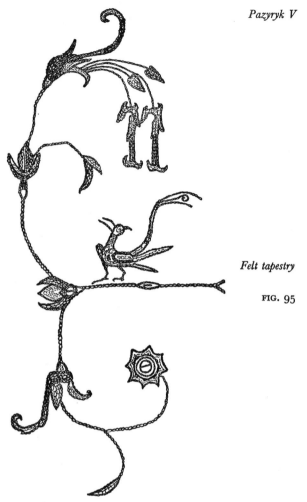

Pazyryk V Kurgan V at Pazyryk turned out to have the usual construction: it had been completely stripped, although pieces of rock weighing almost three tons had been used to fill the shaft beneath the mound. The latter had a crater-like hollow and was normal in diameter but unusual in height.

In this case the tree-trunk sarcophagus contained two corpses: those of a man and a woman. The bodies were still there, although badly battered. Traces of mummification are clearly apparent. Among the surviving contents of the chamber particular mention must be made

Felt tapestry of a fragmentary felt tapestry. When restored, it was found to show a

FIG. 95 fight between a sphinx with antlers and a fabulous bird; this can probably be traced back to Chinese models. Also astonishing is the pot-shaped headgear in wood with a pigtail pointing vertically upwards on top. The remainder of the fittings (a small drum with a skin on one side only, fragments of a stand with six poles and several small tables) can all be explained in terms of the ritual observed in kurgan II. At various sides of the chamber, i.e. buried in an unusual position, were

Horse burial nine horses with iron snaffles, whose harness showed disappointingly little imagination. Four sets are completely identical, the only ornamental motif being the segmented sphere. Two other harnesses exhibit a preference for plain lines, and only in the last three do animal style forms prevail. One horse stands out from the others by reason of its 'mask' and the sheath that contained its mane. Five of them are caparisoned in felt,

FIG. 96 – *Pheasants on a flowering twig. Silk embroidery of Chinese workmanship, used to decorate a saddle-cloth. Cf. p. 116.*

PLATE 18 – Reconstruction of the constantly recurring scene on the tapestry from kurgan V, Pazyryk. It no doubt played an important part in funerary rites, and may have belonged to the tent in which the body was deposited until the kurgan was made ready to receive it. Felt. *Hermitage, Leningrad. Size of entire carpet 4.5 × 6.5 m. Cf. p. 114.*

FIG. 97 – *Reconstruction of a four-wheeled waggon. Presumably this vehicle was built solely for the funerary ceremony, for the front axle is fixed; this would also explain why the vehicle was made so that it could be taken to pieces. It may be based on a Chinese model. Cf. below.*

PLATE P. 113

FIG. 96

FIGS. 97, 100 and one is trimmed with a fabric of Near Eastern origin – as is also its breast-strap. Another saddle-cloth is covered with white silk bearing embroidery of Chinese origin. Together with the horses there was discovered an elegant waggon with four wheels, without any metallic

FIG. 98 – *Carvings on the coffin and coffin-lid in kurgan II, Bashadar. Length of the entire coffin 3.10 m. Cf. p. 119.*

FIG. 99 – *Figure of a griffin from a medallion in the carpet shown in Plate on p. 118. Cf. below.*

FIG. 100 – *Figure of a swan made of appliqué felt intended to decorate the covering of the waggon shown in Fig. 97. The elegance of line points to a Chinese model. Cf. p. 116.*

parts. The superstructure, made of poles, had a felt cover decorated with swans in high relief. Fragments of the crown of a tent were also found, as well as a huge felt carpet. The latter is divided into two friezes, which feature the same scene several times: a horseman in front of a figure seated on a throne holding a highly stylized tree. The clothing of the persons shown is unlike that which one could reconstruct from the fragments that have survived in various kurgans. Outside the burial-chamber there also lay a knotted carpet measuring approximately 2 metres in length and 2 metres in width. It has 36 knots to each square centimetre; thus we may call it a work of medium fineness. The central panel, divided into twenty-four squares, is enclosed by two friezes, which in turn are flanked by ornamental bands. The inner frieze depicts a procession of fallow deer and the outer one horsemen, either mounted or leading their horses on foot. The innermost and outermost decorative bands consist of a row of squares containing griffins.

This brief description may suffice for the present. We shall come back to these kurgans when treating the material analytically.

After Rudenko had concluded the excavation of Pazyryk (three smaller kurgans remain to be discussed later), he turned his attention to the large kurgans at Bashadar, a necropolis situated 180 kilometres further to the west, on a tributary of the Katun. For here had been discovered an apparently undisturbed mound which immediately raised hopes of at last finding gold plates matching those of the Siberian collection.

Felt carpet

Knotted carpet
PLATE P. 118
FIG. 103

FIG. 99

BASHADAR

117

PLATE 19 – Detail of knotted carpet from kurgan V, Pazyryk. The figure of the man leading the horse clearly recalls the tribute-bearers on the reliefs at Persepolis. The figure of the horseman is probably a clumsy development of the same motif. *Hermitage, Leningrad. Size of entire carpet 1.9 × 2 m. Cf. Fig. 103.*

In spite of this the gigantic kurgan II at Bashadar (58 metres in diameter
and 2.7 metres in height) proved to have been stripped bare. The chamber, at an unusual depth about six metres below the surface, was low and of rather simple construction. It consisted merely of a single wall, built of tree-trunks of which the ends projected at the corners. Along the north wall lay fourteen horses, badly mutilated by the grave-robbers. In the chamber there originally stood two sarcophagi, one of which
contained the embalmed body of a man and the other that of a woman. The latter, which stood closer to the centre of the low-roofed chamber, had impeded the robbers in their efforts to approach the man's coffin. They had therefore pulled it half-way up into the shaft and finally thrown it back into the chamber, together with the brutally dismembered mummy of the woman. They also had to prop up the top of the sarcophagus containing the man's body.

On the woman's sarcophagus, which is in an extremely poor condition on account of the rough treatment to which it was subjected, only the lid was painted – with orange-coloured spiral designs. The man's sarcophagus, on the other hand, was lavishly carved. Its lid can easily be reconstructed despite the fact that part of it has been broken off; it depicts a procession of four tigers striding over two boars, two elks (without antlers, i.e. probably females) and three rams. On the south side of the sarcophagus are four other tigers on the march, of which only the FIG. 98
last is treading upon an elk. Perhaps this carving was not completed. It is an excellent work, in which we can distinguish specific points of difference from the prevailing tendency of animal style objects at Pazyryk. The coat of the tiger is rendered by flame-shaped lines; the bodies of the other animals are filled in with a systematic arrangement of volutes and spiral scrolls. In the chamber the robbers had torn down the felt hangings from the walls, but had hardly paid any attention to the bronze nails. Apparently they were less eager to obtain metal than was the case with robbers further to the east. It has even been observed that from one bronze object they only removed the gold-leaf, scorning the material underneath. They evinced much greater interest in fabrics and furs. In spite of this,
two different kinds of footwear can still be recognized: one is a man's boot, the foot of which has a complex pattern of incisions, and a tall leg with a mosaic of fur, in which small rectangles a few square centimetres FIG. 101
in area have been painstakingly joined together. It is reported that clothing produced by the same technique was being worn by the Huns several centuries later. The ancient account seems to have inspired Gottfried Keller, in his *Seven Legends*, to make Knight Mouse, the 'innumerable one', engage in combat with the Madonna, clad in a cloak made up of innumerable small pieces of mouse-skin.

What else has been found in the way of tiny fragments of fabric is enough to show an astonishing variety of weaving techniques. In the decoration

of leather objects we admire the spirited treatment of line. Isolated plaques of bronze and horn have also been preserved. As at Pazyryk II, fragments of a stringed instrument were found. Small tent-poles point to the existence of hashish-burning equipment. Bones of stags and sheep come from the meat dishes placed in the grave as funerary gifts. There is also some evidence of cheese. Clay vessels served to hold liquid nourishment.

Horse burial   The fourteen horses were interred with saddles and harness. The harnesses are badly damaged, but notwithstanding this considerable differences can be observed in the composition of the individual sets. Five horses still wear old-style bronze snaffles; one apparently had a 'mask' with huge ram's horns. The straps were embellished with bronze pendants sheathed in gold, which once again take the form of plant ornaments.

FIG. 102   The saddle was adorned with wooden plaques representing eagles, which were treated with splendid monumental austerity and compactness. The whip-handle shows superb carvings of animals. Huge felt hangings shaped like the heads of carnivorous animals served to decorate the saddles. In the making of one of the saddles, a fragment of carpet of unusual fineness had been used (70 knots per square centimetre). The exquisite piece from kurgan V at Pazyryk, which for a time was regarded as the oldest specimen

Knotted carpet   of knotted carpet work in the world, has thus actually lost the place of eminence it once held.

TUĖKTA   Since kurgan I at Bashadar is assigned – presumably correctly – to the following phase, this logically leads us on to the two huge kurgans at Tuėkta, in a large necropolis situated close by and containing 197 mounds, which Rudenko examined a few years later.

Tuėkta I
 FIG. 104   Tuėkta I has a mound measuring 68 metres in diameter and four metres in height, and is one of the largest specimens of its kind. In a shaft more

FIG. 102 – *Frontal view of a stylized eagle. Wood carving used to decorate a saddle-bow. Width approx. 20 cm. Cf. above.*

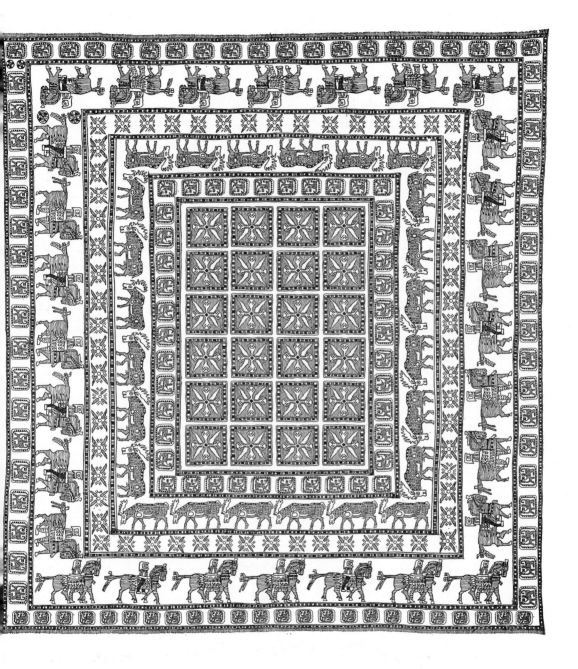

FIG. 103 – *Scheme of composition of the knotted carpet from kurgan V, Pazyryk. Note the initial markings at the bottom right-hand corner, from which it may be inferred that this carpet was used for gaming. Size of carpet 1.9 × 2 m. Cf. Plate on p. 118.*

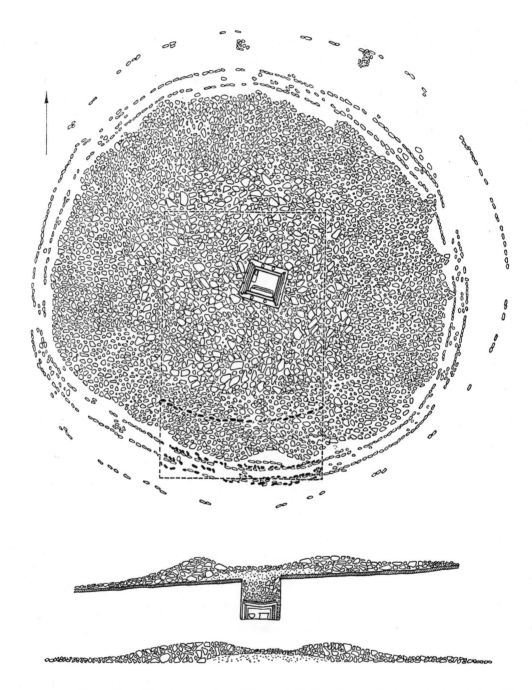

FIG. 104 – *Plan and two different cross-sections of kurgan I, Tuékta. One can clearly see the stone circles which originally marked out the burial-place and were later covered over by the mound (but only partly).Cf. p. 120.*

than seven metres deep was a spacious chamber with a double wall. Although there were no external signs that it had been tampered with, it too had been thoroughly stripped; indeed, in the material used for filling the shaft there were even discovered the 'ladders' down which the robbers had climbed. At one spot the floor of the chamber was charred: here they had lit a fire, possibly to thaw objects that had already frozen hard.

This was the grave of a man. His sarcophagus, preserved in excellent condition, was adorned with spiral designs and tiger silhouettes cut out of birch-bark. The funerary equipment was of the usual type, as is evidenced by small tables and vessels, as well as fragments of hashish-burners. Even the man's clothes can be reconstructed in broad outline. So far as weapons are concerned, there have survived arrow-shafts and the sheath of a dagger, the clamp of which is decorated in animal style, as well as fragments of an iron sword. Presumably the robbers did not take it away for the sole reason that it had been broken already before it was left in the grave.

The eight horses were without any kind of harness. But instead they had many more trappings – at least eighteen saddles and twenty snaffles were discovered between the double walls of the chamber. Evidently these were supplemented by a fairly large number of masks, for eight pairs of wooden horns of varying sizes were found which formed part of them. The saddles were decorated with silhouettes in leather and birch-bark; in both the abstract ornamentation and the pictures of animals one may observe the same love of spirals and volutes. The carvings used to decorate the harness include a frontlet of great artistic interest: it has two eagle-griffins encompassing the buckle in the middle in a magnificent sweeping curve.

One of the peculiarities of this kurgan was the presence in the chamber of an astonishingly well-preserved table almost two metres in length. It lacks any kind of decoration and bears a strong resemblance to an operating-table. For this reason it has been assumed that it was used for embalming the dead, and was disposed of by being left in the grave. On the table, however, there stood a huge bowl with short legs. In view of the fact that the chamber has been stripped, we cannot of course know whether this was the spot where it originally stood.

Kurgan II at Tuėkta is only half the size of its immediate neighbour. Since its mound at one point covers the latter, it must have been erected at a later date. It was plundered in the same mysterious way. The chamber possesses only a single wall, protected by a supporting structure of the usual massive proportions.

The tree-trunk sarcophagus, embellished with the rendering of a procession of stags, contained the body of a woman. Of the jewellery and sumptuous leather clothing she wore, only scanty fragments have survived.

Horse burial

FIG. 105

PLATE P. 124

FIG. 106

Tuėkta II

123

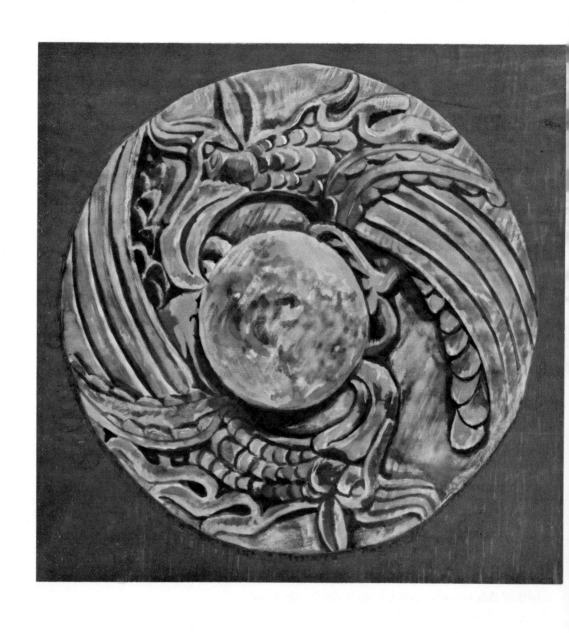

PLATE 20 – Carved frontlet from a horse's headgear from kurgan I, Tuėkta. *Hermitage, Leningrad. Diameter 12 cm. Cf. p. 123.*

124

The eight horses likewise were carefully examined and stripped by the robbers, who took almost all the gold-foil.

By comparison with these large kurgans, other graves, such as those at Aragol, are on a more modest scale and have relatively little to offer in the way of artistic interest. For their stone caps are not large enough to permit conservation by the ice. Yet they have been plundered with the same thoroughness. They are thus of particular interest only to the scholar who seeks information about the social background of the people who built the large kurgans. But even the simpler barrows which can definitely be assigned to this period required a fairly considerable amount of labour. Under a stone cap (which was actually flat) there was dug out a pit deep enough to hold a man, in which had been placed a chest, made from tree-trunks, although it often consisted merely of a single ring of beams. In this the dead man was buried, wearing clothing as lavish as possible, together with gifts of food, and in some cases also of weapons. This wooden structure was carefully covered up. The mount is deposited on the north side. Evidently this was also done with burials of women. Wherever traces of ornaments were found, these followed the same principles as in the large kurgans. There is no basic difference between them and the graves in the foothills of the Altai, which belonged to livestock-raisers (but not to the farmers who also lived there).

There are of course graves which surpass the simple standard type in the design and wealth of interior fittings. In such cases the mound is larger, the chest becomes a chamber and is located at considerable depth, and is now protected from the pressure of the masses of earth above it by layers of beams, which occasionally are supported only by dry walls. Horses are buried wearing harness.

Here mention must be made of three graves opened at Pazyryk: kurgans VI–VIII. One of these, the burial-place of a woman, yielded a broken Chinese mirror as well as remains of lacquer.

This vast material can serve as a good starting-point for a most profitable study of the various techniques of craftsmanship employed. Thus, for example, we know from the large log structures that the Altai tribes had excellent carpenters, who had mastered various forms of mortising.

Other kurgans

FIG. 107

Techniques

FIG. 105 – *Tiger with antlers. Cut-out leather silhouette for decorating a saddle. From Tuëkta I. The role of the curvilinear style is particularly marked here. Cf. p. 123.*

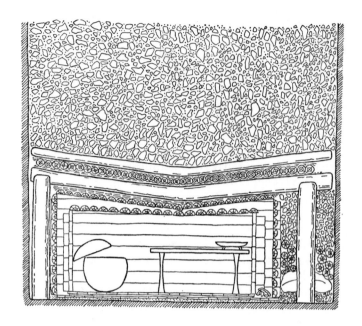

FIG. 106 – *Longitudinal section of chamber in kurgan I, Tuëkta. Cf. p. 123.*

Veritable works of art were produced with the aid of a small socketed celt that was used as an adze. Since the Russians themselves are past masters in this art, it is not surprising that Russian scholars should have investigated this field of study with particular thoroughness.

Weaving is another craft that has been comprehensively studied. The inhabitants of the Altai were masters of practically all the techniques for textile-making known today, including that of working tapestries and genuine knotted carpets.

Very frequently leather was used for purposes that may astonish us, such as the production of three-dimensional carved objects, or in combination with metal foil (gold, tin); even pottery was decorated with leather.

For the rest, we cannot expect ceramics of high quality from the inhabitants of the Altai. Some of the forms produced here may have been derived from western Turkestan.

In spite of the interest taken by the grave-robbers in metal objects, the remains that have survived suffice to show that articles worked in gold contain about 20 per cent silver. This corresponds to the composition of natural deposits in the Altai. The copper used, which had a silver content of 0.1 per cent, also comes from the same region. Only the vessels used for the hashish ritual are made of a bronze with unusual admixtures, so that these pieces can probably be identified as imported.

Economic pattern It is also possible to establish with certainty elementary data about the

FIG. 107 – *Fragment of a bronze mirror of Chinese origin. Kurgan VI, Pazyryk. Diameter 12 cm. Cf. p. 125.*

pattern of economic life. Horses and sheep must have played a predominant role. Oxen were also raised and used as draught animals. Meat and milk products are often found among the foodstuffs deposited in graves. No doubt the high-lying meadows were used as hill pastures for the cattle, which spent the winter months in the lowlands. In the valleys the people probably lived in log houses, as may be inferred from the great skill which they displayed in the working of wood. It is also certain that hunting played an important part in their economy. They had an amazingly wide range of furs, which may have been, along with gold, one of their principal exports.

It also seems beyond doubt that the 'spoils of war' played a significant part in the economy of the Altai people. For war was, so to speak, the 'national industry' of the mounted nomads of Central Asia. Not everything that we recognize as foreign, by means of stylistic analysis or by the nature of the material itself, need have originated from regular trade links. Some objects may have been obtained as booty or tribute, others brought back by men who had served as mercenaries at foreign courts. Rudenko once put forward the bold suggestion that the man interred in kurgan II at Pazyryk had served in the Achaemenid army.

The weapons are amazingly standardized, and correspond fairly closely *Weapons* to those we came across among the Pontic Scythians. As we have seen, the light shields made of small staves, such as have been found in the

127

Altai, were depicted by Greek artists. As in the Pontic steppe, here too bows and arrows were carried in a gorytus and worn on the upper thigh; the short sword corresponds to the akinakes. Only the pick may be an Asiatic speciality, although it caught on in the forests of eastern Europe and is occasionally met with even among the Scythians. The differences evident in the types of harness can easily be explained by the fact that they had to be adapted to a mountainous environment. Here breast- and tail-straps were needed, and the saddle-bows were higher.

We have no idea whether the millet found in Tuëkta I came from locally-grown crops or from tribute levied upon settled neighbours. It is also debatable how the 'vertical nomadism' of the Altai people – i.e., the use, in alternating seasons, of pastures at a higher and lower altitude – worked out in practice, and whether one should not rather speak of semi-nomadism or transhumance. Griaznov holds the view that in spring whole clans moved from their winter stations to the mountains; Rudenko is convinced that only wealthy members of the tribe who had large herds actually moved there. Rudenko uses this as the occasion for a veritable diatribe against the term 'early nomads', coined by Griaznov. 'Neither early nor nomads' is his thesis, the rights and wrongs of which we shall have to examine later.

Social structure There is agreement only on the point that private property existed on an extensive scale. This brings us to one of the fundamental problems: namely, the social order of the Altai people.

In the first place it is certain that there is no sign of an advanced state organization. It is therefore risky to draw comparisons with royal tombs in Asia Minor or China, where deified kings were laid to rest surrounded by members of their court. Even the largest kurgans are situated amidst rows of smaller mounds beneath which less important members of the clan are interred. Nor is there any basic difference between the design of 'rich' and 'poor' graves. The so-called 'chamber' develops out of the simple rectangle of beams. This explains why there is not even the suggestion of a door, and why the ceiling was often inconveniently low. (The grave-robbers might have had a thing or two to say about this.) It would therefore be wrong to draw too close parallels between these graves and the tombs conceived as 'houses for the dead' which are known to have existed in China at this time.

The large kurgans are rather the burial-places of chieftains who, together with their kin, are interred in such a way as to show that they were emerging from the broad mass of the people, their power buttressed by the wealth they acquired or inherited, and maintained by their good fortune in battle – and presumably also by their talent for organization and eloquence.

Clan organization In what way were these kinship groups organized? One naturally thinks first of clans organized on a *patriarchal* basis, although it must be borne in mind that there is clear evidence that in ancient Central Asia women enjoyed independent status and high rank. The Persian king Cyrus lost his life in a battle against a queen of the Massagetae (Massagetians). In the kurgans, in any case, women are no worse adorned than their menfolk. Like them, they could be honoured by having their mounts buried with them. It is on the whole doubtful whether the women found beside men in several kurgans were actually concubines who had been put to death and buried with them, as some believed, their imagination fired by Oriental examples of this custom. The completely equal treatment they received is an argument against this hypothesis; moreover, the practice of mummification, which is known to have existed, made it possible for persons who died at different times to be buried together.

Around the nucleus of the free clans, who interred their chieftains in the large kurgans, there may of course have gathered various kinds of dependent groups, which we shall never be able to identify (possibly *Dependent groups* because they left their dead to decompose above ground). It is in these groups that the grave-robbers are probably to be sought. Perhaps in digging for metal-bearing ore they may have gained experience which stood them in good stead in sinking the shafts into the graves. This would explain how these could sometimes reach a depth of ten metres (for the mound, too, had to be opened). Such dependent clans may also have supplied the costly furs found in the rich graves.

A striking feature is the large number of mounts deposited. Griaznov *Significance of* boldly explains these as tribute paid by the groups dependent on the *horse burials* deceased chieftains, and says that fourteen horses indicates the homage paid by fourteen clans. Since these clans were ritually grouped into two 'wings' (here, seven in each wing), as was the case with nomadic peoples of a later period, they deposited in the grave two emblems, represented by the horses' masks. Thus where, as in Pazyryk II, we encounter seven horses, we must probably regard this man as the chieftain of only one 'wing'. This would also provide a plausible explanation for the fact that in kurgan I at Pazyryk completely different incisions are found in the horses' ears. But unfortunately the hypothesis is not tenable. There is clear evidence of differences of quality among the horses, and this can hardly be reconciled with their function as gifts offered in homage. Moreover, at Pazyryk II more than one mask was found.

Proceeding from a different starting-point, Rudenko has put forward arguments which may well solve this puzzle.

We have noted that kurgan I at Tuékta was rifled in spite of the fact that *Early plundering* its stone covering remained intact. Traces of the grave-robbers were *of graves* found only in the material used for filling the shaft. They had dug their way down exactly at the spot where there were the least number of boulders to hamper them. It was here that the ladder they used was discovered. Dendrochronological analysis shows that the small trees employed for this purpose, which still had stumps of branches on them, were cut no later than the tree-trunks used for the burial-chamber. In the chamber the usual devastation was found, but at ground level all traces of plundering had been carefully removed.

In his explanation of these facts Rudenko gave evidence of his considerable abilities as an amateur detective. He assumed that the grave-robbers had the best opportunity to study the layout of the grave precisely because they had been drafted to perform the heavy work entailed in burials. Thus they were familiar with the weakest points in the shafts. Construction took place in two stages, possibly because the short summer did not allow the work to be brought to completion at once, but possibly because the clans wished to spread the number of slaughtered cattle necessary for the funerary ritual over a longer period of time. While the leading group, still mourning their chieftain, went down to the foothills with their cattle in winter, their subjects, natives of the high-lying areas, realized that the moment of opportunity had come. They thereupon proceeded to dig up what they had just buried with so much effort and ceremony.

Later the unsuspecting nomads raised the mound over the rifled grave, a task which involved shifting some six thousand cubic metres of soil. Rudenko assumes correctly that this tremendous labour was carried out, not by slaves, but by those who congregated at the site and who were *Funeral feasts* allowed to partake in the grandiose funeral feast. By way of comparison Rudenko relates almost nostalgically how he witnessed, on September 21–23, 1927, the funeral ceremony held for a wealthy Kazakh who had died on March 25 of the same year. Fifteen felt tents were used for entertaining the population; entire auls arrived to take part; four horses, six oxen and twenty-five sheep were slaughtered; and a further twenty-five sheep were offered by relatives; at every turn there were dishes piled high with meat and filled to the brim with rich steaming broth. Only the sporting contests that had previously been customary had to be omitted; for the Soviet authorities were already preparing to put an end to such reactionary high living.

Of other peoples, such as the Kafirs of the Hindukush and the Nagas of Assam, we know that the erection of massive stone monuments, the so-called megaliths, was frequently connected with funerary rites of this kind. They testify to the exuberant power of the community celebrating the feast; they perpetuate the glory of the dead man, and at the same time that of his clan, which survives him. Frequently it is believed that the ceremony will benefit the dead in the beyond, assuring them continuation of life in their proper status, or conferring upon them a greater degree of immortality.

And indeed in the culture of our kurgan-builders, too, the erection of stones seems to have played a large part. Only recently it has been noted that the kurgans are surrounded by lines of menhirs, some of them several hundred metres in length. Circles of stones are to be found not only surrounding the kurgans, but also under the mounds. Obviously they corresponded to intermediate phases in the ritual. The bones of horses found beneath mounds of stones are believed to be remains from such ceremonial banquets.

No doubt this splendid extravagance is rooted in the burning ambition of members of clans who lived side by side with one another in prosperity and proud independence. But this ambition is – so to speak – directed along paths with resting-points at regular intervals, and is not permitted to go beyond the limits of the community. When these intermediate stages are reached, the powerful man's accumulated wealth is poured into 'feasts of merit'. In this way, possessions which might lead to a chieftain forming a retinue of followers, and thus acquiring paramountcy, are put at the service of the needy.

Tribes subjected to such a powerful regulating code of honour usually apply strict rules to the conduct of war, at least among members of the same ethnic group. Heroism becomes more important than mere victory, the symbolic trophy more desirable than the destruction of the enemy.

Once again the material evidence fits the general picture. From Herodotus' account of the Pontic Scythians we heard that they performed rites in honour of warriors who had proved their worth in battle and greatly esteemed the scalp as a symbol of victory; and here in kurgan II at Pazyryk there was found the body of a man on whom this gruesome rite had been carried out.

If, however, there was a tendency toward gradated symbols of prestige, this would at once explain the practice of depositing a varying number of horses with the dead. They are an expression of the status he had attained and a sign of rank. In the funeral procession they were probably led along in pairs, with the most precious animals at the head, distinguished from the rest by a kind of decoration which we now inaccurately refer to as a mask.

It is clear that the accentuation of tangible symbols of success was the basis of the heightened desire for ornamentation. In addition to this, artistic creation was evidently held in high esteem for its own sake. Little is known about the persons responsible for the works produced in the Altai, but they can hardly have belonged to a class of foreigners such as the Greek artisans employed by the Pontic Scythians. It is much more probable that in each clan there were men who had developed particular skill in treating a special material, or possibly several materials, and had thereby acquired honour and prestige. It is helpful to bear in mind the nature of Oceanic art at the time of the great voyages of discovery. Moreover, the situation must have been similar in Europe during the Viking period, when the term 'smith' simply meant a man skilled in art of any kind. We cannot tell whether such craftsmen lived under the protection of powerful chieftains and devoted themselves wholly to their service. We may presume that many of them had at their disposal only a limited repertoire of ornamental designs, some of which they had adopted in the course of their work, while others were inherited. It may be taken as certain that a very large proportion of this work was performed by men; in this respect there is a marked difference from the practice of modern Central Asian peoples. The latter have traditional domestic handicrafts which are carried on by the womenfolk, or alternatively commercial art produced in the bazaar which is offered for sale to anyone. Only to a limited extent has anything survived comparable to what we have been discussing here – for example, among the Kirghiz tribes, who also possess a multiplicity of narrative designs.

Griaznov's analysis This social basis must presumably be given its due weight if we are to understand Griaznov's ideas about Altai art. He observed a startlingly broad spectrum of artistic genres: modelling and work in high relief, linear drawing and silhouette all come into their own and are combined in a most exciting way. Thereby materials of the most varied kind are treated in an analogous fashion, and their inherent possibilities exploited to the utmost degree. In some cases it can be said that excessive demands are made upon the material – as, for example, in the case of certain carvings in thick leather.

A genuine sculpture is most likely to be successful where a rod constitutes the basic form. This can be translated into the elongated figure of an animal – as, for example, in the case of whip-handles and small table-legs. Most of the sculptures may be seen as two plaques in relief which, when opened out so that they lie end to end in a single plane, would produce a symmetrical figure. The two principles – rod and relief – are combined where, for example, a head projects vertically from a plaque.

Reliefs are always executed in a strictly frontal manner, elegant curves being achieved by the use of the 'Schrägschnitt' previously mentioned. In spite of this one gains an impression of the utmost dynamism, since details represented as seen from the side may be curved round through an angle of 90° or 180° (see Figs. 80, 82). This is known as torsion or inversion. In each case, therefore, there is no base-line.

The other basic form seems to be the silhouette. As in relief works, there is a preference for a frontal or a strict side view. Actually, silhouettes also occur wherever several colours are employed. These are completely unrelated to the colours found in real life; nor do we find any half-tints. Griaznov further points out that elegance of composition is confined to the individual decorative object, whereas in arrangement one is aware of a certain ungainliness. Magnificent plaques thinly covered with gold and tin hang down from the straps of the harness in long rows, without any attempt at rhythm, or any noteworthy intensification. There is a complete lack of that quality of suggesting something that transcends the object itself, a feature which is so characteristic of Upper Palaeolithic art. This has been overlooked hitherto, since we have only had available small objects detached from their context.

It is all the more astonishing that in each instance the proportions are reproduced so skilfully, or else are deliberately distorted with even greater dexterity. It is this which accounts for the celebrated realism of the animal figures.

If we try to make sense of this, we could speak of a subjective art. What is considered vital is not the final result, the use to which the work is put – in the process the details being relegated to a subordinate role, but the individual object itself, as it is when it leaves the artist's hands. This corresponds to the interests of the person who commissions the work, who merely seeks to obtain merit by decking himself out with works of art as though they were trophies. One can appreciate the sense of aesthetic enjoyment felt by the modern collector: he is familiar with no more than the fragment, which was what actually counted at the time. We also observe the contrast between this and the *Machtkunst* (art designed to express secular power, to use Strzygowski's expression) of the later nomads, who obtained tremendous effects by the use of simple stereotyped basic forms.

Such is the perspicacious analysis of Griaznov, which we have had to develop further only in regard to a few isolated points; against it Rudenko can set only the familiar formulae normally employed to explain the animal style. His merit lies in the comprehensiveness with which he lists the motifs, but his findings had already been anticipated in some brief notes made by Griaznov. The motifs may be classified as follows: *Rudenko's list of motifs*

1. Simple geometrical forms, cones, spheres, etc., culminating in the twisted rod.

2. Ornamentation with spirals and volutes. The favourite figure here is the spiral, and frequently the whorl.

3. Motifs representing in a schematic way plant forms such as the blossom, palmette, lotus or geometrical scroll.

4. Schematic renderings of animal attributes, such as the ram's horn, stag's antlers, boar's tusk, or the claws of wild beasts.

5. Realistic animal scenes, or parts of them. Their range is vast. Among those authenticated are fish, birds, cervids (reindeer, stag, fallow deer and elk), as well as the antelope, wild sheep, mountain goat and wild boar; there are, however, only rare specimens of hare. We often meet wild beasts: wolf, tiger, lion and snow leopard. Among birds of prey, the most important is the eagle. Domestic animals, on the other hand, are almost completely absent; only the cock and more especially the horse are given an equal place with wild beasts.

6. There is a whole range of animal combinations, i.e., fantastic creatures some of which can be described as 'lion-griffin', 'eagle-griffin', etc.

7. Men play a very insignificant role. There are stylized human heads, a few clothed figures, and some creatures that are half human and half animal.

8. Animals in particular are put together to form larger compositions: as a frieze, arranged in heraldic fashion, or forming a circle like *yang* and *yin*. Of particular importance are the combat scenes, in most of which a wild beast is seen pouncing upon a grazing animal. Scenes in which human beings appear, on the other hand, seem to be portrayed with an entirely different sense of style.

Origin of motifs The problem which now confronts us is the nature of the development that these groups of motifs may have undergone. Where do their origins lie? In what sequence did they appear? How long did this whole development take?

A very high proportion definitely originated in other areas. It is clear that the lotus-blossom cannot have been thought up in the Altai; like the palmette, this was adopted from the Near East. Also of Near Eastern origin is the very idea of scenes depicting beasts locked in combat, as well as specific kinds of animals: lions and fallow deer, of course, are not to be found in the environs of the Altai. The cock, too, which plays such a large part in Iranian mythology, can only have come to the Altai as a symbol introduced from a foreign culture. The entire group of fabulous creatures is the product of the fertile imagination of the peoples of the Near East, even though during the process of adoption the former acquired many northern attributes, such as reindeer antlers.

Even scenes depicted upon the felt tapestry from kurgan V at Pazyryk are probably taken from southern Central Asia, if not from further afield, together with their religious associations. The best evidence of this is furnished by the fact that both the costume of the persons portrayed and the trimming of the horses' manes do not correspond to those actually observable in the Altai. In the hangings on the walls of kurgan V at Pazyryk one can furthermore detect signs of Chinese influence. To what extent this also motivates the symmetrical design of some ornamental plaques is an open question.

Chronology More difficult is the problem of the relationship between animal figures and spiral ornamentation. Those scholars who, so to speak, have remained loyal to the classical phase of research into animal style have a simple principle of classification ready to hand. For in his day Schefold stated that, as they developed, all animal motifs became ever further removed from nature and less recognizable, until they finally became transformed into ornamental designs. Since there is no doubt that volutes have the same curvature as is found in animals, it seems tempting to interpret them as ornamentalized derivations from the latter. Since at Pazyryk there are already a considerable number of such abstract patterns, these designs were assigned to a late period; the newly discovered kurgans at Tuėkta and Bashadar, which had an even greater number, must therefore be still more recent. E. Dittrich has attempted to buttress this classification by drawing comparisons with ancient China.

In spite of this the traditional view is not convincing here. If one went by its abstract designs, Bashadar II would have to be ascribed to a late period, whereas the realistic animal carvings suggest an early date. In a letter written shortly before his death Minns compared them enthusiastically with Kelermes, and even with Ziwiye. This can only be understood if one accepts the assumption that no chronological gradation is possible, and that animal style and spiral ornamentation developed side by side in the Altai from the start. Today advocates of the early dating of Bashadar II (and thus of the Tuėkta kurgans) can base their case on scientific methods of investigation which, following the American model, have been carried out on well-preserved tree-trunks in the graves. The first of these methods is dendrochronology, i.e. the comparison of sequences of rings in the cross-section of a tree-trunk. It has a good reputation, but can supply only relative dates. With the aid of this method it is possible to distinguish two principal chronological phases. The kurgans of the first phase which have been most thoroughly investigated (Bashadar II, Tuėkta I and II) are some one hundred and thirty years older than the earliest large kurgans of the second group (Pazyryk I, II); Pazyryk IV was erected seven years later, and Pazyryk III thirty years after that. Between the latter and kurgan V there is another period of eleven years, so that the mounds belonging to the second phase can be fitted into half a century. Absolute dating by means of the radiocarbon method, i.e. according to the rate of decay of radioactive carbon (C_{14}) accumulated only in living matter, suggested for Bashadar II and Tuėkta I a date of 520 B.C., and 390 B.C. in the case of Pazyryk II (expressed as mean values); in other words, once again we have a difference of one hundred and thirty years – confirmation that is almost too good to be true. Rudenko eagerly takes his stand on these dates, stating that the kurgans were indeed constructed between the sixth and fourth centuries B.C. Griaznov, on the other hand, resolutely postdates these sites by one century – which is quite justified in this case, in view of the great margin of error involved in the radio-carbon method (on the average $\pm$ 130 years). For the rest he bases his later dating upon typological affinities, e.g. with snaffles and arrow-heads from southern Russia. With rare unanimity both scholars oppose those who advocate a still later dating, and would place the most important kurgans in the period when the steppe lands were already under the dominion of the Hsiung-nu.

It is in any case certain that spiral ornamentation is of independent origin and has a long prehistory in the steppe zone. Griaznov emphasizes the fact that meander patterns were already to be found in the decoration on ceramics of the Andronovo culture at the beginning of the first

Radiocarbon dating

135

millennium B.C. In his view, this is a spiral ornamentation which was fragmented into a series of short straight lines by the tool used, the comb-toothed stamp. As a matter of fact, we have already come across it in the Altai, in the Maiemir phase. The existence in the southern steppe of a style composed of spirals and volutes is probably connected with finds made in the distant region of Seistan of button-shaped discs bearing similar designs; and perhaps even with the fact that in approximately 500 B.C. Darius had the wooden columns of a hall erected at Persepolis painted with continuous series of spiral patterns.

Imported objects In our survey we have frequently pointed out objects in which the material used could be recognized as imported. In the first place one thinks, of course, of silks. Their Chinese origin is beyond doubt and is brought out still more plainly by the stylistic characteristics of the designs. Imported goods from the area of Achaemenid culture, on the other hand, can be identified only by the subjects depicted on the textiles. Women are shown standing in prayer before a sacrificial altar, the form of which recurs on the reliefs at Persepolis as well as on cylinder seals. It is tempting to use these objects for purposes of dating, although unfortunately comparisons on the basis of the Chinese material are rendered less valuable by the fact that this is itself of fairly problematical date. (For this reason Lubo-Lesnichenko approaches the matter from the opposite direction. He takes the steppe finds as the basis of his chronology.) But the connections with the west support a dating in Achaemenid times.

It is interesting that these imported goods are unevenly distributed in time and space. The artistic influences observable in the various kurgans also differ considerably in these respects. This means first of all that the various clans which buried their dead in the high-lying valleys of the Altai were independent, and that not all of them were linked with the same foreign lands, or had the same points of contact with them. The men buried at Tuëkta and Bashadar evidently are more closely connected with the western part of Middle Asia, such as Khorezm. In the necropolis at Pazyryk this is typical only of the latest kurgan, Pazyryk V, which moreover has a sudden abundance of goods imported from China. It is as though a door had been opened to the east – perhaps as a result of some warlike events.

Ethnic composition From earlier finds it was already clear that the Altai population combined the characteristics of two great races, as is the case with many Turanian peoples of the present day. Recent investigations show that the Mongoloid element was unexpectedly strong and began to appear at an early date. It is now believed that immigration took place from the northern part of what is now Mongolia. The immigrants had ample opportunity to rise high among the aristocratic warriors of the steppe lands, who did not yet form a closed society. Indeed, the chieftain interred in kurgan II at Pazyryk looks like a Tungus. He may have been given a beard in order to make him appear more like a native dignitary. The woman buried with him is completely Europoid in type.

In spite of this, we still have no idea what kind of language was spoken in the Altai at that time. Was it an Iranian dialect? Are we dealing with a proto-Turkic idiom spoken by immigrants from the east? All possibilities are still open.

If we now seek to extract from the material substantial evidence about the religious beliefs of the population, the first point to note is that the burial rite makes it clear that the after-life was imagined to be none too different from earthly existence – with considerable differences of rank; the people hoped to influence a man's social position after death by endowing him with gifts befitting his merits. The embalming carried out on all the dead was apparently also regarded as a means of preserving their immortality. In this connection we may note that it also served a different function: the preservation of the body during the period that elapsed while the grave was being prepared.

Religious beliefs

Mummification turns out, on closer inspection, to have been a complicated operation which took greatly varying forms. In all cases an opening was made in the skull and abdominal cavity to remove the substances that decompose most rapidly. On other parts of the body incisions were made, and a liquid with preserving properties applied. Frequently entire bundles of muscular tissue were removed as well, so that in an extreme case (Pazyryk V) nothing remained but a skeleton covered with skin. In this connection one may recall the popular belief, widespread in modern Central Asia, that resurrection begins with one's skin and bones.

Other problems arise from the finding of sets of hashish-burning equipment. Was this substance used only for enjoyment? It is much more reasonable to assume that it was employed in religious ceremonies, as with the Pontic Scythians, among whom, however, it had its place in an act of collective ritual. Are we dealing here with a preliminary stage of shamanism, which later used the hypnotic trance in a highly skilful fashion, and employed it, so to speak, as a psychotherapeutic method? Presumably this was the case. Ecstasy had not yet become the prerogative of a priest, i.e. an individual with specialized religious functions, as distinct from those who wielded military or political power.

Hashish-burning

Wiesner observed a most curious phenomenon on a knotted carpet from kurgan V at Pazyryk. Along three of the border friezes he noted markings such as may be found on the boards of our dice games to indicate the starting-point. From this he inferred that they were employed in an analogous way, i.e. for playing games. But in early times the ground plan for almost any game may represent a cosmic picture; as the dice are cast, a door is opened to the irrational. For this reason it may be employed as an aid in a ritual act, especially for the purposes of prophecy.

Here it was probably also used in this way, as is also suggested by the curious and significant numerical relationship noticeable in the arrangement of the objects depicted. It is interesting that the carpet should feature fallow deer which did not exist at all in the Altai, although a few years ago this type of rather ungainly-looking deer was rediscovered in Iran not far from Persepolis, where the same animal figures in the famous reliefs. In Persepolis we also meet the motif of a rider walking beside his horse. The horse-riders on the Pazyryk carpet are but a somewhat clumsy variant of the same figure.

Deities Who were the deities whose benevolence people wished to ascertain in this way? It is thought by some that the image depicted on the felt carpet in kurgan V at Pazyryk is that of a female goddess. Since the very same figure was also found in the Pontic area, some Russian scholars hold it to be the Iranian deity known in the lands of the Medes and Persians as Anahita.

The fact that animals do not represent gods of high rank is evident from their use as ornaments. But it is possible that they symbolize certain lower-ranking supernatural powers believed to confer blessing. Corroborative evidence of this has been seen in the lavish tattooing of the man in kurgan II at Pazyryk. Griaznov holds the view that certain animals were believed to correspond to the various strata of the cosmos – the higher and lower worlds. This would open up interesting perspectives as regards both the carpet just mentioned and certain other compositions, such as the head of a stag carried in the jaws of a fantastic animal.

OTHER KURGANS In our survey we have so far left out of consideration a whole number of large kurgans: Berel' and Katanda, which gave Radloff the first inkling of the archaeological marvels hidden in the Altai, as well as Shibe and Bashadar I. These graves are regarded as of more recent date; and Griaznov has assigned them to his 'Shibinsk phase'.

Shibe The kurgan at Shibe is of considerable size, measuring 45 metres in diameter and 2 metres in height. The large shaft, seven metres deep, has at the bottom the familiar chamber with a double wall; along the north side lay fourteen horses, and above it there rose the usual structure, with thirteen layers of tree-trunks, designed to afford support and protection. Two corpses, those of a man and a child, had originally been interred in a tree-trunk sarcophagus. They had been mummified in an extremely thorough manner; most of the muscular tissue had been removed and the cavity filled instead with a vegetable substance.

In the chamber were found a number of small pieces of wood for sewing on to garments; they were covered with gold, and some were very simple in form. Remains of iron objects bore damascened work in gold. A lacquered bowl is also said to have been discovered. Among the horse burials were found objects such as *psalia* executed in animal style.

When this inventory is compared with those of the preceding phase, no real difference in ritual is observed. Especially striking are the affinities with Pazyryk V, which is probably the most recent monument of the late Pazyryk phase. Here, too, one finds embalming carried out with similar thoroughness.

A certain discrepancy occurs only in the abundance of lamellae sewn on to garments, markedly simple in form. The question is whether this suffices to justify our regarding this as a separate phase. At first sight, such a view can be explained only by reference to the history of discovery: Pazyryk I and Shibe were unearthed almost simultaneously, at the same time as Noin Ula. At that time it was tempting to regard Shibe as an intermediate link between these two extremes. For it was not yet known that Chinese imports would also be encountered in the Pazyryk group.

With other barrows, however, the differences are clearer. Berel', for *Berel', Katanda,* example, has many horses, but almost half of them lack harness. Katanda *Bashadar I* contains not a tree-trunk sarcophagus, but only wooden biers. Bashadar I has a relatively small chamber, on the south side of which a quiver was found. Mummification was carried out here in a most curious way: holes were bored into the marrow-bones, which were then filled with a fluid. Other kurgans, such as Iakonur, no longer possess a stone covering. The ceramic ware found in them varies markedly and is more elaborate. Rudenko, in this case not without reason, is prepared to designate only this latter group, where the mound consists solely of earth, as dating from a late period. The majority of archaeologists, however, follow Griaznov in his clear-cut and now well-established classification. Many smaller kurgans are ascribed to this group: Kurai, Iakonur, Karakol', Kurota. Expressed *Kurai, Iakonur,* in simple terms, the period after Pazyryk V may be characterized by *Karakol', Kurota* increasing differentiation and degradation of ritual among the different tribes. In equipping the graves, quality gives way to quantity, for example in the case of the horses. Achaemenid influence disappears, whereas Chinese imports continue to be available.

No individual artistic achievement of this late phase has been given anything like the same amount of attention as have the objects from the kurgans at Pazyryk, except perhaps the garment from the Katanda kurgan exhibited in the Historical Museum in Moscow. This is due not only to the poor quality of the publications on the subject, but also to a certain decline that occurred in the animal style which, especially in the *Decline of animal style* so-called earth kurgans, is replaced by unimaginative trimmings consisting of simpler plaques covered with gold.

The abstract decoration which occurs at Tuėkta and Bashadar II has been seen as the beginning of this decline, but this is presumably wrong. The shield-shaped plates of the late period never occur in the early kurgans. It is not necessary to derive them from spiral or volute ornaments. Wherever we find designs of whorls in the latest earth kurgans, they probably did not develop as a direct continuation of the 'early' spirals or volutes but rather as a result of Chinese influence.

The dating, which has not yet been corroborated by scientific analysis, is doubtful. Pazyryk V, built only fifty years after Pazyryk I, probably allows us to locate the beginning of the Shibinsk phase in the third century, and not in the second century B.C. as proposed by Griaznov. Whether we must assume that the period lasted into the Christian era is likewise doubtful. Rudenko has protested firmly against this.

Break in continuity The claim which I put forward in 1952, in opposition to the views of some Soviet scholars, that there was no logical continuation of this phase, has proved its validity. The next graves in the High Altai are several centuries later and at best can only be said to be a pale reflection of the former glories of the animal style. Perhaps the clans that had dominated the population of the High Altai had long since left the area; perhaps they only adopted a different kind of burial rite. In any case the further evolution of the animal style has to be examined on the basis of different material.

IX. THE HSIUNG-NU IN TRANSBAIKALIA AND NORTHERN MONGOLIA

It is most fitting to proceed directly to the area north of the Gobi desert: to Transbaikalia and northern Mongolia. This was for many years a province of Russian scholarship; only in recent times have Mongolian archaeologists emerged, trained on the Soviet pattern.

HISTORY OF DISCOVERY

Graves and other archaeological remains were described as early as the eighteenth century. In the nineteenth century several excavations were carried out by amateurs working separately and by local museums. But the main interest was naturally centred upon much more recent monuments such as those that bore the justly famous Turkic runic inscriptions. This was also true of the Orchon Expedition organized by the Imperial Russian Academy of Sciences.

The situation changed all of a sudden when Kozlov, leader of the Mongolian-Tibetan Expedition of 1924, heard of the finds that had been made already in 1912 by the engineer Ballod in the mountains of Noin Ula, north of Ulan Bator. With the support of such eminent scholars as Borovka and Teploukhov, he discovered graves of which the construction must have required an enormous expenditure of labour. At the bottom of the shafts, some of them as much as eight metres deep, were found – despite the fact that the graves had been rifled in the usual fashion – costly textiles dating approximately from the time of the birth of Christ; some of them were of Chinese and others of Western origin. The rest of the inventory, too, contained many Chinese imports. Thus at this early date the view already prevailed that these were royal graves of the Hsiung-nu, that mighty people whose battles with the Chinese are repeatedly recorded in Chinese sources of the Han era.

Kozlov

The findings of these excavations were at first published only in an extremely fragmentary form; too many members of the expedition met their end in the purges. Nevertheless the short account by Camilla Trever was at least well illustrated. Today we have a systematic work from the pen of the indefatigable S. I. Rudenko – which unfortunately has wretched illustrations.

Although the reports on these excavations are few and of poor quality, the results were sensational enough to warrant further excavations in Mongolia, although again none of the findings were published. The situation was better in the Soviet Union, where Sosnovsky investigated, as well as a cemetery, settlements of the same people that had built the large kurgans. His work was continued after his death, although once again with a fair degree of secrecy. Only the most recent researches carried

PLATE 21 – The central area of the ancient Hsiung-nu empire is today inhabited by Mongols. This people retained its empire for a long time, but then lost much of its political importance in China. The surplus population was absorbed by Buddhist monasteries. In spite of this, even in our day photographs have been taken which evoke the life led by these warrior horsemen of the steppe. They carried lassos suspended from long poles.

out in Mongolia, in which native scholars participated, have been at all adequately published, in Mongolian as well as in Russian. Nevertheless, a tolerably comprehensive picture can be gained only on the basis of the excavations carried out in Soviet territory.

In the wooded steppe south-east of Lake Baikal, especially on the Selenga, we may distinguish two distinct groups of finds. The first one, which is Bronze Age in character, consists exclusively of burial-grounds. The individual graves, which are fairly uniform in size, are marked by stone slabs and layers of stones; hence the name 'slab-grave culture'. Almost the entire inventory has been rifled. The sparse remains reveal that the weapons and implements used were similar to those of the nomadic cultures of the western steppe. Among the bronzes are some roughly shaped pieces which can with difficulty be recognized as animal sculptures. Certain types belong to an eastern tradition descended from the impressive metallurgical industry of China. Iron remains a rarity. The few skulls to have survived indicate that the builders of the 'slab graves' were Mongoloid in type, not unlike the Tungus of the present day; they were certainly related to the inhabitants of the neighbouring forest regions. No settlements are known, and the graves yielded bones of horses, cattle and sheep, so that these people are taken to have been nomads – mounted nomads, as is suggested by the fact that fragments of harness have been found. During the late period, the external marking of the graves displays greater variety. It is thought that the 'slab-grave culture' lasted from approximately 800 B.C. to the middle of the second century B.C. *'Slab-grave culture'*

It is superseded by a cultural group which is distinguished not only by a different kind of burial rite but, in particular, by a large quantity of goods imported from China; this circumstance makes it possible to assign it to the Han period. Literary sources make it clear that here, as with analogous monuments in northern Mongolia, we are dealing with archaeological vestiges of the Hsiung-nu. *Hsiung-nu*

As we know from Chinese sources, the history of the feudal states was an eventful one: from the eighth century onwards they were held together only very loosely by the power of the inefficient Chou dynasty, and in the north-west neighbouring tribes of non-Chinese stock often made trouble. Nor should the influence which they exerted in artistic matters be overlooked. Among these tribes there emerge, towards the end of the Chou dynasty, the Yüe-chih, a nomadic people obviously of western origin.

During the third century B.C. the situation changed radically. China attained political unity under the power of a short-lived dynasty, but so did the nomads of the north-west: Mao-tun founded the steppe empire of the Hsiung-nu. Later a lengthy prehistory was invented for these people who, it was claimed, were linked with earlier Chinese dynasties. Even today Soviet authors maintain that the name appears as early as the eighth century B.C., whereas the only certain fact is their sudden violent rise to power, paralleled by that of many other steppe peoples. Their actual origin is still a mystery.

At the end of the third century and the beginning of the second century B.C. the Han dynasty, which was more stable, succeeded to power in

China, but the Hsiung-nu also registered successes. They drove the Yüe-chih to the west and for some time exacted tribute from the Han. In the wars that followed, which dragged on for decades, it was the Chinese, who were better organized and had enormous reserves of manpower, who gained the upper hand. They learned military tactics from their neighbours and combined them with better strategy. Gradually the *Decline of Hsiung-nu* Hsiung-nu lost their hold over the pastures along the southern fringe of the Gobi; and even their firmly-based centre of power to the north of the desert belt was subject to enemy attack. China secured control over the Tarim basin and thus over the trade-route to the west, the famous 'silk road'. Among the nomads new groupings appeared, led by tribes whose vitality was still undiminished. Although repeatedly victorious in battle, a large part of the fairly heterogeneous population of the Hsiung-nu empire was finally driven off westwards; these migrants, it is believed, went to make up the people known in Europe as Huns, who set in motion the Great Migrations.

It was only after the decline of the second Han dynasty, which also meant the end of a strong central government in China, that the tables again began to turn. Daring groups of the Hsiung-nu people, who had now split up, gained a footing in north China, and their leaders founded Chinese dynasties.

This picture, as it is presented by Chinese historians, is modified in a curious way by archaeological finds. In Transbaikalia, and today in *Earthworks* Mongolia as well, there have been found earthworks dating from the Hsiung-nu period. They probably served them as military bases in the campaigns fought against hostile forest tribes. The one that has been examined most thoroughly was in any case destroyed by enemies and burned down shortly after it had been erected. Its inhabitants had built permanent houses, evidently on the Chinese pattern. They not only engaged in agriculture, as is indicated by finds of ploughshares, but also devoted themselves to pottery and furthermore to metal-working, which played such an important role from the military point of view. All this would be very odd for a population of mounted nomads. It is probable, however, that the inhabitants of these bases were simply Chinese, either prisoners of war or deserters.

The 'forest tribes' mentioned above may have consisted for the most part of peoples who had formerly lived in the steppe proper or in the wooded steppe, but had been driven out by the Hsiung-nu. The Soviet archae-*'Slab graves'* ologist Okladnikov discovered typical 'slab graves' far to the north, in a small island of steppe amidst the taiga of Cisbaikalia.

The graves of the Hsiung-nu themselves provide evidence of sharp social differentiation. The simplest type can be recognized only by the presence of a circle of stones; the body rests upon a bed of stones, and is only rarely placed in a protective log structure. People of higher social status were given a rectangle of stones when they were not interred beneath flat mounds of earth. Later the oblong log structure became obligatory. The end at which the head rests is now a little broader, and occasionally the longitudinal sides are slightly concave in shape. This produces the same geometrical form that is often observed in the surface markings of the slab graves. The dead were buried with victuals, various kinds of implements, weapons and horses' harness. Instead of burying whole horses, as had been the practice hitherto, now only their heads were deposited, and of these not more than four. Silks, jade and fragments of mirrors of Chinese origin reveal the great role which Chinese handicrafts played in the lives even of the broad mass of the population. In the grave of one chieftain there was discovered a copper seal bearing an inscription in Chinese, probably a symbol of office. Perhaps even more characteristic of the prevailing Chinese influence is the occurrence of chopsticks. A typically nomadic utensil, on the other hand, is the bronze cauldron; only fragments of these cauldrons, however, have been found in graves – *pars pro toto*. Reinforcing plates of bone point to the use of the double curved bow, the terrible weapon of the steppe warriors.

Chinese influence

Such other products by native artists as one encounters besides these are few and of poor quality. There are two small statuettes of horses and bronze plaques covered with gold-plate. Small heads of griffins are distorted to form cloud designs on the Chinese pattern. Everything is remarkably indistinct and lacking in vigour and intensity. Only the early burial-ground at Derestui (second–first century B.C.) yielded two bronze plaques in open-work featuring animals locked in combat, a buckle in the form of a buffalo head, and even a gold plaque showing a griffin attacking a mountain sheep. For this reason the hopes of archaeologists were all the more keenly concentrated upon the large kurgans in the mountains at Noin Ula. These are situated approximately 1500 metres above sea-level; their mounds, which are relatively low, are shaped like the frustum of a pyramid. Beneath the mound is a shaft, often of astonishing depth (as much as 10 metres); at the bottom of this is the wooden burial-chamber. On the east, south and west side it has a double wall with an intervening space, and its four sides face in directions exactly corresponding to the four principal points of the compass. The similarity to the rich graves in the Altai strikes us immediately. In the eyes of the modern observer it is further accentuated by the fact that here, too, only the perishable part of the inventory has survived, owing to the combination of destructive operations by grave-robbers and the conserving action of frost. The graves, however, lie so deep that the chamber is located below the lens of permafrost. In most cases it was completely filled with ground-water. But for this very reason the textiles have retained an amazing freshness.

On closer examination, however, considerable differences can be observed.

Native products

FIG. 108

Noin Ula

PLATE 22 – Herd of camels grazing in the steppe lands of the Mongolian
People's Republic. The external conditions of life here have changed but little
over the millennia. At first this led scholars to the premature conclusion that the
forms of social organization also remained the same. The twin-humped 'Bactrian'

camel was of great economic importance to the nomads of Central Asia;
nevertheless (or possibly for this reason) only isolated representations of them
in animal style have survived. Exceptions are to be found in Peter the Great's
treasure. *Cf. also the plate on p. 218. Photo by Burda.*

FIG. 108 – *Gold plaque with scene of one animal attacking another, from the Derestui cemetery. Overall width approx. 10 cm. Cf. p. 145.*

The mound consists only of earth – and extends over 1200 square metres at the most. It is covered with rows of stones forming a lattice-like pattern. But a particular feature is a wall of earth tapering towards the north; below this is a sloping ramp that leads into the depths of the shaft. The material heaped up in the shaft yielded animal bones, probably the remains of a funerary feast.

Funerary chamber The chamber, which lacks the shield of tree-trunks usually found in the Altai and is protected merely by its amazing depth, can almost be called delicate in its mode of construction. In most cases planks were used which were well polished on both sides and covered with cloth. The sarcophagus, too, is not simply a hollowed-out tree-trunk but consists of boards skilfully dovetailed together. This was presumably the work of Chinese craftsmen.

Waggons Fragments of waggons of Chinese make were also found, as well as skulls of horses, but there is not the slightest indication of impressive processions of horses such as the Altai people had, with their masks and costly harnesses. What has been found in the way of saddles and bridles was only just sufficient for the 'personal needs' of the dead man. Rudenko believes that he can also identify pack-saddles, but as yet this has not been confirmed.

Pigtails Only in the case of women's thick pigtails was the supply of funerary equipment anything like as massive. Eighty-five of these, neatly placed in *étuis*, were discovered in one grave. Rudenko surmises that in this form the complete harem symbolically followed its master into the grave. The women themselves were probably allowed to remain alive, but were so to speak already pledged for the afterlife. As is known, a custom of this kind has been authenticated in the Iranian area, where even children from a woman's later marriage are assigned to her first husband. Rudenko explains the two different ways in which the hair is plaited by saying that the women originated from two different ethnic groups, perhaps from two moieties.

Parasols were used as emblems of rank – exactly on the Chinese pattern – and their fittings again suggest Chinese workmanship. A similar function may have been fulfilled by the numerous banners: bands of material divided into two pointed tips at the ends, and decorated with sewn-on triangles. These banners may have been affixed to the bronze tops of poles. Pieces of jade may have served as symbols of office.

Domestic objects

The domestic objects are amazingly varied. We find small tables, carpets, kettles, many lacquered bowls of Chinese origin, and also primitive-looking fire-making equipment consisting of a little board and a drill, and finally a money-belt. The deposit of tufts of hair and finger-nails no doubt had some magic significance – being regarded either as amulets or as means of preventing other people from using them for magic purposes against the owner. Mirrors, too, which we invariably find only in fragmentary form, presumably did not serve cosmetic purposes, but were put into the grave on account of their magic power. Among the weapons there are double curved bows measuring one and a half metres in length. Metal rods are interpreted by Rudenko (not very convincingly) as clubs. Bronze plates are thought to have been used as arm-guards, and not as frontlets for horses, as was formerly assumed.

Weapons

In the graves human bones, condyles in particular, were found only occasionally. It is by no means clear whether they derive from the main burial and to what extent the body had decomposed under the curious conditions that prevailed at this depth. Rudenko is silent on this point. The plunderers may have deliberately dismembered the body and dragged parts of it to the surface; in this case the rifling would have to be seen as a magic act with a political flavour. From Chinese accounts we know that the graves of the Hsiung-nu rulers were purposely destroyed by hostile neighbours when their empire declined.

The inventory is completed by shreds of textiles, sometimes torn in almost grotesque fashion, by articles of clothing that are relatively well preserved, by small ornamental plaques in gold, bronze and silver which had apparently escaped unnoticed, and fragments of various boxes and caskets. In conclusion we may say that we are undoubtedly dealing here with the graves of high-ranking Hsiung-nu nobles, and possibly even with the tombs of the supreme rulers, the Shan-Yü. To satisfy their needs, they made extensive use of the services of Chinese craftsmen. Gifts from the Chinese court, a camouflaged form of tribute – today we would speak of 'aid for economic development' – provided much of the material used. The textiles, especially the silk, found here and in the cemetery at Il'-movaia pad' have now at last been comprehensively studied; they represent a valuable contribution to the history of the applied arts during

Textiles
FIG. 109

FIG. 109 – *Silk hood, originally crimson in colour, reinforced with felt and stiffened with birch-bark. From kurgan VI, Noin Ula. Height 34 cm. Cf. above.*

FIG. 110 – *Fragment of a dark red woollen fabric. The embroidery, executed in brown and yellowish tones, shows the face of a man and recalls the portraits of Kushan kings. Presumably this, too, is an import from the western part of Middle Asia. Kurgan XXV, Noin Ula. Approx. 14 × 20 cm. Cf. below.*

the Han period. We cannot but admire the elegant play of lines so characteristic of this phase.

The lacquer employed in the decoration of many objects is of Chinese origin, and so also are the numerous lacquered bowls. One of these bears an easily legible inscription which enables kurgan VI to be ascribed to the first decades of the first century A.D. This is probably a fair estimate of the average date of the entire necropolis. But also the metal objects, especially the larger bronze vessels, and the finer ceramic ware are probably imports or – what is still more likely – the work of deported artisans.

One group of woollen fabrics, on the other hand, shows scenes of characteristically Hellenistic style such as we find, for example, at Kerch'. One might conclude that these were pieces that had found their way to the east along the 'silk road', and had been 'diverted', so to speak, by the Hsiung-nu during those happy times when they controlled this trade-route. But it is not absolutely certain that all of them originated so far to the west. From kurgan XXV comes some exquisite embroidery depicting heads of men with moustaches, whose facial features and expressions recall royal statues of the Kushana period. Two horsemen shown behind their noble steeds have also been identified as Iranians. In any case

FIG. 110

PLATE 23 – A yak standing between two fir-trees, on two rows of small mountain peaks. Round silver plaque with embossed work. Kurgan VI, Noin Ula. *Diameter 14 cm. Cf. p. 154.*

PLATE 24 – Fantastic animal with body of a wolverine attacking an elk. Appliqué work on felt carpet from kurgan VI, Noin Ula.

In the lower part of the picture one can recognize a piece of Chinese silk sewn on to the carpet. *Height of the figures approx. 25 cm. Cf. p. 154.*

Rudenko holds the view that textiles of this kind were produced in Middle Asia, which was influenced by Hellenistic trends, and that they may even have been created by artisans summoned to the court of the Hsiung-nu prince.

Metal objects Objects in precious metal, which we can but regard as a poor relic of the original inventory, show hardly any features of animal style. Among gold pieces embellished with granulation is the small head of an ox; another animal head is inlaid with precious stones. But in the main we are dealing

PLATE P. 151 here with embossed work; of this the most important items are two silver plaques which depict a yak upon symbolically represented mountain peaks in front of some trees, surrounded by braid decoration. A similar piece features a stag. One should also mention here a cylindrical seal in bone depicting a winged wolf. With none of these pieces can Chinese workmanship be ruled out for certain. Trees and symbols of mountains are in any case alien to the animal style.

In spite of this much has been written about the scenes of animals in combat found in the Noin Ula kurgans; the animal style of the Hsiung-nu has had to withstand many attempts at profound interpretation that allegedly sprang from superior insight.

Carpets The appliqué work found on two carpets forms the very limited basis for all these wild speculations. The larger of these two specimens, which measures 2.60 by 1.95 metres, has been far better preserved and published; it once covered the floor of the antechamber in kurgan VI.

This felt carpet has a central panel consisting of a continuous pattern of twenty-four spirals, the spaces between which are filled in with tongue-shaped volutes. The monochrome centre, adorned only with stitching, is surrounded by a crudely designed border, and this in turn by a frieze in which tree symbols alternate with scenes of animals in combat. One of these scenes depicts a yak butting a fabulous creature, which is trying to bite its attacker. The beast has the body of a tiger and a mane; its antlers and tail terminate in birds' heads. The next scene in most cases represents a glutton with birds' wings and bird's tail attacking a fleeing cervid, probably an elk. On the bodies one sees ornamental curves, presumably Chinese in inspiration.

Animal style In spite of their dynamism and realism, which are most marked, one may note some major changes by comparison with the large kurgans of the Altai. We no longer find here strict adherence to the principle whereby the picture is rendered either in frontal view or in profile, or else by combining both at right angles. One could even detect a certain attempt at perspective. It is no longer the tension before movement that is rendered but the act of movement itself. We no longer have large areas

PLATES PP. 152–3 filled in with motifs originating in the Near East (patterns of dots and commas), and spiral-like whirls are also lacking. Instead of these there is a tendency towards the use of concentric arcs, as though the work had

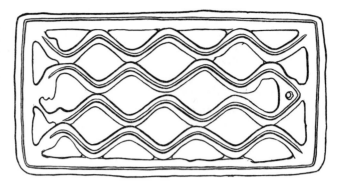

FIG. 111 – *Open-work plaque showing serpents, from the walled fort on the Ivolga. Here one can already see the transition to the abstract forms that were to prevail in later centuries. Length approx. 16 cm.*

been done with a burin. The silhouette principle has disappeared; to distinguish various parts of the body different colours are used. On closer examination it is noticeable that some of these characteristics are also to be found in the few pieces known to us from Derestui, especially the scene depicted on the gold plate featuring a griffin attacking a mountain sheep.

The best proof that this is indeed a later phase of animal style is afforded by a comparison with the later Altai kurgans of the Shibe phase, which have hitherto been given little attention. The Kumurtuk kurgan in the Altai still contains, for example, a bronze dagger of archaic form, but alongside this a plate which has the same parallel curves in the rendering of griffins' heads. Similar details are also to be found on Siberian gold plaques.

It is perhaps no accident that in the poorer and more conservative Derestui such motifs should still occur in metal, whereas at Noin Ula they only appear on felt carpets (produced by the more traditionally-minded womenfolk). The metalworkers were already giving preference to a different stylistic trend, which we may glimpse in their embossed silver plaques. This would explain why in many kurgans so few objects in animal style have been discovered.

Another consideration would be relevant here. The felt rug bears a vague resemblance to the knotted carpet from Pazyryk V, so far as its composition is concerned (friezes arranged around a panel consisting of twenty-four identical figures). Perhaps it has some ritual background as well. If this is so, it would be quite plausible that on an object of religious significance we should find symbols belonging to a stylistic tradition that had already become obsolete in everyday use, or had simply become taboo.

In any case it is hardly advisable to assume that there was a general 'preponderance' of animal style art during the heyday of the Hsiung-nu empire.

Presumably the social prerequisites for this art no longer existed. The large amount of goods imported and the employment of Chinese artisans gradually relegated native art into the background. But artistic interests, too, had shifted. The 'agonal' principle no longer prevailed; we no longer encounter free clans with equal rights, striving after fame and immortality and glorifying themselves in their art, but instead the subjects of a great empire; their rulers were separated from the people by an unbridgeable religious divide, and had adopted a good deal from their neighbours in organizational matters. Among the latter, from the Ch'in dynasty onwards, government was carried on according to rational, almost Macchiavellian, principles.

The Huns of Europe have been regarded as the first people whose art was based upon a concept of power *(Machtkunst)*. But in this respect they were only obedient disciples of their Far Eastern predecessors. The principle of animal style may at this time have been no more than a powerful relic from a bygone age. The Hsiung-nu empire still kept up the ritual use of motifs which in the preceding period had been freely adopted or produced, modified or totally transformed.

X. ORDOS BRONZES

We have now learned enough about Mongolia and its adjacent areas to be able to enter into a discussion of the Ordos bronzes.

Very few of these famous bronzes are still left today in the stocks of dealers; most of them have long since found their way into museums and private collections. They are mute witnesses to an archaeological scandal of the first order. This was due to the highly-developed trade carried on by the Chinese in antiquities, to the absence of any effective state control over this trade, and especially to the fact that, after the First World War, objects executed in animal style attracted lively attention everywhere. As soon as these bronzes were found north of the Great Wall, therefore, people immediately showed interest in them – in contrast to the pre-war period, when the few pieces that had been exhibited at the Burlington Club evoked no response. Now, however, the British Museum made the first purchases. The breakthrough occurred in Paris with an exhibition at the Musée Cernuschi. Prices rose; the supply of finds made on the surface was no longer sufficient; and therefore grave-robbers hastened to meet the demand to the best of their ability. The extent to which forgers also took advantage of this favourable state of affairs has not yet been fully investigated.

Understandably enough, the existence of the new finds attracted the interest of J. G. Andersson, the indefatigable curator of the Museum of Far Eastern Antiquities in Stockholm, who at that time was almost the only scholar extending knowledge in the field of Chinese prehistory. He acquired a lavish, but of course completely undocumented, collection and published it in a number of well-illustrated articles, the titles of which were calculated to arouse interest among patrons of the arts, whose aid

Appearance on the market

PLATE P. 159

FIG. 112 – *Mounted ape. An Ordos bronze of whimsical shape. Exner Collection, Museum für Völkerkunde, Vienna. Cf. p. 158.*

Andersson needed if he was to be able to continue his Sisyphean labours: 'The Route across the Steppes' was followed by 'Hunting Magic in the Animal Style'. Minns had the dubious good fortune to coin an attractive term for this group, which had hitherto either been named after the province of Suiyüan or, to denote the relationship, 'Sino-Siberian': he called them 'Ordos bronzes'. (Ordos is the name given to the steppe country situated between the northward loop of the Yellow River (Hwangho) and the Great Wall.) Other scholars pointed out mysterious connections with the Hallstatt culture. It could not be denied that there were curious affinities with practically all regions where the animal style flourished.

Meanwhile bronzes kept pouring on to the market. Following the scent of money, they found their way to New York and Paris, where the dealers Loo and Wannieck built up magnificent collections for sale, and were finally dispersed in dozens of private collections, large and small, among them such well-known ones as those of Stoclet and David-Weill. Some came into the possession of museums, either by direct purchase or by bequests. Gradually people came to know the most common types of object. There were knives, daggers, axes, socketed celts, bridles, hook-clasps, pole-tops and hollow animal figures whose purpose was unknown; but above all else there were mounted bronze ornaments and pendants. At every turn one found animals, sometimes treated in a magnificently austere fashion, such as those of the Pontic area and the Altai, but sometimes almost playfully deformed and combined. There were beasts of prey with heads that were detachable or did not fit the body at all (e.g., a wolf with the placid face of a ram), highly erotic scenes, and also much that was blurred, indistinct and decadent. Human figures played a considerable part. All in all a range of possible forms was opened up such as did not exist in any other province of animal style.

The flow only began to dry up when the fighting that broke out in the 1930s with the Japanese penetration into northern China put an end to these sales. The extent of the damage caused in the meantime can be deduced from the fact that not a single complex of finds came to hand intact. Only the Swedish scholar Arne made an attempt to reconstruct two grave inventories on the basis of statements by peasants. Despite the close proximity of centres of ancient Chinese civilization, not one single

Chief types
PLATE P. 160

FIG. 112

PLATE 25 – Representative selection of ornamental plaques from the Ordos region. The lower piece has parallels in Peter the Great's treasure; the yak *(top left)* is akin to those depicted at Noin Ula; the piece showing two animals of the equine family grazing resembles the fragment of belt-plaque from Minusinsk reproduced on p. 79. Portrayed from an oblique angle, the ram *(top right)* is of a type that is not found within the usual range of animal style. *British Museum. Cf. pp. 157, 183.*

PLATE 26 – Pole-top of the standard type occurring in the steppe
area. *British Museum. Slightly
reduced in size. Cf. p. 158.*

*Controversy over
classification*

specimen bore an inscription. There was thus nothing else that could be
done but to apply the methods of stylistic analysis and comparison.
Many scholars, including Minns, distinguished two broad groups. They
maintained that one of them was Chinese, but influenced by some foreign
element in its form and decoration. The other was called 'barbarian'.
Certain types are so strongly reminiscent of Scythian works in animal
style that they were confidently ascribed to the last few centuries B.C.
Working on this assumption, ethnic classification seemed fairly easy.
Chinese historical works mentioning the life-and-death struggles waged
by the two Han dynasties against the Hsiung-nu were published on a

FIG. 113 – *This pick has Chinese decoration, but its shape points to the steppe area. The reverse combination is much more frequent. Museum für Völkerkunde, Munich. Length 20 cm.*

fairly extensive scale. The finds at Noin Ula had just aroused the interest of scholars in this people. The Hsiung-nu had also held sway over the Ordos steppe south of the Gobi. Why should they not have been responsible for these curious bronzes as well?

Incidentally, views of this kind were calculated to increase still further the market value of the bronzes. Only occasionally was surprise expressed at the fact that the European Huns, who were after all thought to be descended from the Hsiung-nu, had turned out to be such complete failures so far as the animal style was concerned. But then the route from Noin Ula to the Catalaunian Plains was long and dangerous, and many cultural traits might have been lost en route.

As late as 1962 Rudenko wrote a book about Noin Ula that is in complete conformity with this thesis. He borrows some of the Ordos bronzes, as it were, so that he can claim for the Hsiung-nu the animal style so scantily represented in northern Mongolia and Transbaikalia.

Recent excavations carried out under the Communist régime in north China do indeed support the theory that such a link existed. On the southern fringe of the Gobi desert there have been discovered cemeteries from the Han period which are not Chinese in character. They may therefore probably be ascribed to the Hsiung-nu, especially since some of them were situated close by an earthwork which resembled those north of the Gobi. And in the graves were discovered open-work bronze plaques bearing animal figures such as had hitherto only been known from surface finds. But these specimens – at least those illustrated in Soviet publications – are blurred and rather indistinct, and are not very impressive.

It is true that, as Miss M. von Dewall kindly informs me, in the meantime more representative finds have been made in graves whose other contents belong to the Han period, but may be even more recent. Even within the borders of the Chinese settlement area proper, one can point to some graves containing Ordos bronzes – again dating by and large from the Han period.

But the real question is whether this solves the problem of the Ordos bronzes, or whether it has not far more complex aspects. Are all the various types of Ordos bronzes represented in these late burial-places? In the case of the large number of bronze knives and daggers reproduced by Loehr, for example, this is extremely doubtful. The use of this alloy at so late a stage is in itself unlikely, except for ornamental or cultic purposes. Miss von Dewall does in fact mention at one place an iron knife in a grave of the Han period.

Massive knives in particular (those with marked articulation of the cutting

Recent excavations

Various types

FIG. 114 – *Ordos knife terminating in an animal's head. End of 2nd millennium B.C. Length 18 cm. Cf. below.*

FIG. 38
FIG. 114 edge and handle, and with terminals shaped like bells or animal heads) have often been assigned to the late second millennium, partly on the basis of links via southern Siberia as far afield as Turbino and Seima in the eastern part of European Russia, and partly on the basis of links with An-yang. In An-yang, the centre of the Shang empire, as Miss von Dewall argues, they are particularly popular as funerary gifts placed in the graves of charioteers, who belonged to a small group of nobles closely attached to the court.

Since the An-yang complex is undoubtedly from the end of the second millennium B.C., this might mean that we have to postulate a sub-group of Ordos bronzes from a much earlier chronological phase, characterized by austere forms. But, as mentioned above, in this phase we already find animals used as decorative motifs.

Karlgren's theory H. Kühn was the first to point out the implications of this for the history of animal style. Karlgren almost reluctantly drew the unavoidable conclusion and put forward the hypothesis that in view of the relative antiquity of these pieces, the entire animal style of the steppe lands might have been derived from Shang art, and have then slowly trickled westwards, reaching the Black Sea area some five hundred years later.

In favour of Karlgren's view one may argue that the important part played by north China as a metallurgical centre has been brought out ever more clearly by the excavations carried out in China over the last few years. Necropolises have been unearthed which can be accurately dated by inscriptions found on bronzes. They show that China did not only draw inspiration from the West, but also introduced to Europe the socketed celt and the so-called 'cruciform buttons' of the Hallstatt area along routes that are still unknown, so that it is hardly any longer a matter for surprise that genuine silk should have been found in a princely grave of the Hallstatt period near the Heuneburg, in south-western Germany.

Important evidence in favour of Karlgren's thesis is provided by the above-mentioned occurrence of Sinid skulls in graves of the Karasuk culture in the Minusinsk district. Here we were able to point out influences from the Far East on the shapes of metal objects. At that time the Chinese borderlands were no doubt partly inhabited by sheep-raising tribes who were presumably the ancestors of the nomads of Tibet. It has been supposed that such a group was once driven off towards the Enisei. *Sub-group from Chou period* Other evidence suggests that a further sub-group dates from the last few centuries of the Chou period. In his discussion of Ordos bronzes Rudenko

PLATE 27 – The piece shown above is magnificently modelled, whereas that below is flat and schematic. It cannot, however, be seen as a degenerate work on that account. There are links with the large round plaques in Peter the Great's treasure. Chou period. *British Museum. Slightly reduced in size.*

reveals almost in passing that there were among them figures of tigers whose coat is depicted as a pattern of flame-like forms similar to that of the tigers featured in the 'procession' on the sarcophagus lid at Bashadar II. But the latter, according to our reckoning, belongs to the fifth century B.C.; and Rudenko has even assigned it to the sixth century. Further clues of this kind could be mentioned. There are, for examples, Ordos plaques whose western counterparts are Pontic works of the fifth century B.C. The Viennese scholar Griessmaier has already drawn attention to the existence of these pieces in his work on the interesting Van der Heydt Collection, which was lost in those chaotic days toward the end of the Second World War.

This suspicion will be confirmed when scholars finally come to study those Ordos bronzes which at present are lying unnoticed in the collections of American and European museums. Most of them are not even published because, being made to serve purely practical purposes, they were of no interest to the aesthetes. Stockholm, for example, possesses bridle-bits with stirrup-shaped ends, to which the reins were attached. This type is well known in the steppe area, during the phase which is contemporaneous with the Ch'un-ch'iu period in Chinese history (722–481 B.C.). It would be surprising if animal style bronzes were not present among the complexes of finds which contain bridle-bits of this kind.

These early steppe neighbours of the Chinese were sedentary, in spite of their links with the west and north. They surround China like a protective belt through which outsiders only occasionally penetrated, which explains why the main areas of the Chou civilization retained the old-fashioned chariot for so long. This was definitively established by the research of Miss M. von Dewall.

Those tribes, however, which troubled the Chinese by their raids towards the end of the Chou period were most probably nomadic in character. Presumably the Yüeh-chih and the Wu-sun, the most typical representatives of this new way of life, came from a region far to the west, from Central Asia. Their appearance in the borderlands of western China may have had repercussions on their native areas, which may be traced in the civilizations of the Sakian tribes north of the Tian'-shan' and the Altai (at Pazyryk V). Some of the animal style bronzes found on the Chinese border may be attributed to these truly nomadic peoples.

Bronzes from Han period Even the Ordos bronzes belonging to the Han period itself could be subdivided. Those specimens that correspond to the Derestui material might belong to the early Han period; and those bronzes with patterns which never occur in the Altai would then have to be ascribed to a later phase. Among these are, for example, pseudo-buckles with square borders and relatively strict treatment of lines, frequently without actual animal figures. A predilection for symmetrical treatment and a curious blurring of contours may also be typical features of the late period. It

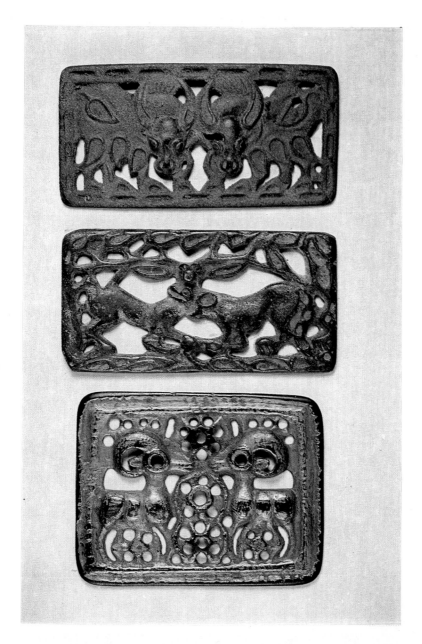

PLATE 28 – These ornamental plaques may be immediately classified as belonging to the later group on account of their symmetrical structure, evident even in the scene showing animals fighting *(centre)*. This date is confirmed by the presence of the yak *(top)*, which plays a great part in Hsiung-nu art. The depiction of wheels on the lowest plaque has been attributed to Buddhist influences. *British Museum. Approx. life-size. Cf. p. 164.*

was probably in the late period that the prevalent taste, which was already displaying a tendency towards the ornamental styles of the later nomads, was overlaid by foreign Chinese influences.

Of great assistance in classifying this group is the Tashtyk culture in the Minusinsk district, which in the meantime has been investigated more thoroughly. In this group animal representations are used in rites but also, as we have seen, in an almost humorous manner (e.g., birds with movable beaks). This could explain the figures with movable heads to which we referred earlier. In general one often gains the impression that one is dealing not with ornamental objects but with amulets – and this fits our general picture of the Tashtyk culture.

Latest group Another group of Ordos bronzes may perhaps be even later in date and thus already belong to the successors of the Hsiung-nu. Bronze was employed to produce small ornaments until well into the Iron Age. We have drawn attention earlier to the skill displayed by the nomadic tribes of Central Asia in the art of casting metal, making use of the most primitive devices, with cattle dung serving them as fuel.

PLATE 29 – Wolf with the horns of an ibex. Hybrid animals composed of wholly realistic individual elements also appear in the Tashtyk culture, which is further evidence of its late date. *British Museum.*

XI. TUVA: AN AREA OF WITHDRAWAL

Proceeding now to consider those provinces of animal style that have only *Geographical setting* recently been discovered and have not yet been examined thoroughly, we may most conveniently begin with Tuva. This region was wrenched from China as early as the Tsarist era, and for a long time its status was unclear; it now forms part of the Soviet Union. The history of research and excavation in this region also took its own peculiar course. It is an inaccessible area situated at the sources of the Enisei, intersected by ridges and surrounded by lofty wooded mountain ranges. It is bordered on the north by the Western Saian, which separate it from the Minusinsk basin. This confined space is the natural habitat of animals which one would hardly expect to find together elsewhere: not only the reindeer and the wild horse (possibly the *koulan*) but also the wild yak and the wild camel. For this reason it has been suggested that it may have been one of the areas where livestock-breeding first developed. It is also situated close to the great route taken by the migrant peoples, a route which runs from east to west by way of the Dzungarian Gate.

Here, too, the first and most effective excavations were carried out by *History of discovery* Adrianov (1915–6) and Teploukhov (1926, 1927 and 1929). Unfortunately both were denied the opportunity to publish their results, a gap that has not been filled to this very day. After several isolated attempts and reconnaissance journeys had been undertaken, digging was begun by Kyzlasov, who was also the first to study systematically the material gathered by his predecessors. In close connection with this work, the human skulls found were studied by Debets and later by Alekseev.

Kyzlasov was a member of an expedition mounted by Moscow University. He produced only a very telescoped summary of his findings. The researches conducted by the 'Tuvinian Complex Expedition' sponsored by the Institute of Ethnography of the Academy of Sciences, led by Potapov, are published much more extensively. It may, however, be noted that very little attention is paid to the views of Kyzlasov, who took his revenge in a critical review. The upshot is that we are still dependent upon his views, since most of the recently excavated material belongs to later phases.

Kyzlasov distinguishes a Bronze Age extending from the beginning of the

FIG. 115 – *Bronze knife from Tuva. Stray find. Possibly from the 6th century B.C. Cf. p. 168.*

second millennium B.C. to the end of the eighth century B.C., the development of which takes a roughly similar course to that in the Altai and the Minusinsk district. Of special interest is the large number of mines exploited for ore.

Uiuk culture:
first phase The period between the seventh and third centuries B.C. he designates by the term Uiuk culture. To its first phase, extending into the fifth century B.C., Kyzlasov can only assign a very unrewarding earth kurgan containing a chamber timbered with tree-trunks. On the basis of comparisons with adjacent areas, however, several stray finds can be classified FIG. 115 here, among them a knife of early Tagarian form, its handle decorated with images of stags and its pommel crowned with a standing animal.

'Stag slabs' The nature of the animal style is more easily grasped when we consider the so-called 'stag slabs'. These stelae originally stood near graves and were spread over an area that extended from the Altai to Transbaikalia and included Tuva and northern Mongolia. On some of these, especially the earliest, it is possible to identify a crudely worked belt with weapons attached to it, as well as ornamental objects, so that they can almost certainly be identified as figures of warriors. On the sides, however, are several pictures of stags, often placed at irregular angles one above the other. This form of decoration seems to assume ever greater importance as time goes on. These pictures of stags are not of a uniform character. In one type the animals are rendered with legs outstretched, as on a mirror from the Altai reproduced by Borovka (Fig. 50), while in another the extremities are drawn under the body and joined – i.e., the posture normally found in Minusinsk bronzes. The form observed in southern Tuva, on the other hand, is curiously mannered: the head projects far forward and has two branches of antlers. It is found again in eastern Mongolia and Transbaikalia, but also in eastern Kazakhstan, on petroglyphs in Fergana, and finally among the bronzes of the late Koban culture in the northern Caucasus. Chlenova, who has studied representations of cervids from the Scythian period, is of the opinion that the pattern of distribution shows that this type was originally developed by the Saka peoples of Central Asia. She believes that where they ruled, at least as a narrowly restricted upper class, statues commemorating their chieftains bore this symbol, which represented the totem animal of the whole people. According to one Soviet philologist, the basic meaning of 'Saka' was 'stag'. In this connection it is of interest that links in fact existed between Tuva and eastern Europe. Among the chance finds is a dagger with a hilt formed of rings linked together in one plane. This peculiar feature is found again in eastern Europe as well as in the Caucasus.

FIG. 116 – *Stele featuring stags and other animals, from Tuva. The weapons worn suspended from the belt are clearly recognizable. Cf. above.*

The second phase is characterized by an astonishing variety of types of *Second phase*
graves: Kyzlasov distinguishes no less than six. Some of them are quite
similar to those dating from this period in the Minusinsk district: the
grave timbering was burned down before it was finally sealed, and
instead of weapons only miniatures were deposited. Even the animal style
objects found in these graves are similar to those of the Minusinsk basin.
According to the few accounts available, other grave complexes have
their counterparts in north-western Mongolia. Kyzlasov takes the view
that these are the graves of immigrants who had to join a confederation
of tribes led by native chieftains. The latter were interred beneath massive
earth kurgans, and it is these that yield by far the greatest proportion of
the objects decorated in animal style. Unfortunately neither reproductions
nor descriptions of them are available. Other groups yielded much less
material. In any case we can see that different stylistic principles obtained
among the tribes which, after an embittered struggle to maintain their
position in the steppe area, took refuge in the valleys of the Saian range.
The skulls show considerable racial intermingling. As well as an ancient
Europoid element, there is a stronger Mongoloid one, evidently originating
from the forest areas in the north rather than the steppe lands.

In the subsequent Shurmak culture (second century B.C.–fifth century *Shurmak culture*
A.D.) the variety of burial rites continues. Generally speaking, there are
considerable affinities with Tashtyk. The influence of the Hsiung-nu, who
apparently ruled this region over a long period of time, is much in evidence. It is all the more curious that a greater proportion of the skulls
that are known should be Europoid than was the case in the preceding
phase. It may be that, under pressure from the expanding empire to the
east, steppe tribes of this racial character fell back to take refuge in the
mountains. Henceforth there is no longer any mention of animal style.
Apparently, as in the adjoining Minusinsk district, it had nearly reached
the end of its dominance.

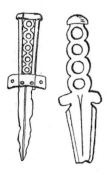

FIG. 117 – *Daggers with hilts composed of a number
of rings placed end to end. Left: from Matra, Hungary;
right: from Tuva. Stray finds. Cf. pp. 168, 216.*

XII. THE SAKA IN MIDDLE ASIA

Geographical setting We still have to consider a vast area which, although extremely important for our topic, is not particularly productive. Between the Kirghiz steppe and the northern rim of the Iranian plateau there lie regions referred to in current Soviet literature as 'Middle Asia' – so as to avoid the politically loaded term 'western Turkestan'; this is not the same as Central Asia, which is a larger territory. This is an area of vast deserts: Kara-Kum, Kyzyl-Kum and Bet-Pak-Dala. It is bordered on the east by high mountain ranges but contains scattered fertile oases and inviting grazing-grounds.

As a result the population has from the earliest times been divided into hard-working peasants and warlike nomads.

The Greek historians have handed down to us not only all manner of names from this area but also concrete events and ethnographical data; much of their knowledge was derived from the Persians. At the height of their power the Achaemenids controlled an area extending from the Aral Sea to the foothills of the Tian'-shan'. Their royal inscriptions are another important source of knowledge for modern scholars. Alexander's campaign then provides a further body of authentic information.

A string of oases stretches along the rim of the Iranian plateau. Here were situated the lands of Hyrcania, Parthia, Areya, Margiana and Bactria. They also encompass, of course, the head-waters of the rivers that feed these oases. In an exposed position to the north of this chain of oases, lie Khorezm (on the lower reaches of the Amu-Dar'ia, the classical Oxus) and Sogdiana (Transoxiana) with Fergana.

Ethnic composition There must have been nomads in the territory between these isolated oases, too, but most of them lived in the region north of Sogdiana, along the lower reaches of the Syr-Dar'ia (Jaxartes) and the northern slopes of the Tian'-shan'. These are the Massagetae referred to in Greek sources.

PLATE P. 171 The Persian inscriptions only mention the Saka as existing in this region. Evidently this is a collective term; the Greeks employed the term 'Scythians' in the same general way, perhaps also 'Massagetae'. To the north of the Parthians lived the Dahae, who are referred to as nomads, although now permanent settlements have been found which are claimed to be theirs.

The ethnographical data contain some surprises: in this area agriculture is not known, but only livestock-raising and fishing. The status of women is very high, as with the Sauromatians. Of a people living close by to the north, the Issedones, it is recorded that their womenfolk were owned in

PLATE 30 – The Oxus treasure provides valuable information to supplement the data given in ancient sources about this area. A model of a waggon in gold shows that two-wheeled vehicles were used in battle and on ceremonial occasions. Details of the clothing worn by the two passengers are clearly discernible. *British Museum. Length 18.8 cm. Cf. p. 170.*

common. The killing of old men once they had become unfit for work is also mentioned, as is the ceremonial eating of the dead by their closest relatives.

These are all peculiarities that do not easily fit into the usual picture of Indo-European peoples. In spite of this not only the settled peoples, but evidently the greater part of the nomads as well, spoke an Iranian tongue. The oldest parts of the Avesta make it clear that the relationship between nomads and peasants was by no means always friendly and peaceful. Excavations carried out in the southern belt of oases, including the area nowadays called Turkmenia, has resurrected before our eyes an agricultural civilization that has its origins deep in a very remote past. In Khorezm, Tolstov has unearthed – in addition to sites of early and very early date – vast cities which already existed in classical antiquity. In the

Archaeological discoveries

FIG. 118 – *Bronze altar for burnt offerings, the upper part crowned by thirteen panther figures. This piece belongs to the hoard discovered by Lake Issyk-Kul' in 1937, now in the Hermitage, Leningrad. Overall height 19 cm. Cf. pp. 173, 217.*

east, where the mountains lie, the principal expeditions were directed by Bernshtam, who unfortunately published his findings in very schematic form. In recent times the Academies of Sciences of the various Republics of the Soviet Union have carried on an astonishing amount of excavation work. The fact that the inter-Republican boundaries are so tortuous renders it difficult to obtain a clear picture of this activity.

We can definitely assign to nomads the graves that have been opened up in large numbers on the northern edge of the Tian'-shan' and in Semirech'e. In the mountainous areas they extend a long way to the south, as far as the Altai and Pamirs. They are referred to collectively by the term 'Saka culture', which may even be an appropriate designation.

Dzhuvantobe The earliest phase of this culture is represented by the kurgans recently opened in the district of Alma-Ata. A kurgan in the Dzhuvantobe field of barrows, for example, has two pits under a low mound. In one was the horse, in the other the horseman. The man's burial contained only a comb and a knife; by the horse were found remains of the harness, including crossed tubes and a bronze snaffle of very archaic form, as well as a small horse's head carved in bone. It was concluded that it belonged to the seventh or sixth century B.C. Later graves of the same culture have beneath their mounds pits of which the sides are reinforced by dry stone walls. The roofing consists of stone slabs and, in later graves, of layers of beams. It was a regular practice to deposit small bowls with rounded bases; the weapons found were arrow-heads and – on one occasion – a dagger in the shape of an akinakes.

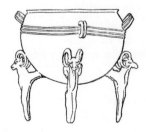

FIG. 119 – *Bronze cauldron with four handles and three legs representing the fore parts of wild sheep. From Semirech'e. Alma-Ata Museum. Height 55 cm. Cf. p. 173.*

PLATE 31 – Armlets and fragment of an armlet *(centre, top)* from the Oxus treasure, showing great differences in the stylization of animal forms, some of which were originally decorated with enamel. The smooth open silver ring of the lower piece is a modern addition. *British Museum. Diameter of largest specimen (right) 8.6 cm. Cf. pp. 175, 187.*

These necropolises would tell us little about the local animal style: much more information is provided by the treasure hoards. These consist almost exclusively of curious altar-tables used for burnt offerings, and cauldrons which were presumably also employed in rites. The decoration usually takes the form of three-dimensional animal figures. Ibexes or goats crown the rim or embellish the sides of the legs. But lion-griffins and panthers are to be found as well. FIG. 118 FIG. 119

The austere element which very frequently characterizes animal style is wholly absent. The animals are conceived in terms of modelling, not of

PLATE 32 – Small golden figure of a griffin from the Oxus treasure. Possibly the ornament for a hood; at the rear are two pins for securing it. It also has cells for coloured inlays; the tip of the tail is leaf-shaped. *British Museum. Overall length only 6.15 cm. Cf. p. 175.*

wood-carving. On the other hand they are sometimes decorated with S-shaped spirals in unexpected places: this we see, for example, on a recumbent yak which no doubt formed part of a cultic object. In this connection we may recall that spiral designs appear on the comb found at Dzhuvantobe. There are, in addition, small sculptures of human beings which are combined with animals so as to form whole scenes.

Whence are these singular features, so unusual in the steppe areas, derived? The answer is apparent when we compare these bronzes with the art of their sedentary neighbours, about whom our information comes mainly from the famous Oxus treasure, found somewhere in Bactria as long ago as 1877. It contains fine realistic sculptures of human beings and animals, and also magnificent highly stylized animal sculptures with small hollowed-out depressions to hold an inlay of paste and coloured stones. We are already familiar with the designs used in this cloisonné work – dot and comma – from the Altai, but here their forms are much more regular. Once again we come across fabulous animals based on models from the ancient Orient. *Oxus treasure.*

PLATES PP. 173, 174

If we compare these sculptures with the reliefs at Persepolis and the large number of finds recently made on the Iranian plateau, it becomes evident that the Oxus treasure marks the transition to a vast region of great artistic importance. This region encompasses the Achaemenid empire, but was probably already built up syncretistically from many elements under the rule of the Medes. The affinities which it bore to steppe art will be discussed later; here we need only say that we are dealing with an art that was most closely related to animal style. Of course we do not find in Achaemenid ornaments the spontaneous vigour of the nomadic works; at every turn one can sense here the presence of the powerful rulers who commissioned such works, and who demanded clear smooth lines that were aesthetically perfect. *Links with Iran*

The Saka tribes did not, however, maintain cultural relations with the south alone. There is significance in the mere fact that they chose cast iron as well as bronze as the material for their sacrificial tables and cauldrons. Cast iron was known in China – and almost only in China – from pre-Christian times onwards; in Europe it did not become important until almost two thousand years later. There are some affinities in form as well. Recently Maenchen-Helfen has proved that Chinese bronzes display distinct Middle Asian influences; for example, they show the same designs on the muscular parts of their bodies as we have already observed so clearly and regularly in the Oxus treasure. Even here animal figures may have had some magic protective function. This conception may have given rise to the animal-shaped handle, which served to shield from evil influences the contents of the vessel to which it was affixed; later on it is to be found throughout almost the entire steppe area. *Chinese influence*

More closely related to the familiar distinctive features of the animal style is a form of decoration that has now been found mainly in the Syr-Dar'ia area, east of the Aral Sea. The basic motifs, such as the small schematized griffin's head, are familiar, but in this case they are arranged close together, covering the object almost like scales. From stray finds we have long been acquainted with objects decorated in a similar way – for example a psalion. The graveyards near which such objects have recently been discovered show an extremely interesting variety of burial rites. Massive low circular towers were built, which contain only a few chambers *Syr-Dar'ia kurgans*

FIG. 120

FIG. 120 – *Bronze clasp. Part of harness. From kurgan VIII, Uigarak. Overall width approx. 12 cm. Cf. p. 175.*

and from outside are somewhat reminiscent of 'towers of silence'. On these towers huts or pavilions were sometimes erected, in which the dead were cremated together with their funerary gifts. Beneath the kurgans, too, there were found the ground-plans of such 'houses' for the dead which had been burned down. Besides these, there were probably structures in which the uncremated bodies were simply exposed and allowed to decay. Tolstov attempted to describe the entire range of combinations of the various highly specialized forms. He assumes that the differing rituals were first practised by various Sakian tribes. Zoroastrian literature contains reminiscences of such heterodox burial rituals. The well-known wall-painting at Pendzhikent presumably represents cremation in the pavilion. Exposure of the dead for the birds of prey to devour in open towers was evidently characteristic only of a very limited part of Middle Asia.

Besshatyr VI Of the utmost interest is kurgan VI at Besshatyr, 180 kilometres east of Alma-Ata. It contains a wooden chamber which in size does not fall short of the structures at Pazyryk; but it has not been let into the soil, which has remained intact, and is constructed in an entirely different way. It was preserved only on account of the extraordinary dryness of the climate, but has been rifled with regrettable thoroughness. Below, in the virgin soil, curious catacombs have been discovered which served for the depositing of sacrificial gifts by the tribe. Nevertheless we can obtain some idea of the wealth that has been lost to us as a result of plundering.

It has already been mentioned that Sakian necropolises are to be found scattered through the mountain valleys far to the south. Evidently the nomads advanced from one high-lying pasture to another, much as the Kirghiz do today. One characteristic feature of these burial-grounds is that the mounds of the kurgans form a chain – and in some cases, a single long rampart.

In Fergana, which during the preceding period was already inhabited by tribes who came from the steppes, nomadic culture fused with that

FIG. 121 – *Bronze cauldron from Alikhur cemetery, in the Pamirs. The affixed griffin's head and circular handle distinguish this piece from the well-known types of cauldron; all the more important, therefore, is the occurrence of a kindred piece in the Karakorum Mts. Cf. below.*

of peasants whose way of life had preserved extremely ancient characteristics and who perhaps even still spoke a pre-Indo-European language. Even in the high-lying valleys of the eastern Pamirs there are 'Sakian' graves. Some of them belong to a late period, to the centuries before and after the birth of Christ. Among these late finds is a bronze vessel of most singular shape, with an animal head affixed to it. An exact counterpart exists, surprisingly enough, south of the Karakorum range, in the Gilgit Agency, i.e. in what is today the Pakistani area of Kashmir. Litvinskii believes that he has here positive evidence of one of the Sakian invasions of north-western India, which he claims took place by way of the mountain passes.

Graves in Pamirs

FIG. 121

But in the Pamirs there are also still more ancient graves of nomads. In one of those the pit was sealed off by a layer of huge wild sheep's horns, as though to ward off demonic influences. Next to the dead man were deposited parts of a horse's harness. The bridle-bit, its ends formed in the shape of a stirrup, suggests an early dating – almost to pre-Scythian times. This is emphasized by the buttons for fixing cross-straps, which are of

FIG. 122 – *Ibex leaping. Cast bronze plaque. It has a loop on the reverse, and formed the decoration on a bow-case. Pamirskaia I cemetery, kurgan X. Width approx. 6 cm. Cf. pp. 178, 228.*

FIG. 122
'Thraco-Cimmerian' form. Cast bronze ornaments for the straps depict animals, an ibex and a bear. The bear in particular shows a striking affinity with the 'standing animal' of the Minusinsk area. The ibex, too, has the heavy and squat character of southern Siberian cast bronzes. One might almost think that a tribe had been driven into this area from the north.

Sarmatian occupation During the centuries that followed the birth of Christ there appear over very wide areas of Middle Asia 'catacombs', i.e., shafts with lateral niches, covered by kurgans. In the niches are deposited the bodies of Europoids or even Mongoloids with deformed skulls. They are found even at oases where no graves whatsoever from earlier periods had been found; here PLATE BELOW the settled population had presumably exposed their dead. It is supposed that the whole region was under the sway of a Sarmatian ruling group, which came from the Volga area, but had previously absorbed some immigrants from the east. The animal forms of this period resemble the Sarmatian ones in character. The vessels consistently retain animal handles throughout.

PLATE 33 – Gold bracelet with Scythian motifs. An analogous specimen is to be found in the Römisch-Germanisches Museum, Cologne. In spite of the rather archaic execution of the lion's body this is a late piece. It could have belonged to a chieftain of the nomadic warriors who invaded north-western India by way of Bactria during the 2nd century B.C. *Peshawar Museum, Pakistan. Diameter 7 cm. Cf. above.*

XIII. SIBERIAN GOLD: THE STEPPES OF
NORTHERN AND EASTERN KAZAKHSTAN

Now, at the end of our journey across the steppes, in the course of our survey of the problems raised by new areas of animal style, it is necessary to return to the steppes of northern and eastern Kazakhstan – to the region where the grave-robbers first began their operations.

Russian peasants who crossed the Urals and settled along the banks of the Ishim river are said to have been the first to follow this profession, which was no less dangerous than prospecting for gold in the lands of the American Indians. For the steppes, with their enticing rounded mounds of earth, were by no means under the control of the Tsar. For many years they remained the grazing-grounds of Kazakh and Kalmuck horsemen, arch-enemies of the Russian colonists. *Grave-robbery*

But who was frightened of these perils if he could obtain from such a kurgan five, six or even seven pounds of silver and gold (as the German Messerschmidt records in his diary on March 25, 1721)? Thus in Tobol'sk, Tomsk or other towns expeditions would be formed: in the spring, so long as the sledge-tracks were still in good condition, parties of two to three hundred men would set out into the steppe; coming to a line of intact kurgans, they would split up into groups, but remaining within sight of one another and keeping their rifles ready – for only too often lone treasure-seekers were attacked and killed.

Sometimes these groups had bad luck and found no more than bronzes and corroded iron. In most cases, however, the yield was remunerative – to such an extent that many pieces of jewellery made in this period were worked from the gold found in graves, which fetched a steady price from dealers. Of course it was necessary for the grave-robbers to press on ever further eastward, and to advance more and more boldly into the steppe – as much as twenty days' journey from their starting-point.

Probably all these gold riches would have disappeared without trace had it not been for the intervention of Peter the Great. All the gold and silver vessels, idols, chains, neck-rings and bangles, belt-plaques and buckles would have ended in the melting-pot without anyone noticing. As we know, this was eventually the fate that befell even the wonderful collection obtained from Russia in 1716 by Peter's Dutch friend and intimate, Witsen.

As it chanced, however, the Tsar's attention was drawn to the mysterious objects from the 'Tartar' graves in the dramatic circumstances which we have recorded in our introduction. His zeal led to the formation of the splendid Imperial collection, which as early as 1726 comprised two *Imperial collection*

179

hundred and fifty gold objects, with a total weight of 74 pounds. At that time it consisted of the Demidov presentation and the consignments despatched by two governors of Siberia, Gagarin and Cherkasskii. On his expedition to Siberia the German scholar Müller was still able to acquire a few pieces, but these were only odd gleanings. The gold rush had come to a sudden end with the exhaustion of all accessible cemeteries. Only very foolhardy pioneers ventured further on into the steppe, in the direction of Dzungaria. This was such a dangerous enterprise that in 1764 it was found necessary to prohibit such journeys by special decree. From 1726 onwards the objects were housed in the newly founded Cabinet of Curios (Kunstkammer), and in 1859 they were transferred to the Hermitage, where the finest pieces are still exhibited today in one of the two gold treasuries. When one enters this room – after wandering for some time through this vast labyrinth of a museum (to visit all the rooms

PLATE 34 – Lion-griffin attacking a horse, which has already collapsed. Ornamental plaque, one of a pair; one part could be used as a spike for attaching a leather strap. Dated 4th century B.C. *Hermitage, Leningrad. Width approx. 12 cm., weight of the pair 307 gr. Cf. p. 191.*

would involve walking thirty-five kilometres), one automatically falls into the solemn mood befitting its mysterious splendour.

Inventories

During the course of the last two and a half centuries a number of inventories have been produced, which makes it quite easy to trace the history of each object. Attempts at publication have, however, been dogged by misfortune. The first plan to produce an illustrated catalogue could not be realized because some of the plates that had already been engraved were lost during the Kunstkammer fire in 1747. In the nineteenth century studies appeared by Linas and by Tolstoi and Kondakov; but they only cover a selection of the works. The catalogue compiled by Kieseritzky in 1904 remained unpublished, possibly because it was written in German. Of great importance were the books of Spitsyn (1901, 1906); these contained an attempt at dating which was well received by scholars. From that time onward interest never flagged; indeed, in the years after the Second World War it became more intense than ever. Fettich has succeeded in making some interesting observations, and Salmony has given some datings which are not always convincing. Roes, Haskins and Dittrich have added further interesting studies to the literature on the subject.

In 1962 the long overdue publication surveying the whole range of 'Siberian gold' appeared as part of a comprehensive inventory of all archaeological monuments in the U.S.S.R. Since it had in the meantime become evident that the Altai kurgans contained the key to dating, the signal honour of writing the text was given to the man who had excavated these same kurgans.

One may hope that this edition will not be the last, for the coloured plates are appalling, and are in striking contrast to the amazing technical abilities of the Russian people, which we have occasion to admire each time a rocket space probe is launched. Above all, on closer examination we see that it is not a complete edition at all. Rudenko has excluded those objects which, though of Siberian origin, 'fall outside the scope of the basic collection'. Among these are a drinking-horn dating from the Achaemenid period and the group of so-called Bactrian objects. On the other hand some finds made later are included, although they undoubtedly come from 'contemporary and analogous' graves.

Why Rudenko carried out this 'purge' and why it is unacceptable is not difficult to see.

Gold plaques
PLATE P. 184

The most important group – and the heaviest in weight – is that of the gold plaques, which are as much as one pound in weight. These evidently always occurred in pairs in the grave; with every pair, each plaque is an exact and symmetrical replica of the other. Naturally not all the sets are still complete; oddly enough, one missing piece was reproduced by Witsen – and thus formed part of the collection which he smuggled abroad.

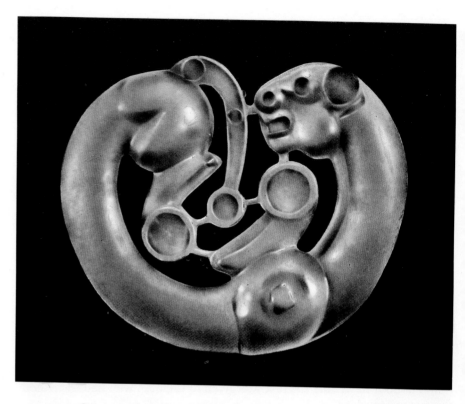

PLATE 35 – Ornamental plaque of thick gold plate, in the form of a curled felid. The cells were used for coloured inlays. *Hermitage, Leningrad. Overall diameter approx. 11 cm., weight 221 gr. Cf. below and p. 189.*

Some plates are rectangular or round; others have the form of a rounded arch with an adjoining shoulder resembling the shape of the letter B one of whose loops has been flattened off. All of them are executed in open-work. Some of these pairs were no doubt used as belt-clasps, but it is quite out of the question that the plaques with high arches should have been employed for such a purpose. Rudenko therefore assumes that they were used to fasten together ornamental robes and thus were worn on the chest. Fettich has put forward the ingenious suggestion that, from a typological point of view, most of the gold plaques are to be regarded as having evolved from the side-pieces attached to the scabbards of Scythian swords, which became independent ornaments in their own right.

PLATE ABOVE   Besides a magnificent curled-up animal, which forms the theme of one circular plaque, the main motif is that of animals fighting. As is only to

182

be expected in such a jumbled accumulation of material, it is possible to distinguish several groups on the basis of subject-matter, quite apart from the considerable differences in artistic quality that are observable. The biggest group has parallels in the Altai kurgans excavated by Rudenko. *Three groups* Presumably these also contained similar pieces, either in massive gold or in wood covered with gold-foil.

Another group consists of compositions of unusual animals, modelled in a magnificent manner: for example, a yak or a gigantic snake.

A third group is distinguished by strictly symmetrical structure. The nearest parallels are to be found among the Ordos bronzes, with which they are also linked by the dragon's heads, whose shape is reminiscent of Chinese specimens. PLATES PP. 159, 193

PLATE P. 231

A further group has been called 'anecdotal'. It cannot be classified under the heading 'animal style'. To our astonishment we see a hunting scene in a wooded tract of country, then again two people seated under a tree FIGS. 123, 126 who appear to be guarding a man lying on the ground and possibly wounded; next to them two horses are waiting. Griaznov has made a striking comment on this. In a short article he points out that the head-gear of one of these two persons must be identical with the curious wooden helmet worn by the woman interred in Pazyryk V. A tall spike was affixed to a truncated cone, and to this spike the woman's pigtail was tied. We recall that a huge felt tapestry which likewise bore scenic compositions was found in the same kurgan. Incidentally, the horseman depicted on this tapestry is wearing a costume that was unusual in the Altai; and the mane of his horse, too, was not cut in the fashion typical of this region.

It may be that besides the ruler interred in this kurgan there was buried

FIG. 123 – *Gold plaque (companion-piece extant) showing a group of people resting (or possibly a lament for the dead?). Two loops on the reverse. Hermitage, Leningrad. Length approx. 16 cm. Cf. above.*

183

a princess belonging to a people whose cultural tradition included the creation of narrative compositions depicting several figures; for her people had closer contact than his with settled tribes which produced wall-paintings. This people may also have acted as an intermediary in transmitting the articles imported from China which are to be found in this same kurgan. Possibly it was they who produced these naturalistic anecdotal gold plaques.

We should of course never lose sight of the fact that we are familiar with only one section of the vast range of works that must once have existed and which found their way into the melting-pot. Thus there appears in Witsen's volume a copper engraving of two belt-plaques in which the figures of the wild beasts are distinguished by sharp curving edges. No doubt these pieces were representative of a whole group which has been lost.

Very often we find gaily coloured inlays, consisting of pastes, turquoises, coral and in particular amber. One round plaque is literally studded with

PLATE 36 – Gold plaque, one of a pair, showing a 'mythical' wolf fighting a tiger. On the reverse side the metal has the appearance of a fabric. It has pins with which it can be affixed, but no loops. *Hermitage, Leningrad. Length approx. 16 cm., weight 526 gr. Cf. pp. 181, 191.*

such inlays; it depicts a stag, whose body forms a circle, surrounded by PLATE P. 190 scenes of animals in combat. The scenes show beasts of prey attacking a boar.

Many of the plaques have a singular feature that is due to technical *Plaques with fabric impress* factors and has led to lively speculation. The convex reverse side has a rough surface corresponding exactly to the structure of a coarse fabric. Meister thought that he could identify traces of embossed work here. This is out of the question: the thickness alone indicates that these pieces must have been cast. Recently Jisl made an interesting attempt to reconstruct the method by which they were manufactured. First of all a die was produced in the usual way, based upon a model carved in wood; this was covered with a piece of fabric identical in outline with the object in question; on to this clay was pressed, which was then fired; it thus formed a counter-die, but of course bore the impress of the fabric. According to Rudenko, this cannot be correct either. The thickness of the plaques is irregular and greater than would correspond to the thickness of a fabric. We recall that in this way pieces weighing as much as one pound were cast. For this reason Rudenko assumes that, in modelling the counter-die, the hollow space which was to remain was filled in with wax, which was covered over with fabric. Personally I believe that this covering was necessary for the simple reason that the material employed was not wax (perhaps nomadic tribes did not always have access to it), but a different, less suitable substance – possibly clay.

There are also ornaments with an onyx in the centre of a very prominent gold mounting, which are again covered with scenes of animals in combat; these, too, Rudenko believes to have been used to ornament clothing.

A plaque on which an eagle-griffin is shown in frontal view gripping an PLATE P. 186 ibex in its talons was already interpreted by Tolstoi and Kondakov as a crest of barbaric splendour worn on the head-dress. The griffin's head stands out sharply from the surface in a manner reminiscent of the composite wood-carvings of the Altai area.

The next large group includes the necklets. Some of them have the shape *Necklets* of an almost complete ring, but frequently they are spiral-shaped; the terminals, however, are invariably in the form of animal bodies or of animal heads. The grandiose manner in which they are fashioned follows the principles we observed in studying the gold plaques.

Other torques have hinges affixed in such a way as to divide them into two parts of unequal length. In most cases they still look essentially like spirals. With this type the rings can be multiplied or combined in such a way as to form collars, which are then further modified. The gaps in between are filled with ornamentation. The upper edge may be crowned with several animal figures. Most of the pieces showing the greatest artistic skill are, however, of simpler construction. The figures at the FIG. 124 terminals are richly embellished with inlays.

PLATE 37 – Eagle-griffin striking an ibex. Ornamentation on a hood. Made of pressed and worked gold plates, and decorated with inlays in coloured enamel, of which only parts have survived. *Hermitage, Leningrad. Photograph of an electrotype in the Victoria and Albert Museum, London. Overall width 16 cm. Cf. p. 185.*

FIG. 124 – *Recumbent lion, its tail terminating in a small griffin head. Cast in gold; the cells were inlaid with amber (and coral?). The figure (length approx. 4 cm.) forms part of a massive two-piece torque (diameter approx. 18 cm., weight 618 gr.). Hermitage, Leningrad. Cf. p. 185.*

Rudenko includes bangles in the same group of objects. Most of these, too, consist of wire coiled into a spiral. Occasionally the animal head on the terminals is replaced by an entire composition depicting a beast of prey attacking a stag. An unusual item is a broad armlet cast in open-work, the surface of which is divided into three horizontal zones, all of which feature fighting animals. Wolves are shown attacking a horse and wild sheep. Animals also decorate the open ends of the bangle.

Bangles
PLATE P. 173

There is an extremely wide range of finger-rings. Only one of these, on the face of which a crouching wild goat is depicted, is cast in one piece; this national technique was evidently associated with animal style in the minds of the people. The others have in their mountings coloured stones or pastes, and in one instance also a pearl; otherwise they have small discs, either decorated or plain. Here extensive use was made of granulation and pseudo-granulation, techniques which we have not encountered hitherto. One open ring is decorated with a lotus palmette which must be of Near Eastern origin.

Finger-rings

There is a very wide selection of ear-pendants, apparently worn by women on both ears but by men on one only – a distinctive custom which can be observed even in Central Europe today. Some pieces must have been used as amulets, since on one occasion we also find as a pendant a human tooth, hanging on a simple little chain. A piece of this kind is also reproduced by Witsen. In another case we find, likewise suspended from a chain, a plain double hook, and elsewhere a small head or gold beads decorated with granulation. Other specimens have several of these small chains. Yet others feature funnels, rings and golden berries; and small shields filled with coloured paste occur. In one particularly lavish type the lower part of the pendant is flattened out in the shape of a horseshoe and may display various kinds of ornaments.

Ear-pendants

FIG. 70

The treasure contains numerous other small pieces on which one may identify filigree, granulation, engraving and cloisonné work. Much of this may likewise have formed part of ear-pendants. There are some pretty miniature vessels, which, Rudenko speculates, may have served to hold either aromatic substances or even poison for arrow-heads.

One small group, which is, however, of great artistic excellence, may have been used, Rudenko suggests, to decorate horses' harness. We find buttons which were presumably fixed on to strap intersections, and gold imitations of boars' tusks. Here, too, massive casting and animal style preponderate.

Harness decoration

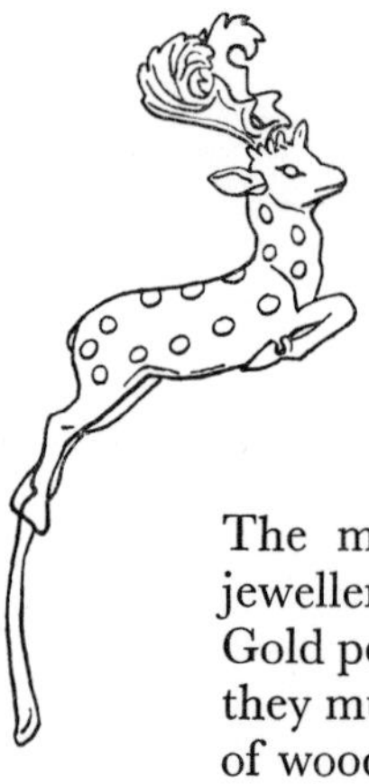

FIG. 125 – *Fallow deer. This naturalistic sculpture may have served as the handle of a vessel. Silver; spots on the coat and hooves gilded. It is one of the few pieces in the Siberian collection whose origin is known for certain. It was dug up by soldiers on the Bukhtarma river and was later acquired by Müller from Captain Bashmakov. Hermitage, Leningrad. Width of figure approx. 8 cm.; weight 222 gr.*

The more delicate techniques employed in the making of personal jewellery are less in evidence.

Gold pendants are so heavy that, if we may follow Rudenko's explanation, they must have formed part of the saddle – although similar objects made of wood and only sheathed with gold-plate have been found on belts in Altai kurgans.

Outside these large groups is a very fine small horse's head, which may possibly have formed the terminal of a whetstone; the handle of a knife that was once lavishly decorated with inlays; and above all the thin metal sheathing of a four-sided staff. The latter depicts a group of mounted warriors who are evidently bringing back home, slung across their saddles, men who have been killed in battle. This piece thus corresponds to the anecdotal gold plaques. We do not know what purpose was served by some small animal sculptures treated in a fairly realistic manner.

Bowl Rudenko discusses in detail a fine bowl with a horizontally fluted body, and handles shaped like animals. He identifies this piece as an import from the Achaemenid empire. It is all the more difficult to understand why he should not mention other pieces which he believes to have come from the same source.

The full significance of these incredible marvels of the goldsmith's art cannot be grasped as long as the problem of dating remains unsolved; and the converse is also true.

As long as scholars reassured themselves that animal style had evolved out of a barbarization of Ionic forms, it was logical to assume that its offshoots in Siberia must be of considerably more recent date. In Witsen's plates we find reproduced coins of Roman emperors such as Gordian and Nero; and this seemed to clinch the argument.

Dating Another possible dating, based on less superficial considerations, seemed to offer itself when scholars began to distinguish a later, polychrome phase of animal style.

The gold plaques are lavishly decorated with inlaid work; they frequently exhibit a fanciful play of lines; indeed, so far as their form is concerned, it is possible to establish some direct parallels with finds from the Kuban' area (Novocherkassk). Thus what was more natural than to classify them, too, in the Sarmatian phase? We have already seen that, on the basis of this assumption, a skilful forger succeeded in reconstructing further Kuban' finds which then lent weight to the prevailing theory.

The theory of Sarmatian animal style also implies that early Scythian forms must have lived on in Central Asia. Near Eastern cloisonné techniques, it was alleged, had long influenced this area. One could thus postulate that the plaques were made long before the polychrome style had any influence on southern Russia.

Parallels with Altai

This view became plausible when excavations were recommenced in the Altai, and the opinion came to prevail that the discoveries made there were of an early date. For in the Altai objects were found corresponding to many well-known pieces in the Siberian gold treasure, but on these same objects we observe motifs that are undoubtedly of Achaemenid origin. It is understandable that Rudenko should have been particularly proud of this aspect of his excavations. Immediately after his discovery of the tattooed body he declared that the riddle of the Siberian gold had at long last been solved. He naturally made this view his starting-point when he was given the task of undertaking a scholarly examination of the treasure in the Hermitage.

Rudenko's classification and chronology

According to Rudenko both groups are distinguished by a similar variety of artistic tendencies. Naturalistic pieces stand cheek by jowl with fanciful ones; the degree of stylization fluctuates constantly. The range of motifs includes realistically observed animals as well as human beings and fabulous beasts. In the treatment of detail, too, affinities are continually found. In both cases 'Schrägschnitt' is employed. The animal's coat is rendered by flame-shaped lines and the mane by scales. Animals' snouts, ears and paws are standardized, as though rendered by logograms. Designs are added to the muscular parts to suggest animation; most commonly these consist of dots, commas or arcs.

Contour lines which give the figure its elegant curves are accentuated by a band of short hatched strokes. If the artist desires to contrast one plane with another, he achieves this either by simple dotted designs or by applying cloisonné. Even in the details there are identical forms, as for instance in the curvature of griffins' wings. Some of these affinities, extending to minutiae (e.g., articulation of large body surfaces by means of cloisonné enamelling) recur on objects from the Oxus treasure.

Since it is now possible to distinguish chronological phases in Altai art, something similar must also be feasible in the case of the Siberian collection, particularly if one makes comparisons with the Oxus treasure, as well as with Scythian and Sarmatian antiquities. This is the line Rudenko attempts to follow, and as a result he is continually discussing and assessing the opinions of his forerunners Fettich and Salmony.

PLATE P. 182
6th century B.C.
PLATE P. 34

Rudenko believes that a heavy gold breast-piece in the shape of a curled animal belongs to the beginning of the sixth century B.C. It is comparable with the curled animals which form the paws and tail of the well-known

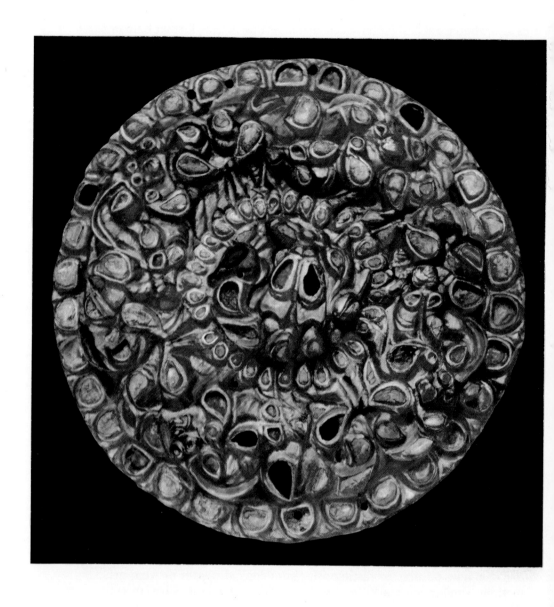

PLATE 38 – This gold plaque, like the others reproduced here, was probably the ornament on a ceremonial robe (a companion-piece is extant). The animals represented have rich inlays of turquoise, and eyes of black stone (or paste). *Hermitage, Leningrad. Diameter approx. 12 cm. Cf. pp. 185, 191.*

panther from Kelermes, as well as a bronze of the Maiemir culture. He PLATE P. 184 ascribes to the middle of the 6th century those plaques featuring combatant animals whose coat is rendered by flame-shaped lines and whose mane is suggested by scales; for these singular features already occur in Bashadar II.

He believes that the magnificent round plaque with its lavish inlays and 5th century B.C. a curled stag in the centre belongs to the fifth century B.C. In his view, PLATE P. 190 a key to dating is provided by the form given to the nostrils. Rudenko assigns to the same century objects which are reminiscent of pieces in the Oxus treasure: in both cases there is a certain smoothness of form and much use of such filling-in motifs as the dot, comma and bean. In this category he also includes armlets and necklets made of strong gold wire, the pendants we have already mentioned, and also a very fine gold button depicting an elk being attacked by a wild beast. To the same period, he thinks, belong hinged necklets and the golden bowl which is so strongly reminiscent of Achaemenid art. Nor does he hesitate to assign to such an early date those finger-rings and ear-pendants which are more static in form.

On the basis of parallels in the Altai, Rudenko assigns to the beginning Early 4th century B.C. of the next (fourth) century, or possibly to the middle of that century, PLATE P. 180 the plaque showing a lion-griffin attacking a horse, which has often been reproduced on account of its elegance; also the scene of a fight between three animals, set in a rectangular frame; and finally a cast armlet the three zones of which each feature combatant animals. Comparison with the Oxus treasure also induces him to include in this transitional period the most splendid necklets, richly ornamented with cloisonné enamelling; and also the famous *cap agraffe*, although Roes does not find another toothed crest on a griffin's head until Greek art of the fourth century B.C. This late appearance is of no consequence, according to Rudenko; it was just an Oriental element that was only gradually adopted by the West. In spite of the objections raised by other scholars, he assigns to this early date the naturalistic anecdotal plaque depicting a hunt, as well as that showing men bringing home those killed in battle. He is not disturbed by the fact that on the plaque featuring the hunt one can observe a sword-fastening which differs from that used by the Scythians. Maenchen-Helfen has indeed recognized in this a feature characteristic of warriors in the southern part of Central Asia.

The period of time covered by this intermediary group (end of fifth – beginning of fourth century B.C.) must however be taken as evidence of some uncertainty on Rudenko's part, for not much now remains for the fourth century proper – at the most those plaques with symmetrically 4th century B.C. arranged figures inside a rectangular framework; this whole dating is based upon very vague affinities with the kurgans at Pazyryk. According to Rudenko we must also attribute to this place collar-shaped necklets the ends of which terminate in animal figures that are still comparatively simple. A congestion of objects occurs once more in a transitional group dating from the beginning of the third century B.C. This is the period of origin suggested by Rudenko for all those plaques cast in gold whose outlines are blurred, or which are unusual in their choice of subject. Thus, for example, in one case we have camels fighting a double-headed animal which has the foreparts of two wolves combined. Also to be classified here are a monster with a wolf's head and antlers which terminate in small griffins' heads; furthermore, those ungainly rectangular plaques depicting a wolf fighting a snake; and lastly the naturalistic anecdotal plaque showing a wounded man being cared for or commiserated with under a tree. Rudenko classifies in this group the sharp-edged belt-plaques reproduced only by Witsen. Some necklets are also included on the strength of parallels drawn between them and Sarmatian works.

To the third, or even to the second, century is assigned that boldly curving plaque which depicts a snake attacking a wolf. The inlays that are elsewhere treated in such a schematic manner are in this case wholly incorporated into the composition. In the same group, the latest in date, is a gold casting depicting griffins, which is unmistakably linked with the Sarmatian area.

Thus, in sum, this attempt to provide a dating finally assigns the treasure of Peter the Great to the period between the fifth and third centuries B.C., with some pieces falling outside these limits.

It is striking that, in order to prove his point, Rudenko does not draw upon the affinities which undoubtedly existed with Transbaikalian and Mongolian finds of the Hsiung-nu period. Not even the gold plaque found at Verkhneudinsk in 1844 seems to him a fixed point, although it deserves to be incorporated not only for its motifs but also on the strength of its outlines alone. But others have made such attempts.

The most recent is by E. Dittrich, who has endeavoured to establish a chronological classification by approaching the problem from the reverse direction, from the east. She seeks to distinguish in the gold treasure stylistic groups, two of which correspond to stages in Altai art (but with Pazyryk occurring before Bashadar!); two others, however, she considers to be 'localized in the area of northern Mongolia and Lake Baikal'; the earlier one, attested by finds 'in Noin Ula and its environs', is characterized by polychrome compositions and the use of certain artistic devices (three-quarter profile of overlapping animal bodies); in the later Mongolian and Baikal group at Derestui there occur compositions featuring three animals or more.

These two eastern stylistic groups are thought by Dittrich to have marked the chronological limits of a stratum which, geographically speaking, runs right across the steppe area, and to which the Novocherkassk treasure also belongs.

Early 3rd century B.C.

PLATE P. 196

3rd or 2nd century B.C.
PLATE P. 15

Dittrich's classification

In fact Derestui is probably considerably earlier than is presumed here. *Dittrich refuted* Burials in the Hsiung-nu cemeteries in Transbaikalia cease at an early date, at the very same time that the forts succumb to attacks by barbarian neighbours. On the other hand Noin Ula is later, and must be dated about the beginning of the Christian era. But in fact what happened in the case of the Hsiung-nu was that certain motifs became petrified through their use in magic and were therefore preserved for a long time. We have been able to show that the mainstream of artistic development had already long been flowing into another direction. At Derestui, too, no more than degenerate offshoots of the glorious old tradition were found. These objects indicate that the heyday of animal representations was over.

In the Ordos area the process of disintegration took a different course:

PLATE 39 – Gold ornamental plaque, lavishly decorated with inlays of coloured paste. (Companion-piece extant, made into a buckle by the addition of a hook.) It depicts two serpent-dragons with goat-like heads flanking a 'tree of life'. Borovka was the first to point out parallels in Chinese works of art. *Hermitage, Leningrad. Approx. width 15 cm., weight 353 gr. Cf. pp. 183, 194.*

here degeneration led to playfulness; possibly these late pieces were used as amulets.

Thus for the time being Rudenko's classification remains more serviceable. It is at least consistent. If he excludes the finds made in Mongolia and the Baikal area from the material on which he bases his comparative dating, this is only because he believes that these were the result of influences whose spread had been retarded. The bronze plaques from the Minusinsk area he regards as intermediate links between these late products and the main works from artistic centres, e.g. in the Altai.

PLATE P. 193

But he is unconvincing when he denies that even the rectangular plaques with symmetrical representations are derived from the east. In this case a centre in the Chinese border area may indeed have played a part; but it was situated further to the south and presumably flowered before the period when the Hsiung-nu consolidated their power.

Nevertheless comparison with such pieces from the east does not mean that the dates provided by Rudenko have to be put forward very significantly. If we are to incorporate any of the objects from this treasure into the later period of Hsiung-nu rule, then at the most we can do so in regard to a small insignificant-looking buckle on which there are no animals but instead only rectangular lattice-work.

But one certainly could argue that the dates taken by Rudenko as his starting-point are too early. We have already seen that he ascribes the Altai finds to a date up to one hundred years earlier than that which a comparison of styles would require. If we amend this, then of course the age of Peter the Great's treasure would also have to be altered: its mean date would then be the fourth or third century B.C. Fettich's reasonable and sober view is thus again shown to be valid.

Fettich's chronology validated

Can we now say who produced these gold objects? Herodotus mentions a number of peoples living to the east of the Sarmatians. Of these the Argippaei and Arimaspi, for example, come to mind in this connection, as do perhaps the Issedones, whereas the 'gold-guarding griffins', a purely legendary term, have been identified with the inhabitants of the Altai. Most of the best pieces were probably not produced by the Saka, for their totem animal was the stag which, as we have seen, played but a minor part as a motif.

Ethnic ascription

But these are unfortunately all names which tell us little. Therefore we must once more turn to archaeology for assistance, only to discover that it, too, has little to offer in the way of information about northern and central Kazakhstan, the areas which are of the greatest interest for our purpose.

Kurgans in northern Kazakhstan

In 1956 Griaznov described kurgans in northern Kazakhstan which had ramparts of stone shaped like tongs leading off from them – hence the graphic name 'kurgans with a moustache'. He established that they belong to the Scythian phase. In the same year, the Kazakh Academy of Sciences also began to publish a series which contained regular reports by Kazakh archaeologists on their work. Thus today we know that kurgans of less striking construction were also erected at the same time. Apparently this area was inhabited by two rather large tribes living side by side: what the nature of their relationship was we do not know.

An important fact is that stray finds made in modern times are continually testifying to the prevalence of animal style in this region. We can observe well-established links with the Sarmatians in the west, and also with the Altai and the Enisei area in the east. One fine unique object is a pick, the neck of which is decorated with the figure of a ram also cast in bronze. The small gold head of a saiga antelope with horns shaped in the form of a lyre exactly resembles a work of art well known from an engraving in Witsen's work. Bronze snaffles are reminiscent of those known in the Maiemir culture of the Altai. A bronze dagger is embellished with volutes and a succession of linked spirals. Griaznov points out parallels to this found both in the region that is now Uzbekistan, and also in the Anan'ino culture.

The present archaeological situation and the knowledge that plunderers undertook expeditions involving up to twenty days' journey naturally give rise to the question whether these grave-robbers who accumulated the Siberian gold treasure may not also have operated in the area around

Kurgans in eastern Kazakhstan

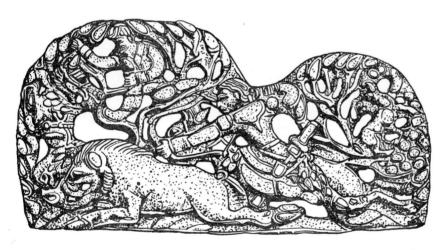

FIG. 126 – *Anecdotal gold plaque (companion-piece extant) inlaid with amber and coral. Eyes of black glass or stone. Hunter on horseback in a wooded mountainous landscape. Centre: slaying of a boar; top left: man in a tree-top holding his horse on a tight rein; right: an ibex, evidently being hunted. The man killing the boar wears his sword suspended by a loop on the side of the sheath – a fashion common in southern Central Asia, whence it radiated westwards and eastwards (even to India with the Kushan). Hermitage, Leningrad. Width of base approx. 19 cm.; weight 464 gr. Cf. pp. 183, 196.*

Lake Zaisan, in what is nowadays eastern Kazakhstan. At any rate, in this region huge cemeteries have very recently been discovered which belong to the last centuries before the birth of Christ. Regional differences in ritual show that here, too, several tribes must have existed alongside one another. As well as normal burials of nomadic freemen there are gigantic kurgans which, as a rule, have been stripped bare. One group, at Chilikty, bears a remarkable resemblance to some of the enormous Scythian kurgans in southern Russia. In spite of all the destruction that took place, the graves in this area, which date from as early as the sixth century B.C., have yielded several gold objects: curled panthers, stags, and thin gold-foil plates which once covered wood carvings showing boars in relief.

Here we find ourselves in the immediate neighbourhood of the Dzungarian Gate. Whoever held sway over these grazing-grounds was virtually predestined to maintain contacts with tribes on all sides. It is tempting to assume that the gold plaques in which intercourse with the east found particularly clear expression – and also those which display distinct affinities with the oases of Middle Asia – were found in this area. Into this region people of Mongoloid appearance may have migrated at an early stage; and it is they who are thought to have been represented in

FIG. 126

PLATE 40 – Gold plaque showing a wolf and a large serpent in combat. The coloured inlays in the hollowed-out cavities are missing. The reverse side has the appearance of a fabric and bears traces of repair (also noticeable in the illustration). The tongue and slit make this plaque a pseudo-clasp; these features are lacking in the companion-piece. Long narrow pairs of plaques such as these might, however, have been used as belt-clasps. *Hermitage, Leningrad. Length 16 cm., weight 222.7 gr. Cf. p. 192.*

the naturalistic anecdotal plaque showing two people guarding a man who appears to be wounded. The bulk of the population, on the other hand, were Europoid; their skulls make it clear that descendants of the Andronovo population were still dominant everywhere.

In any case we have to see the whole treasure against the background of a highly complex ethnic pattern, involving a large number of tribes whose names we shall probably never learn.

Many tribes responsible

Now it has, of course, been maintained that this complexity does not matter very much so far as artistic developments are concerned, and that the broad movements of taste and manners in each period everywhere asserted themselves in a very uniform and rigorous fashion. But the actual concrete material found refutes this contention. In discussing the Minusinsk district we have already noted that, during the second stage of the Tagar culture, the stag was represented with many singular features which had long since become obsolete in the Pontic area. Thus in various regions people clung with differing degrees of tenacity to what had become outdated. Only in this way is it possible to explain that problem of retardation which is connoted by the term 'Sarmatian animal style'.

XIV. THE AFTERMATH

Arguments in favour There used to be a tendency to regard animal style as having developed out of the art inherited by hunters from the Palaeolithic, and as the culminating achievement of the barbarian world; it was therefore tempting to suppose that its effects lived on for a lengthy period of time. The stimuli it imparted seem to have evoked a ready response wherever a daemonic attitude to life prompted willing self-abandonment to fate, and sought urgently to express the inarticulate forces of heroism latent within it. Fettich, who with true zeal devoted a lifetime of study to this barbarian world, which existed alongside and in defiance of the advanced civilizations, formulated the problem as follows:

> 'Among all the barbarian peoples, from the seventh century onwards, the inhabitants of southern Russia, the Scythians of Iranian origin, are the most important, judged by their prowess in producing small-scale works of sculpture. Their art, a combination of various barbarian and classical elements, exerted a great influence upon their barbarian neighbours in every respect. From Scythian basic forms there evolved, at various places and times, one new animal style after another, all of them agreeing only in that they shared the characteristic qualities of barbarian art: a departure from naturalism, and correspondingly a geometric variation of the forms to be found in nature, or a predilection for entirely fanciful compositions.'

Europe:
Germanic styles It is striking that these views were expounded mainly with reference to European material. Ancient Germanic animal decoration used to be regarded as a quite legitimate, if rather western, offspring of Scythian animal style. The so-called 'second Germanic style' was also traced back to the ancient culture of southern Russia, despite the chronological and geographical gap between the two. Brønsted and Fettich and many others collaborated to provide an interpretation of this mysterious network of links between Europe and the east.

It is understandable that scholars should have been keen to regard the Huns, who were charged with having lived 'in a world filled with mythical images', as leading representatives of animal decoration in applied art. The legend that tells of their immigration, ostensibly in pursuit of a stag, was interpreted to this effect. Bronzes in animal style from various areas were used as a means of familiarizing the unsuspecting reader with what was supposed to be the Huns' mentality. When it could no longer be doubted that this view was based only upon very scanty material evidence (animal figures are very rare in the works produced by the Huns in Europe) the line of argument changed, and it was claimed that the punched scaliform designs on the Huns' gold sheets actually portrayed the plumage of a bird of prey.

Such attempts at interpretation would be much easier with the so-called *Huns* late Hunnish work in metal. Fettich links the Martinovka culture with Hunnish tribes which had withdrawn to the region of the Dnieper. In the applied art they produced he distinguishes one component which he boldly calls 'neo-Scythian'. Then, according to Fettich, when the invading Avars broke into the Carpathian basin in A.D. 568, they absorbed ethnic elements which carried on the traditions of the Martinovka culture. This **PLATE BELOW** would explain why the bronze casting from the latter half of the Avar *Avars* period represented this 'neo-Scythian' stylistic trend in grandiose fashion, 'within the general cultural pattern of the early Middle Ages'. What specialists refer to as the 'Keszthely culture' he claims to be virtually identical with this new flowering of the old tradition.

Others working on Scythian culture have endeavoured to trace these threads further still. T. Talbot Rice believes she has detected Scythian

PLATE 41 – Decoration on a strap, showing a griffin. From the territory of the Avars. *Göbl Collection, Vienna. Cf. above.*

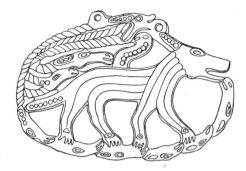

FIG. 127 – *Cast bronze plaque with zoomorphic juncture. Still strongly influenced by the animal style of the steppe, despite its fairly late date. Discovered in the Enisei Canal at the mouth of the Iazeva. Collection of Tomsk University. Cf. p. 202.*

influences on Anglo-Saxon stone stelae of the eleventh century. She assumes that nomadic elements were widely disseminated in Slavic folk art; even a towel made by Lithuanian peasants in the nineteenth century affords material for comparison.

The more popular the level of the work, the more extensive does the legacy attributed to the Scythians become. Even large numbers of medieval illuminated manuscripts have been cited in this connection.

It is thus not surprising that many experts should have expressed doubts about such a late Scythian expansion. Time and time again they have pointed out that late Roman or Byzantine influences could equally well have produced similar results. It has also been argued that the parallel features could have developed simply on the basis of similar attitudes of mind.

Asia In this connection it is instructive to consider the general situation in the vast expanses of Asia. Here, too, animal style is said to have continued up to the present day or at least until the not so distant past.

Roerich, who himself belonged to a family of artists, found a recurrence of animal style among the nomadic tribes of northern Tibet. Okladnikov identified last traces of it in the decoration of Iakut saddle-bows. Not long ago Lopatin maintained that animal style still existed among the

FIG. 128 – *Wild goose, cast in bronze, evidently a realistic piece of late date. Vologda district.*

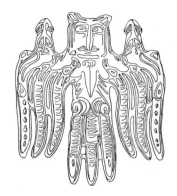

FIG. 129 – *Fantastic creature with a bird's body and human face. It was certainly meant to represent some important religious conception. Kungursk Collection, Hermitage, Leningrad. Cf. p. 203.*

Tungus of the Amur region. The art of the Goldi tribe, who were influenced by the Altai people in the fifth century, came within the domain of animal style. Even today, he claimed, it contained a modified survival of the classical phase of animal art.

Just as its tradition still lingered on in Europe, so – as Fettich himself has stated – it persisted in Korea and Japan as well.

PLATE P. 202

Perm' area

The best, and most carefully studied, picture of such a legacy is furnished by the forest and tundra areas on either side of the Urals, especially the well-known rich region of Perm'. Here impressive finds were made as early as the nineteenth century, which at first were classified, without any attempt at chronological arrangement, under the heading 'Permian-Scythian ornamental style'. Most of these finds consisted of small cast-bronze plaques depicting animals, or in rare instances human beings, in a realistic yet fanciful manner. Very frequently we find fabulous creatures, as well as elaborately composed scenes. In investigating their significance and purpose, scholars took as their starting-point the current popular beliefs and customs of the Ugrian tribes, all or some of which once lived to the west of the Urals. They employed similar pieces to decorate their clothing, for use as votive gifts, or to drape their idols. But it is not likely, as was thought in one romantic phase of research, that they were gener-

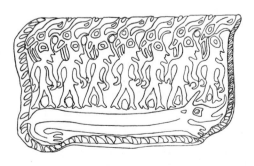

FIG. 130 – *Plaque of 'mythological' content, showing a typical repetition of like figures. In this case, too, there is no lack of animal attributes; at the bottom lies an enormous lizard. Cf. pp. 202, 203.*

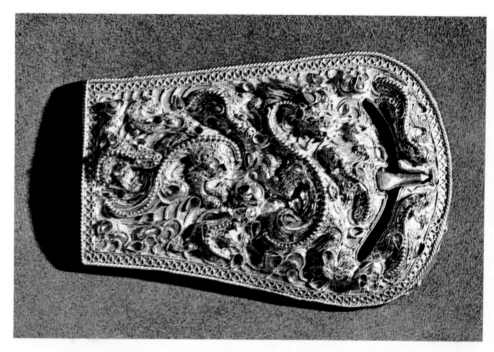

PLATE 42 – Belt-clasp, gold and turquoise, from Lo-lang (Korea). It probably belonged to a Chinese officer whose equipment partly resembled that of China's traditional enemies in the steppe. Animal motifs from the steppe lands are here combined harmoniously with typically Chinese decoration, whose techniques (filigree and granulation), however, originate in the west. 1st–2nd century A.D. *National Museum of Korea, Seoul. Cf. p. 201.*

FIGS. 127, 130 ally part of the costume worn by shamans (hence the term 'Shamanist bronzes').

As time went on, we began to obtain a fuller picture of the historical process in the course of which these curious works came into being.

On account of its mineral wealth, the Perm' district was a target for invaders from as early as the Bronze Age. The metallurgy that developed here absorbed stimuli from very distant areas (such as the Caucasus) and passed them on deep into the forest zone.

It was upon this basis that there developed, in an area that included Perm' (as well as other areas), the Anan'ino culture with which we are already familiar; it acted as a centre of dissemination for Scythian motifs and ideas to north-eastern Europe and western Siberia. At that time, under southern influence, animal figures, which had hitherto been wholly reserved for the ritual sphere, came to be employed in works of applied art. This however does not exclude the possibility that notions of magic may have played a part.

At the time when the Sarmatians were masters of the steppe lands, there developed, as the immediate successor of Anan'ino, the P'ianobor culture, which lasted into the fifth century A.D. The fact that, under pressure from nomadic horsemen, the central area of settlement had to be transferred further to the north was of the utmost importance for this culture. The P'ianobor people broke away, as it were, from the mainstream of development, in order to lead an extremely rich life of their own, in which they expanded and differentiated the cultural legacy they had inherited. *P'ianobor culture*

This formula also makes it possible to understand the course of their artistic evolution. Some motifs originating in the Scythian period were now modified and combined afresh, with an ever-increasing degree of freedom. Human figures and faces were added. As well as occasional realistic animal pictures, probably used by these hunters for magic rituals, we encounter hybrid beings furnished with animal and human attributes. They might represent the deities or heroes of whom Ugrian folk-lore tells. Repetition or symmetrical arrangement almost become the rule. The element of plasticity is reduced, and sometimes one has an impression of plaiting. Particularly characteristic is a bird with outstretched wings and a human face on its chest. Understandably enough, forest animals, such as the bear, play a prominent part. FIG. 130 FIG. 129

A very similar variation upon the old-established tradition is encountered in the Pechora and Ob' districts, where implements from the steppe lands were eagerly collected, employed in rites, and finally preserved at places of sacrifice which remained in being for centuries. As a curious result of this squirrel-like hoarding, the archaeologist finds himself faced with unusual difficulties in assigning dates to western Siberian culture; opinions on this point differ by whole centuries.

In Perm' the culture that follows is that of Lomatovo, which extends into the ninth century A.D. Its hoards contain Byzantine and Sassanid imports, transmitted by nomadic tribes. From an artistic point of view this is a period of gradual decline. By the tenth and eleventh centuries only a few types are left, but they are at least distinguished by their pronounced realism. Some traditions continue until Russian colonization sets in. *Lomatovo culture* FIG. 131

Beyond the Urals, too, old traditions were equally faithfully preserved. Sassanid silver vessels were hoarded in great quantities as religious symbols, until they finally found their way into the Hermitage. These same impressive specimens confirm the principle suggested by finds: that the surviving samples of animal style art are evidently not to be found in the steppe region itself, but in remote peripheral areas. In the centres of political power we are restricted to very few animal pictures, which are

FIG. 131 – *This silver bowl, found at Perm', served cultic purposes, like the specimens from Siberia. It is of Sassanid origin, and has a secondary decoration of animals and dancers. The pointed heads indicate that these are figures of spirits. Sludka, Stroganov Collection. Cf. p. 203.*

FIG. 132 continually reproduced and cited – such as the saddle-bow from Kudyrge in the Altai (fourth century A.D.) which, in an engraved hunting scene, even shows an inversion of the animal's body.

One might almost assume that this scanty evidence of after-effects in the steppe lands is due to the fact that this theme has not yet been treated by a scholar deeply interested in the question. For there are as yet no stylistic analyses that could be compared with those made by Scandinavian, German and Hungarian scholars. Those who have examined this matter have, so to speak, looked at it with untrained eyes and have given priority to quite different questions.

Fettich's view This assumption becomes almost a certainty if we bear in mind that Fettich had no difficulty in finding Asiatic material from Russian excavations for comparison with the European survivals of animal style which he described. In his work, *Bronzeguss und Nomadenkunst*, he devoted a lengthy and highly stimulating chapter to this aspect of the subject.

Soviet scholars' views Nevertheless it does not seem as though it is only a failure to see the broader picture that prevents Soviet scholars from joining in the hunt PLATE P. 206 for surviving animal style motifs in which many of their European colleagues are engaged. They evidently lack that 'romantic enthusiasm for the nomads' which was able to develop most easily in such cramped areas as Central Europe, and among Hungarian scholars of German origin. Perhaps Soviet scholars had a greater sense of the differences that existed because they were concerned in their everyday activity with the magnificent works of the early nomads. They were also familiar with the modern Turkic peoples and their art, and thus were constantly reminded of the great gulf that separates the past from the present.

An extreme position in this matter is taken up by Griaznov, whose

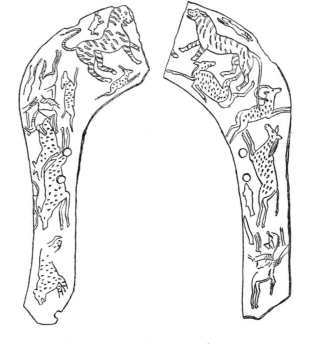

FIG. 132 – *Drawings on the saddle-bow from Kudyrge, Altai. Cf. p. 204.*

intellectual integrity we have had many occasions to note. He stresses the fact that early nomadic art was a splendid and unique achievement that was never again repeated.

The position of Rudenko is more moderate. He shows us the connections which lead from the applied arts of the huge Altai kurgans right up to the handicrafts of those who inhabit this area today, but he emphasizes above all those lines of development which run parallel to animal decoration proper: it is the plant and abstract designs which already appear at Pazyryk that are pregnant with things to come.

In any case this means that, although there were some features reminiscent of past greatness, no further evolution took place in the steppes that could be even remotely compared to the heyday of Germanic animal ornamentation. Even Hunnic art was already different from it. The studies of Alföldi and Werner have enabled us to form a clearer idea of this, and we now know that it was dominated by an abstract principle. It was this principle and the so-called geometric scroll, not surviving elements of animal style, that were to remain of crucial importance in the centuries that followed.

One can now raise the question what it was that caused this change in values and shift of emphasis.

The background of the transformation can be grasped only if we know what was the real essence of early nomadic art and are familiar with its ethnic and social setting. We have already said something about these problems but must now, in our final chapter, consider them in wider perspective.

PLATE 43 – Shield-boss from Herpály, Hungary. The shape of this piece is Germanic and its decoration Sarmatian. It belongs to equipment used solely for ceremonial purposes, not in war. Gilt
bronze. *Original in Hungarian National Museum, Budapest. Photograph of an electrotype in the Victoria and
Albert Museum, London. Cf. p. 204.*

XV. THE RISE OF THE MOUNTED WARRIORS
AND THE BIRTH OF ANIMAL STYLE

In planning this volume we proceeded from the belief, nurtured by numerous general works, that during the last centuries before the birth of Christ the art of the Eurasian steppe had a uniform character. *Uniform character of steppe art*

This view has withstood the test of our study of the material. As we have seen, a common and universal feature was a repertoire of animal motifs, some of them of a complex nature, employed in a specific ornamental manner usually referred to as 'animal style'. We have also confirmed the old hypothesis that this art was the work of equestrian peoples who gained their livelihood by nomadic livestock-breeding. Where it extends further into the wooded steppe, this can be explained as due to the influence exerted by nomads. The huge kurgans in the high-lying valleys of the Altai, and the graves in the Tian'-shan' and Pamirs, do not alter this picture radically either. Until recent times the mountain pastures were used during the summer months by people living in the steppe.

More disturbing is the absence of finds in animal style between the Aral and Caspian Seas; but one could point to the fact that the environment here was extremely unfavourable to the preservation of such works, and that the area has as yet not been thoroughly explored. In the case of the Tarim basin, which likewise fails to fit into the general picture, it is much easier to find an explanation. Chinese accounts from the Han era mention farmers living in oases in this region, and this evidence has been substantiated by modern discoveries made possible by the extreme aridity of the area. Grain and a kind of porridge made from it were among the most important funerary gifts, so that the predominantly agrarian character of the population is beyond doubt. FIG. 133

In more than one chapter of this volume we have found ourselves unable to solve problems of origin. The fact that the animal style begins in one uniform chronological phase points on one hand to a certain kinship between the various 'provinces', but on the other hand makes it extremely difficult to locate the initial centre from which diffusion took place. *Unsolved problem*

We were also unable to explain why early nomadic art should show such a marked preference for depicting beasts of prey and wild game, and almost always avoids the animals that were of the utmost importance in the nomad economy. In the meantime we have learnt from a study by Mrs Il'inskaia that there is one exception to this rule – but only in a very restricted area. The idea that there was some necessary link between the nomadic way of life and the use of this particular motif is, in any

FIG. 133 – *Desiccated mummy of an old woman. From a grave in the delta of the Qum-Dar'ia, opened by Sven Hedin. Finds of this kind convey an idea of the physical and cultural characteristics of the settled population of the Tarim basin, who apparently maintained their Bronze Age traditions for a very long time. Cf. p. 207.*

case, not very convincing when we consider the fact that completely different means of self-expression were found in later periods.

Need for wider view It is, however, tempting to make another effort to solve these problems by looking at the stylistic development of steppe art against a wider background, considering neighbouring cultures as well.

The excavations carried out by Soviet scholars during recent years have produced new evidence of fundamental importance which has as yet hardly been properly evaluated. But they, too, only make it possible to construct a hypothesis – akin to those sketches which so many other writers have already attempted. The reader should always bear in mind on what shifting grounds an advance in knowledge is made in this field.

Pre-nomadic period We have to set out from the assumption that the early and middle Bronze Age, up to approximately 1200 B.C., must have been a relatively tranquil period in the steppes proper. The large-scale excavations which Soviet scholars have carried out in the wooded steppe zone have not yet, at any rate, disclosed at any point the existence of nomadic horsemen who had anything like the expansive urge of their later successors. In this period the dynamic population movement lay further south; for example in what is today Turkmenistan. There the cattle-breeding tribes congregated whose invasion of India can be reconstructed from the Vedic texts.

North of the fortieth parallel, in the vast stretch of land that extends from southern Russia to the Dzungarian Gate, the prevailing form of economy was agrarian. Wherever conditions were even moderately favourable, permanent settlements arose. Their inhabitants, who belonged to an ancient Europoid type, gained their livelihood by cultivating millet and wheat as well as by livestock-breeding. Horses provided above all a source of food: in some graves, horses' ribs have been found which were apparently the remains of 'cutlets' deposited as funerary gifts. In addition to this mares were milked, as Homer already records.

Certain subdivisions may be identified within this huge area: in the area of the river Ural begins the 'Andronovo culture', on the southern rim of which one may again distinguish several sub-groups, which have certain fairly well-marked individual features.

208

Probably the economy was based upon a precise division of labour between the sexes, with all members of the community working closely together. The menfolk, or possibly only the young unmarried men, took the livestock out to the pastures, while the women of the village tilled the soil. The Andronovo culture is the most extensive homogeneous Bronze Age complex within the territory of what is today the U.S.S.R. This was apparently due to the following system: the men with their herds of livestock were continually looking for new areas which they could hope to settle permanently. As a result of contact between individual groups of herdsmen, cultural innovations spread quickly and evenly. There must also have been some trade with distant parts whereby, for example, tin from the Altai found its way to Europe. The peasants of the steppe, however, had as yet no serious enemies. More backward sections of the population, whose economy was based to a greater extent on hunting, may have withdrawn to the mountains.

Only to the east of Dzungaria did there begin a new cultural area which *Eastern area of steppe* we are endeavouring to reconstruct on the basis of stray finds from the Gobi desert. Presumably these people were Mongoloid livestock-breeders and hunters. Most of their settlements have been irretrievably destroyed by erosion. It is therefore difficult to make any definite statements about their political and economic level of attainment. Stone implements continue to be used for a long time. From the position of finds in the sites and the primitive equipment, archaeologists believe they can deduce that here hunters gradually went over to cattle-breeding. In this process the influence of Chinese agrarian culture played no small part.

East of the Chingan range one might expect to find a more rapid rate of evolution. As early as the third millennium B.C. various cultures in this area came into mutual contact and overlapped. In the second millennium local cultures formed, under Chinese influence, in which intensive horse-breeding was carried on, as well as the cultivation of millet. The sites of permanent settlements are known to us.

From the fusion of the various regional cultures in the second millennium an enormous uniform culture-area was then formed. The dead were now buried in stone cists, which may perhaps be due to the influence of practices coming from the West.

In contrast to Sosnovsky's view, this slab-grave culture seems to develop *Evolution of nomadism* in the direction of a nomadic way of life only at a later stage. We must accordingly seek the true source of disturbance not here, but at the other end of the steppe belt.

In the west the continuity of anthropological type in the early and late Bronze Age graves makes it clear that the greater part of the subsequent nomadic population was descended from these ancient and relatively peaceful peasants of the steppe zone. This is also true of the Iranian-speaking peoples whom we have already met as the most powerful: the

Saka beyond the Jaxartes and the Pontic Scythians. An internal transformation of the economic structure and way of life must therefore have taken place, rather than the influx of a new ethnic element.

Griaznov's theory Griaznov claims to have succeeded in detecting the transition to nomadic life in one particular place *in flagrante*, as it were – namely, among the tribes of the foothills of the Altai – and points to the inevitable consequence of this: the plundering and subjection of those elements of the population that were unable or unwilling to join in this transformation in good time. He argues that economic development in the steppes compelled the formation of ever more complex economic units, as well as the creation of larger confederations between them. At first there were only small scattered settlements in the vicinity of which was sufficient grazing land to keep the few cattle that served as a source of milk and meat, and also as draught animals. Gradually other kinds of livestock came to be raised as well, especially sheep and horses, which, when combined with agriculture, required a large number of labourers. For this reason economic life was carried on in larger units, whose leaders already needed to have considerable authority. This stage, which was reached by the beginning of the first millennium B.C., is reflected in those settlements from the late Andronovo culture that contained houses, and probably also stables, half sunk into the ground; when these were constructed, up to 300 cubic metres of earth had to be shifted. The chieftains of these settlements lie buried in huge lavishly furnished kurgans. The economic pattern was already beginning to show a distinct tendency towards greater mobility, towards semi-nomadism.

From this form, he claims, there was a fairly sudden transition to extensive grazing of broad expanses of steppe. This occurred with such remarkable rapidity that archaeological sources only record the *fait accompli*. All that was necessary was to give up fixed settlements and to follow the herds out into the heart of the steppe. However, it was at this moment that it became necessary to divide up all the existing pastures; this was done according to the principle of 'might is right'. By now horse-breeding had been greatly intensified, and thus for the first time large numbers of horsemen fought each other for land.

As it was now necessary to make the entire population mobile, even the women and children moved into waggons resembling caravans, ungainly vehicles drawn by oxen. Thus there soon developed the way of life described by Herodotus from the accounts of his trusted informants. It spread quickly, as if by a kind of chain reaction.

One must readily admit that this theoretical model has the virtues of plausibility and consistency. In its favour is the fact that we have two *New World parallels* examples of a similar course of development in the New World: in the North American prairies and the South American pampas. With the introduction of the horse, the Indians succeeded in conquering the steppe land in an amazingly short time and went over to new forms of economy. In the prairies the area under cultivation was rapidly reduced, and there was a shift to the collective hunting of buffalo.

But this very comparison shows the need for scepticism in approaching Griaznov's scheme – which has been so widely accepted in the Soviet Union (only Rudenko flatly rejects it) that the whole subsequent era is officially called 'the period of the early nomads'. It would not have been possible for the social and economic changes in the New World to have taken place so quickly and radically unless this had been a phase of cultural contact on a truly intercontinental scale, stimulated in the last resort by intellectual development in Europe and the resultant colonial expansion.

It appears that the transition of the steppe peoples to a nomadic way of life took place during a similar period of disturbance.

The existence of a period of unrest in Europe is clearly documented. It is known (following Wiesner) as 'the age of the great migrations', and its earliest phase is dated between 1250 and 1100 B.C. At that time foreign peoples from the Balkans were troubling the whole of the eastern Mediterranean by sea and land. The Philistines crossed the Aegean and threatened Egypt; Palestine today still bears their name. Other attacks were directed against Asia Minor: the Hittite empire fell victim to them, and the area was settled by Enetae, Mysians and Phrygians. Also involved in this movement were the Armenians, who do not appear in the sources until later. *Age of great migrations*

A similar process changed the ethnic situation in Iran. Hitherto the enemies who menaced the advanced cultures of Iran had lived in the neighbouring mountain ranges, as for example the Kassites in the Zagros hills; now, however, new trouble-makers appear whose central tribal areas lie in the depths of the Iranian plateau. At Sialk Ghirshman has excavated a fort and cemetery that bear witness to their presence there. We are presumably already dealing here with ancestors of the Medes and Persians, who were Iranians. *Iran*

It may be that eastern Asia, too, was not spared the visitations of such guests. Foreign elements may already have been involved in assisting the Chou dynasty to seize power. This is even more likely to have been the case with the barbarian invasions which in 770 B.C. compelled the Chou to move their capital to the east. *China*

The question naturally arises what prompted this tremendous dynamism. In the first place it has been established that in Iran at least, but presumably in Europe as well, the striking power of the newcomers was no longer based on squadrons of war-chariots – a complicated and delicate weapon, which had hitherto been in the possession of a highly specialized class of nobles – but that instead they had cavalry, employed in a much cruder and almost 'egalitarian' way. The horse no longer served as a *New strategy and equipment*

draught animal but as a mount – although it was still ridden without a stirrup and with a very primitive saddle.

The mounted warrior proved superior to the charioteer. Only China was strong enough to conserve the ancient method of fighting for some centuries to come. The states of the Near East, on the other hand, adopted the new system – especially Urartu and Assyria, which formed the border marches guarding the Near East from dangerous incursions from the north-east.

During the ninth century B.C. they developed a cavalry of their own. A little later the Assyrians used it to conduct a regular strategy of annihilation. They used horsemen to pursue their defeated enemies and to inflict casualties on a scale hitherto unknown.

PLATE P. 213 The gradual change in military tactics from fighting with chariots to fighting on horseback can be followed in Assyrian palace reliefs from the ninth century onwards. Enemy troops are shown mounted as well. It is also symptomatic that the snaffles become ever more 'barbarian' in style, gradually assuming shapes closer to those that existed in Europe at the time. As we have seen, ever stronger forces of barbarians now came to be enlisted as allies by their civilized neighbours.

The striking power of these forces was multiplied when the Phrygians broke the monopoly of iron production hitherto held by the Hittites. From that time onwards the peoples living on the fringes of the area between the Balkans and the Indian border were frequently better equipped with the new metal weapons than the armies of the old-established large states. Iron-ore mining was not restricted to a few places; the complicated trade carried on in tin became superfluous. The trend towards mass armament was thus accentuated.

New religious beliefs But this explanation, namely that technical progress was responsible for the movements of population, is probably only part of the truth. At that time migrations did not occur solely because the acquisition of horses and, later, the use of iron opened up new opportunities. Religious motives must also have prompted this readiness to set out for distant lands. Perhaps, after the early Bronze Age aristocracies collapsed, the peoples came to see themselves for the first time as nationalities in their

PLATE 44 – Mounted archers fleeing before Assyrian war-chariots. One of the barbarians is shooting back in a manner later characteristic of the Scythians, although the gorytus and akinakes are still missing. Rock relief from the palace of Assurnasirpal II (883–859 B.C.). *British Museum. Cf. p. 212.*

own right, instead of as entities tied to a particular village or stretch of territory. This view is supported by the fact that in this period temples were rejected because they placed too great a restriction on mobility. There must have been a vast number of movable shrines. Some of them have survived, thanks to fortunate chance finds (which have been studied by the Soviet scholar Mrs Trever); others can be reconstructed from models. The fact that images of birds were used as symbols in decoration is readily understandable.

As König has pointed out in his acute analysis, similar vehicles used to stand in the assembly-places of the Persians; this people preserved a social organization that guaranteed the cohesion necessary for each movement to a new location and provided a link to unite the various clans and reconcile their conflicting interests.

According to Xenophon's *Cyropaedia*, Persian freemen (who at that time already formed a privileged class) were divided into age grades. When they were sixteen or seventeen years old, boys were enrolled in a group commanded by their own elected leader and capable of operating independently in battle, as a kind of vanguard. At the age of twenty-six they were ceremonially admitted into the group of married men entitled to hold office, who comprised the solid core of the army. At the age of fifty-two they were counted among the elders, whose duties were solely judicial. Originally even the king was subject to this law; at least, he was compelled to give up his military functions at the age of fifty-two.

There can be no doubt that this system really existed and that it was widespread. We encounter it everywhere following the period of unrest. In the state of Urartu it determined the manner in which the army was organized as well as the way in which the kings lived. Even the gods had to comply. The decisive number here was twenty-eight; this made it possible to establish a connection with the rhythm of the lunar month. The Spartans retained the age-grades system for a particularly long time. Of even greater importance is a remnant in Thessaly recorded by Aristotle; in this case we are perhaps near to the source of the system. A whole spectrum of intermediate forms could be identified. It is an open question whether some of the details related in the legend of the foundation of Rome do not point to a similar structure; possibly these features were derived from the Etruscans' contacts with the east, which earned them

the reputation of having originated in Asia Minor. The steppe peoples were undoubtedly linked with this dynamic world; and among them, too, the principle of clan organization receded into the background. It was a system of age groups that provided them with their political and military striking power.

Herodotus explicitly mentions a group of Scythian youths in the legend of the origin of the Sauromatians; the Parni we now know to have been not an independent people but only the young men of the Parthians. Communal ownership of women, ascribed in Greek legend to some peoples of Central Asia, was probably not characteristic of entire peoples, but was rather one of the customs of such groups of young people. Other evidence of this system has been preserved in Iranian religious texts.

It is, however, clear that a shift of emphasis was bound to occur in the steppe area. Where shepherds already led an independent life, it was only logical that it should not be the entire people that migrated, but that bands of young men should set out on military expeditions, as was customary with some tribes in the North American prairies. Age grades

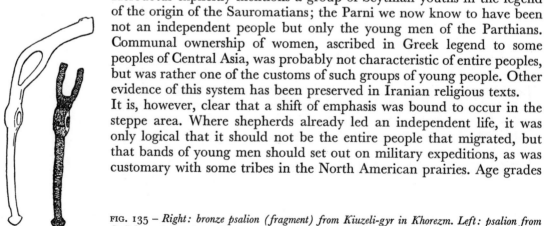

FIG. 135 – *Right: bronze psalion (fragment) from Kiuzeli-gyr in Khorezm. Left: psalion from St Sulpice, Switzerland. Cf. p. 216.*

FIG. 136 – *In Bronze Age Europe it became the common practice to limit the play of the snaffle, made of plaited leather straps, by using antlers as psalia. This arrangement was then executed in metal. At first the psalia had three apertures for the cheek-strap (divided into three tongues). This version remained in use until 500 B.C. The earliest bits made in this novel fashion were found in Sialk B cemetery.*

took on the character of men's societies. When such groups moved south, they entered into the service of the rulers into whose territory they penetrated, and in this way underwent a period of testing. Then, laden with honours and booty, they returned to the more stable conditions of their homeland. There developed a pattern of social and military activity comparable to that which prevailed among the seafaring adventurers of Greek legend; service as mercenaries was both required and limited by ritual.

From this angle we can explain much of the information we have about the Cimmerian and Scythian invasions of the Near East. It has been noted that the length of time which Herodotus says the Scythians spent in the Near East tallies approximately with the length of time a Scythian remained a member of the warrior's age group – namely twenty-six years. A similar movement also occurred further eastwards. It is certain, for example, that mercenaries from Khorezm served the Achaemenids as occupation troops in Egypt. It has even been maintained that the nobleman interred in Pazyryk II had served at an Achaemenid court. On the basis of the ritual known to have existed in the Altai, we have suggested that there were probably bands of warriors which cut across the divisions between clans. The question how the steppe peoples were drawn into this zone of unrest has long ago been plausibly answered. Heine-Geldern, again basing himself on older works, postulated that Thracian, Caucasian and even Germanic forces thrust outwards from

Plundering expeditions in Near East

Heine-Geldern's theory

FIG. 137 – *In early horses' harnesses, the leather straps are kept in place at their point of intersection by means of bronze buttons which have on their reverse side four loops forming a square. This arrangement, too, is found in Sialk B.*

FIG. 138 – *The types of ornamental design that were popular in the homeland of the Cimmerians are illustrated by a horseman's grave in a kurgan near Zol'noe in the Crimea. The bone plaque decorated with its spiral and circle pattern is as much part of the harness as the round open-work bone button; the latter, when viewed from above, represents a Maltese cross (see below). Also highly characteristic is the 'wave-crest' design on a bone cylinder (centre). End of 8th century B.C. Cf. p. 221.*

FIG. 135

FIG. 117

Objections to Heine-Geldern's theory: links with Iran decisive

Europe, disturbed the peaceable peasants of the steppe lands and caused them to mobilize in their own defence. He claims that during the ninth and eighth centuries B.C. an 'ethnic and cultural migration' took place from the Pontic area (hence the term 'Pontic migration') and the northern Caucasus straight across Central Asia to eastern and south-eastern Asia. The survival of an Indo-European language of a western type for two thousand years in Kucha and Qarashahr (oases along the northern rim of the Tarim basin) is explained as due to the settlement there of a group of adventurers who about that time made their way on their swift-footed horses to this distant area in the east. Other groups, repulsed at the Chinese border, fought their way through western China southwards, and left their traces in the curious equestrian features of the Dong-son culture in Indochina. Heine-Geldern regards the motif of circles linked by tangents as having been transmitted by this migration.

On several occasions in my earlier works I have supported this hypothesis, which can in fact be substantiated by evidence that was not available to Heine-Geldern. Thus Tolstov claims to have found pottery of eastern European origin in the Aral Sea area. The discovery in the same region of a psalion that is quite definitely of eastern European make is still more interesting in connection with the theory of a migration by horsemen. Furthermore, a dagger found in Tannu Tuva belongs to a group that occurs in Hungary and the Caucasus. Graves with wooden chambers in central Kazakhstan (Dyndybei) suddenly reveal links with graves of the eastern Hallstatt culture. There are some signs which suggest that the same period of unrest caused the Karasuk culture to migrate as far afield as the Minusinsk basin. Presumably they left their former lands in the Ordos steppe not because they were under pressure from the Chinese, but because other barbarians were on their heels. At any rate the Karasuk inventory does include some evidence of links with the west as well.

Nevertheless, we must today ask ourselves whether this explanation suffices, whether eastern Europe and the Caucasus were really of such crucial importance, and whether it was not rather links with the south,

216

FIG. 139 – *Zoomorphic fibula from the gold treasure at Michalkov, eastern Galicia. The outline of the animal recalls works of the Koban culture. The surface is diversified by the use of medallions. Also 8th century B.C. Cf. p. 221.*

with Iran and Assyria, which set in motion these significant chains of events.

There is no doubt that the Volga area was linked with the territories on the fringe of the Near East. Smirnov has succeeded in proving that some inconspicuous bone implements are actually the cheek-pieces of horses' bits which, on the strength of the prongs on the inside, can be related to a typological group widespread in the Near East. One other relatively late example may be compared with a psalion on a relief of Assurnasirpal II (883–859 B.C.). Small curved bronze poles with an oval aperture may also have been psalia. If one imagines them having leather straps wrapped around them, one obtains one of the forms shown on Assyrian palace reliefs. It is a little later, however, that the most striking parallels appear, in the form of those psalia made from slightly curved antler-points that were used in Assyria under Assurbanipal (668–629 B.C.). The problem arises as to the practical form this kind of contact took, e.g., how we are to interpret the fact that no finds have been made in the intervening area. Possibly bands of adventurers came down the Volga and then began their raids from the southern shore of the Caspian – thus performing a kind of 'migration of seafaring peoples' in miniature. Another link leads from the earliest horsemen on the Iranian plateau – *Links with Sialk B* the Sialk B culture – to the ancestors of the Saka living north of the Tian'-shan'. In the north, for example, moulds have been discovered for casting curious stepped axes such as were later unearthed at Sialk. The arrow-heads also seem to belong to a related type. Cauldrons on tripods and altars can plainly be derived from models which occur among Sialk B ceramics. The altars have the same open-work on part of the leg. In FIG. 118 both areas there occur bronze mirrors with a flat tongue for the handle. It may be that these links would lead further to the north-east, beyond Lake Balkhash. The author has attempted to identify on Assyrian reliefs the forked psalia which occur in the Maiemir culture of the Altai.

Equally, one cannot exclude the possibility that in the eastern part of *Eastern influences* the steppe, too, powerful centres very soon came into existence which

217

PLATE 45 – Before the Cimmerians and the Scythians made their inroads into the Near East, mountain tribes of the Zagros and of the chains south of the Caspian played a similar role. They used elaborate bronzes as symbols of rank and for cult purposes. During the last forty years many of them have been found by grave-robbers, mostly in the province of Luristan, and have been 'exported' to private and public collections all over the world.

This 'tragedy of Iranian archaeology' has permitted a broad spectrum of diverging theories, e.g. that these bronzes, robbed from the temples of the cities of Mesopotamia, were deposited by Cimmerians in the graves of their warriors; to dispose suddenly of such unexpected riches was for them a challenge to develop their own 'animal style'.

In fact, we have so far only a few pieces which indicate that 'northern nomads' settled among the local tribes of Luristan, e.g. this belt-buckle of the steppe type which was shown in the Iranian Exhibition of 1963.

218

FIG. 140 – *Decoration on a metal button covering a strap-intersection. Nadj-i-Ali, Seistan. Possibly 7th century B.C. Cf. p. 221.*

in turn exerted an influence on the west. Thus bronze cauldrons from the Minusinsk area, for example, were exported to southern Russia, where they touched off an interesting development. The cauldrons are based on Chinese models, as can be demonstrated by the mushroom-like protuberances on the handles. Formerly it was assumed that the so-called crossed tubes through which the straps of a horse's harness passed had been brought to eastern Asia by the Pontic migration. Now they have been found in graves of the Shang period, i.e., in China they are older than in Europe. But we do not know whether they were brought so far west as a result of trade, in the form of loot, or by the westward expansion of some eastern equestrian people.

In this situation it is no longer profitable to attempt to interpret the picture in terms of one single chain of cause and effect. It is necessary to retreat to a more cautious formulation: the transition of the steppe peoples to the nomadic horsemen's way of life was caused, or at least influenced, by contact with the entire zone of unrest in the south and west. This is a complex process which we shall never be able to reconstruct in detail, although it extended over a fairly long period of time. Some areas, such as that of the Volga, seem to have had a considerable cultural lead.

It will be understood that in such a transitional period one cannot expect to find an artistic style of imposing coherence and expressive force. At any rate, we do not know of anything that can hold a torch to the works that began to be produced at the end of the seventh and during the sixth centuries B.C. Previously, in the western part of the steppe, spirals and volutes were employed as the principal ornamental motifs; round

Emergence of animal style

FIG. 141 – *A cylinder seal from Sialk features animals with their legs drawn under their bodies. This important 'posture' of the animal style may therefore also have been borrowed from the south.*

219

PLATE 46 – Embossed gold plate. Ziwiye treasure. Part of a larger piece that was divided up by the excavators. The stags and ibexes in the fields bear strikingly Scythian features. The execution of the network corresponds to Urartian taste as manifest in bronze belts found in Armenia. *Fragments in the Archaeological Museum, Teheran. Height approx. 16 cm. Cf. p. 222.*

medallions bearing a Maltese cross were also extremely popular and were FIG. 138 used to embellish schematized silhouette-like figures of animals.

The little we know about Cimmerian art fits in here. The fact that other tribes used similar decorative forms is indicated by the gold treasure found at Michalkov, Galicia. The most splendid artistic development of FIG. 139 such principles, however, occurred in an area outside the steppe: in the Koban culture.

In Middle Asia the situation was no different. Prior to the animal style we encounter abstract whorl designs. The early Iranian site Nadj-i-Ali in FIG. 140

PLATE 47 – Small griffin's head from Ziwiye, possibly one of the four handles of a cauldron. *Archaeological Museum, Teheran. Height approx. 7 cm. Cf. p. 222.*

Seistan has yielded parts of a horse's harness decorated in a marked spiral style.

To the north-east a zone can be identified in which relatively clumsy representations of animals, derived from northern fauna, such as the bear and boar, were used to decorate metal implements. We have already met this phenomenon when discussing the Minusinsk area.

In some parts of the steppe area the angular band seems to have been used copiously as an ornamental motif; it was also modelled in a plastic form.

In the captivating artistic style which is predominant from the close of the seventh century B.C. onwards, these tendencies are not simply continued: the animal style in its fully matured form becomes, as we have seen, much more 'responsive to contact'. It possesses a rich repertoire of motifs of foreign origin which it makes its own by self-confident independent treatment. Only in very early monuments, such as the

FIG. 7

Zhabotin kurgans, has it been possible to distinguish the ancient abstract signs – possibly because they symbolized religious concepts of some kind.

Motifs adopted from Iran

Some of the new motifs introduced may have been European, others even Chinese; most of the innovations, however, were adopted by way of the Iranian plateau. Very frequently they are very ancient Near Eastern motifs which were, of course, passed on by way of the imperial art of the Assyrians.

For this there is a relatively simple explanation. Iran was the most popular and for a long time also the most promising sphere of operations for raiders from the north. People poured into the area from all directions; here it was possible for Cimmerians and Scythians to encounter Saka who came from the steppes at the foot of the Tian'-shan' mountains. Moreover all these tribes were exposed to abundant influences of every kind. Artists of various peoples were prepared to work in the service of powerful individuals and decorate their personal belongings.

Ziwiye treasure PLATES PP. 220, 221, 229

This 'market situation' may be illustrated by the treasure of Ziwiye in Iranian Kurdistan. It need not be analysed in detail here, since it is fully discussed by Edith Porada in another volume in the ART OF THE WORLD series, *Ancient Iran*. It will suffice to point out that the main part of this treasure presumably consisted of the spoils accumulated by a war-lord who had emerged successfully from the struggles between the great powers of the Near East. The gradually accumulated treasure thus comprises works produced by craftsmen of different origin. Among them may have been Assyrians, Urartians, Mannaeans and Medes. Some animal figures, however, are similar to those of the famous Pontic finds of the early sixth century B.C. (e.g. Kelermes) and they evidently belong to the same 'Schrägschnitt' tradition. Especially striking is the occurrence of Assyrian and 'Schrägschnitt' motifs on the same object. A single artist could apparently use several 'pattern books'.

The ivory plaques and other objects belonging to the original finds of the Ziwiye treasure have been dated with considerable exactitude to the period between Tiglathpileser III (745–727 B.C.) and Sargon II (721–705 B.C.).

It has been maintained that the same dating also applies to the metal objects with 'Schrägschnitt' motifs. In that case we would have here the so-called Scythian art prior to the arrival of the Scythians on the scene and could assume that it was originally developed by Mannaean or – even more interestingly – by Median wood-carvers. This would imply that the Scythians only transferred the style to the steppe lands, taking the foreign artisans with them. This tempting solution was proposed by Godard and is now suggested by Nagel in his review of the German edition of this book. Unfortunately the matter is not so simple. The network pattern of the gold embossed sheathing with crouched stags and goats of Scythic type also occurs on bronze belts which, according to Piotrovskii's careful study, belong to a later period, viz. the end of the seventh century B.C. If the psalion from Ziwiye published by Porada is not a later addition by an art dealer, this would be a final proof.

But even if this 'Schrägschnitt' technique of the animal style does not appear so early, it may well be argued that it was developed here, in this breeding-ground for so many artistic trends. Those responsible perhaps were a group of foreign mercenaries whose growing self-awareness prompted a desire for individual expression which was then quickly adopted by other groups who found themselves in a similar position.

Perhaps the Medes who originally used the decorative patterns familiar from Sialk VI (a period now believed by some authors to be rather late, ninth or eighth century B.C.) took over this animal decor from their Scythian overlords and used it not only in the heyday of their power but even later, when they were under the rule of the Persians.

The view that the final phase in the development of the animal style took place on Iranian soil has been substantiated by increased knowledge of ceremonial weapons and ornamentation during the Achaemenid period. This would hold even if we admit that a large part of these fabulous riches were made not by Achaemenid jewellers but by modern forgers catering to the taste of private collectors and some public museums in the United States. In any case, the splendid Exhibition of Iranian Art which toured many European cities showed much genuine material which had an amazing similarity to steppe finds of the same period. One can almost speak of an 'Achaemenid animal style'. To illustrate this, one may mention the interesting fact that objects from the Oxus treasure PLATE P. 225 have alternately been claimed for the Scythian animal style and for jewellery of the Achaemenid period. Nowadays it would almost be possible to see in steppe art a barbarized variant of the incomparably more rigid Achaemenid art – although the former appeals especially to modern taste.

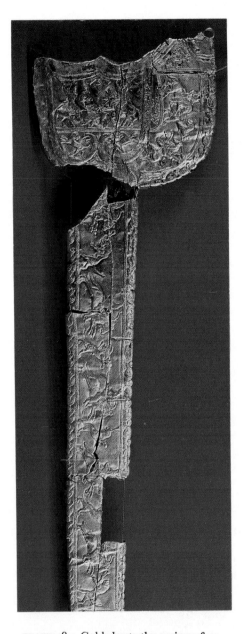

PLATE 48 – Gold sheet: the casing of an akinakes sheath, also from the Oxus treasure. The battle scenes shown do not tally with those depicted by the steppe peoples to the north. *British Museum. Cf. above.*

In both cases we find extensive use of animal figures; certain details, such as the treatment of the mouth or eyes, occur almost in identical form in both – as we have noted, for example, in our discussion of Altai art.

We should not forget that the arms and costume used by the horsemen of the steppe gradually took on stereotyped shapes which, we may assume, received their final form, at least, in Iran. For example, this is true for the akinakes, the short sword, and presumably also of the hood which left only the face uncovered. Altogether, it may be said that the arms and equipment carried by the Scythian horsemen were ingeniously designed for use in a type of warfare in which differently armed troops were also employed, for instance charioteers and infantry.

The study of Persepolis, the most impressive Achaemenid monument, may help us to grasp the spiritual background of the evolution in the steppes. Research carried out during the last few years has shown that this enormous conglomeration of halls and corridors, stairways and terraces was never inhabited permanently. Godard rightly points to the fact that not one of the stone steps was worn. The whole complex forms an enormous framework for a festival, presumably the New Year feast, in which the empire was reflected in all its splendour.

Ghirshman shows that the reliefs only illustrate the function of the individual rooms and stairways. They tell of the arrival of envoys from all the peoples of the empire to offer homage and tribute. Distinguished carefully and deliberately from one another by their arms and costume, they ascended the stairway, saluted the emperor with the *proskynesis*, received his judgment, and then deposited their gifts

PLATE 49 – Armlet from the Oxus treasure. The depressions are for cloisonné inlays that have since been lost. This piece presumably served as a symbol of authority or as a ceremonial gift. *Victoria and Albert Museum, London. Width 11.5 cm. Cf. p. 223.*

in his treasuries. This procedure makes still more sense if it is regarded against the historical background; the period of the great migrations had finally come to an end with the establishment of the stable empires of the Iranian nation, the Medes and Persians. It is as though the aimless wandering, which had for so long been part of the natural order of things, had now reached a conclusion; it had become part of a purposeful design, and had adopted the character of a procession. It terminates in a splendid stone framework that aspires to eternal validity: the former dynamism has given way to an almost megalithic static quality.

From this point of view the destruction of the complex by Alexander the Great takes on a new meaning; it was by no means a haphazard act (the gold decorations of the walls were carefully stripped). His homeland was situated not far from one of the old centres of unrest, and he represents that daemonic world. He did in fact release all those dark forces which the Achaemenids had tried to contain by their campaigns into the steppe. Thus in Achaemenid art, too, the motifs of many peoples came together and were conserved in curiously rigid form. Gestures remain half-poised in the air, as it were; everything remains in a state of the utmost tension. This impression of controlled balance and juxtaposition must have made a great impact upon the steppe peoples. It corresponded to their own

PLATE 50 – Wall-covering of coloured glazed tiles. The fantastic animals depicted on the saddle decoration of the Pazyryk kurgans (Plate p. 93) must have been based on models of this kind. Palace of Artaxerxes II (404–359 B.C.) at Susa. *Louvre, Paris.*

political and social situation. A similar consolidation had taken place in their way of life as well, although not within an imperial framework. Large-scale movements had obviously ceased; they only recommenced after the Hsiung-nu empire was founded, and were then sustained by the dynamism of another race. As we were able to show on the basis of material from the Altai, an ascending scale, regulated and controlled by ritual, lay open to the ambitious. It led primarily to fame, and only secondarily to power. Ambition also found expression in surrounding oneself with objects of beauty. This alone can explain the tremendous creative power which we find in the Altai.

It was only now that men were able to master the overwhelming experience gained through the development of the nomadic horseman's way of life, and could use all those artistic means offered them by contact with advanced cultures.

If we have laid great stress on analogous developments in Iran and Outer Iran, we do not thereby wish to claim that this was the only source of *Earlier local influences* nomadic art during the first centuries B.C. The earlier stylistic trends we have mentioned also continued to exert an influence, especially noticeable in the predilection for spirals and volutes. It is quite clear,

as Wiesner has already noted, that the fondness for inversion derives from a primeval legacy of this kind. The clumsy realism of Karasuk art also continued to make itself felt. It may even have had an effect on the south as a result of isolated population movements. This is suggested by the finds in the Pamirs already mentioned.

FIG. 122

The question now arises whether the tendency to form animal bodies from inclined planes marked off by curves ('Schrägschnitt') should also be traced back to a primeval legacy of this kind, or whether it should simply be attributed to certain techniques practised by the nomadic population and to the influence of the spiral style. Perhaps an ethnic group from the forest zone of the Urals or western Siberia did in fact send mercenaries to the Near East along with those who went there from the steppe; perhaps these men could boast of a superior tradition in carving, and for this reason soon found themselves providing artisans for all the 'expeditions' there, just as men belonging to certain peoples were employed by the Achaemenids for particular kinds of artistic work. Such an explanation would to some extent justify the theory that the nucleus of animal style developed in the northern forest zone. Its diffusion would thus have taken place from Iran.

Forest peoples' influence?

To illustrate this hypothesis one may mention that it has recently been shown that settlers from the early second millennium B.C., the Afanas'evo people, who had been driven off into the forest zone bordering upon the Minusinsk area, survived there and suddenly became active again in approximately 700 B.C., when they sustained the earliest phase of the Tagar culture.

Following up the arguments developed by recent Soviet writers (Chlenova, Terenozhkin), it would even be possible to assume that a preliminary stage of the animal style developed in eastern Kazakhstan, at the point of intersection between southern (spiral and volute), eastern (curled animal), northern (carving tradition) and north-eastern (legacy of Karasuk) influences. The Sakian intermediary stage had already spread far afield, into the Caucasus and southern Russia, by the mid-seventh century, but did not acquire its full expressive power until *after* it had experienced the aesthetic impact of Iran.

Significance of eastern Kazakhstan

It is tempting to ascribe the considerable differences that exist from the beginning between the individual provinces of nomadic art not only to the fact that Oriental influences varied in the effect they exerted in proportion to the remoteness of their source, but rather to the fact that in each case the local legacy must have had a diversifying effect almost from the start. In the Sarmatian area, for example, the spiral element had always been weak, whereas it is all the more marked in the Sakian area of Central Asia. The direction in which the individual forms continued to develop, and the speed with which they did so, must have differed from place to place. A specific variant of the stag motif which manifests

PLATE 51 – Silver bowl covered with gold-foil from the Ziwiye treasure. *Archaeological Museum, Teheran. Diameter 37.5 cm. Cf. p. 222.*

We have seen (p. 138) that the carpet in kurgan V, Pazyryk, served as an aid in divination. If this bowl, which is patterned with similar friezes, served the same purpose, this would explain the enigmatic sign in the border, reminiscent of Hittite hieroglyphs. The animal bodies no doubt also symbolize magic charms.

itself in Ziwiye (as early as the seventh century?) penetrates the Pontic area in the sixth century B.C., where it quickly becomes modified. Suddenly, however, the old forms re-appear in the Minusinsk area in a kind of renaissance. There must therefore have been a permanent centre – probably in Central Asia – whence diffusion took place in a south-westerly direction, then westwards, and finally towards the Enisei.

This unfortunately invalidates the very convenient idea, advanced by some art historians until quite recently, that artistic fashions prevailed in the steppe area which were short-lived but extremely far-reaching. However, the dating is not as simple as that. Later development did not proceed at a uniform rate in the various provinces.

Presumably older groups of motifs outmoded by the animal style, or incorporated into it, survived in the domestic inventory produced and used by the more conservative womenfolk. Of this, usually only the pottery has survived. Where we also have some knowledge of the rest, made from non-durable materials, we stand amazed at the variety of heterogeneous decorative systems they display.

Male and female decorative forms may have been consciously contrasted; this would correspond to the polarity expressed, inter alia, in the division of labour between the sexes.

A similar situation can be observed among primitive peoples of the present day. This did not, of course, prevent a princess or priestess from claiming male prerogatives, and hence a decoration consisting of animal forms.

Significance of motifs Can we now, by thus attempting to incorporate early nomadic art into a historical and social pattern, gain some inkling of the significance of the most important individual motifs?

The animal figures cannot have represented deities. The Pontic-Scythian pantheon, in particular, is well known to us from literary sources, and some of the native deities have been depicted by Greek artists. The Massagetae are said to have worshipped the sun and to have sacrificed horses to it. But even in this case, no mention is made of deities in animal guise analogous to those known in Egypt.

The religious systems of many peoples, however, do contain, subordinate to the pantheon or central divine figure, daemonic forces which like them are venerated or feared, and are believed to intervene in men's lives on certain occasions. Even the highly monotheistic Islam has accepted a rather heterogeneous world of spirits and fairies.

This might also be the case here. The most attractive idea would be that they were individual protective spirits in animal guise, similar to those which young Red Indian warriors in North America acquire by intense concentration of thought and through experiences in dreams. The tutelary spirits invoked by shamans, too, frequently appear in the guise of animals, and fight as 'animal mothers'.

In pursuing this idea further, one admittedly runs into the greatest

PLATE 52 – Belt-plaque from the Ordos area. *British Museum. Approx. life-size.*
A wrestling-match between two heroes, apparently fought according to certain rules. Griaznov has
shown (1961) that such scenes are frequently described in the heroic epics of modern Turkic peoples.
On the basis of further examples he suggests that as a whole these epics go back as far as the first
period of unrest – to the 8th and 7th centuries B.C. Thus the development of the animal style and
the artistic formulation of the epics would have been analogous processes. *Cf. p. 183.*

difficulties. In the Altai it has been ascertained beyond all doubt that
entirely different motifs were combined in a horse's harness or in ceremonial dress. It is not possible to discover any coherent meaning in this
(which also makes it difficult to regard the animals as heraldic figures).
Hitherto scholars have made shift with the assumption that the persons
buried in the large kurgans were furnished with gifts by their comrades-in-
arms. The hypothesis that animal figures were seen as imbued with an
almost anonymous magic power is more promising. People tried to make   *Magical function*
and store as many of them as possible, much as the Tibetans did with
their prayers. A comparison could be drawn with the garments they wore,
which were made up of a mosaic of skins. In Siberian cult practices we
do indeed hear of objects consisting of a number of hunting trophies put
together, which are said to contain the power of all the animals slain.
This would imply that the animal style belonged to a somewhat less
exalted religious sphere, and in support of this view we may again cite

the evidence known to us from Iran. The Achaemenid animal style no doubt primarily catered to the need for personal adornment. It became possible because animals and fantastic creatures had already lost something of their former significance; religious beliefs had become more abstract, and this made such subjects available for non-religious treatment. The situation may have been similar in the steppes as well. This would fit in with Griaznov's analysis of Altai art; he, too, speaks of its subjective and typically additive character. An ornamental button on crossed straps is primarily a craftsman's masterpiece; it may be combined with similar works by other craftsmen to form a somewhat unwieldy set with which the wearer adorns himself as though they were trophies. This could indeed be seen as an almost mechanical accumulation of magic values, which are acquired in the same way as power and prestige. This fact prepares the way for the individual to apply his creative faculties to matters of detail. (Greek art, too, to some extent develops at the expense of its original religious meaning.) As an exception to this general rule, there are combinations of motifs which undoubtedly presuppose myths, such as the stag's head at Pazyryk, depicted in the jaws of a fantastic animal.

FIG. 71

Not all these myths need have been of indigenous origin. Whenever animals were depicted which do not occur at all in the steppe lands (such as fallow deer and large snakes), they have been adopted from elsewhere as part of some wider pattern of ideas. The divination carpet found in the Altai clearly points to the infiltration of ideas from Anatolia. Another striking feature is that certain leitmotifs, such as pictures of stags, are very unevenly distributed over the steppe area. The principal centres are situated in eastern Europe, in the Ordos region and, from a certain point in time onwards, in southern Siberia as well. And there is no doubt that links between the various centres really existed. Chlenova regards the stag as the totem of the Saka tribes. 'Sag' is the word for 'stag' in modern Ossetian, and the Saka are thus said to have called themselves 'the people of the stag'. In fact we have but a few renderings of stags, albeit important ones, in the area east of the Aral Sea where the Saka settled. In Tuva there are so-called stag stelae which no doubt represented human beings – actually famous warriors. This body of religious ideas may explain why white stags (and wolves) were received by the Chinese court as a ceremonial gift from some Central Asian people.

Stag as totem?

The dissemination of the stag image over the vast steppe area – indeed as far as the area nowadays known as Kurdistan – is interpreted by Chlenova as the result of military expeditions, and possibly of the establishment of permanent rule. She claims that other peoples, such as the Sarmatians, who retained their independence, rejected this symbol as it was their enemies' totem, and that it disappeared almost entirely after the Saka went into decline.

PLATE 53 – Parthian coin with the likeness of Phraates III (70–57 B.C.). The Parthians retained nomadic symbols, such as the bow, for a long time. Characteristically, the image of the stag survived among them as a royal attribute, as is proved by the shape of the crown represented here. *Göbl Collection, Vienna.*

These reflections may contain an element of truth. But one should also bear in mind the more complex possibilities raised by our analysis of the social system. Among bands of young men religious groups may have formed which took the stag as their symbol, and maintained relations over wide areas without developing any system of political domination. The end of animal style art has frequently been linked with the fact that the Iranians lost the leading position they had held in the steppe to the Turks and Mongols. It is maintained that the new ruling class brought with it not only a different kind of artistic talent, but also different traditions. *End of animal style*

This cannot be quite accurate. The highly gifted Altai people apparently already included strong elements of Far Eastern origin, possibly Turkic immigrants.

From the conclusions reached in this chapter there emerges a rather different hypothesis: if early nomadic art was the mature product of a *Social changes*

233

phase of consolidation (following upon a period of unrest in which animal motifs were adopted from neighbouring settled cultures), then it is only logical that the subsequent dynamic phase, which disrupted the political balance, should also have deprived the animal style of the basis for its existence.

After this, those principally responsible for the second period of unrest – the Hsiung-nu and their rivals – quickly developed a hierarchy which was far more tightly organized than that of the Scythians, for example. The Turks of the sixth century A.D. are known to have had twenty-nine classes of dignitaries, whose offices were hereditary. There was no longer the same opportunity for the individual to realize his ambitions. Nor was it any longer necessary to give them such an infinitely wide scope. The desire for prestige found its most perfect expression in a minutely regulated and fixed drinking ceremonial. *Machtkunst* was congenial to those with such an attitude of mind, as Strzygowski has rightly observed. The artistic environment, too, had undergone a radical change. The neighbouring advanced cultures no longer offered a repertoire of realistic animal figures; on the contrary, once Islam had triumphed, greater value was attached to abstract ornamentation. Even more marked was the change that took place in internal social conditions. We have seen that the chefs d'oeuvre of Altai art were the work of men who could still hardly be distinguished from the mass of the people, and who were still active as warriors – as were, for example, the smiths of the Vikings. Instructive in this respect is a find at Karmir Blur: an improvised workshop within a Urartian fortress. A man belonging to the Scythian garrison had just carved small griffins' heads from the branch of an antler when suddenly another band of Scythians conquered the fort and interrupted the idyll.

This kind of thing could not have happened several centuries later. The ever-increasing division of labour, and the growing complexity of tasks which the individual shepherd had to perform, meant that the production of weapons and ornaments was entrusted to specialists, most of whom were foreigners. Ever greater importance came to be attached to the bazaars in the large commercial cities that arose on the edge of the steppe. Foreign silk became the standard of wealth. A steppe chieftain could proudly point to the fact that he had no artisans in his vast army; it was enough for each man to be a warrior and a shepherd.

The role of the domestic crafts carried on by the womenfolk hence became all the more important. One could advance the theory that the steppe art of a later period, particularly its most individual creations, the carpets and tapestries, although owing a great deal to countless external influences, also goes back to those primal motifs that existed before the beginnings of the animal style, and which were kept in being by the women of the tribe during its heyday.

One could say that the graceful curves of the geometric scroll, regarded as the quintessence of Turkic art, go back to this ancient spiral and volute ornamentation.

If, however, there were frequent revivals of individual animal style motifs during later centuries, this presumably corresponded to a conservative tendency among the steppe aristocracy, the 'white bones', which had gradually established itself as an exclusive class. To go back to stylistic relics from the distant legendary past was a means of emphasizing the gulf between them and the common people. They willingly accepted stereotyped repetition; comprehensibility of symbol was no longer demanded. It is always a feature of exclusive ruling groups that they seek to retain memories of the more stirring world from which they sprang. *Survival among ruling groups*

A similar development took place in burial rites. The memorials erected to the dead in the centres of the first Turkic empire have ceremonial inscriptions that speak to us in the language of archaic formulae. It is precisely the megalithic character of these structures – the stelae represent the dead and the enemies they slew – that tends to emphasize the ruler's superiority to the mass of the people, the 'black bones'.

Even the high position formerly held by the artisan was retained in symbolic form by this upper class. This explains why the legend of the 'smith king' survived for a long time in Central Asia.

Genghis Khan was not only regarded as the offspring of a wolf and a hind, but also, as his name Temuchin implies, as a smith. Thus the world-conqueror was invested with the ideas and concepts of that distant and already mythical past in which the animal style arose.

APPENDIX

CHRONOLOGICAL TABLE

showing the beginnings and development of animal decoration in the provinces of early steppe art

	Areas decisively influencing the steppe peoples		Pontic Scythia (Chapter II)	Scythian finds in Central Europe (Chapter III)	Caucasia (Chapter IV)	Eastern part of Central Russia (Chapter V)	Volga and Ural Steppe (Chapter VI)
	Iran, Armenia, rest of Near East	China					
900	Assyrian Empire: art rich in figures of animals. Appearance of Iranians	Western Chou Empire: in art, animals used in decoration	Cimmerians predominant: in art, ornamentation with spirals and volutes; few animal images	Animals occasionally portrayed		Boldly stylized animal figures used in ritual	Final stage of timber-grave culture
800	Median Empire founded. Assyria becomes Great Power under Sargon III. Cimmerians threaten Urartu	Barbarian invasions. Transfer of capital from 771 B.C.: Eastern Chou			Koban culture predominant; animal motifs already frequent		Final stage of Andronovo culture; few animal sculpt.
700	Scythians appear in large numbers; decline of Assyria; Neo-Babylonian kingdom. Ziwiye treasure	Rise of feudal states. Circles linked by tangents used in decoration	Scythian rule		First elements of animal style derived from Central Asia (?)	Anan'ino culture; Caucasian influence	
600	Median Empire. 546: Persian Empire. 514: Darius I's campaign against Pontic Scythians	Flowering of an art rich in animal figures	Kelermes: animal art at its height; Oriental, later Greek influences	Scythian raids; Settlement (?) in central Hungary, Transylvania and central Bulgaria	Penetration of Scythian animal style; local settlements of Pontic Scythians	Adoption of Pontic-Scythian and Sauromatian animal style	Animal style. Sauromatian phase
500	Persian expansion towards middle Asia; Imperial art develops legacy of Assyria. Animal ornamentation	from 481: Chan-Kuo 'Warring Kingdoms' Huai style	Royal kurgans Solokha, Chertomlyk				
400	Decline. 334: Alexander's campaign	Dissolution of feudal system	Degeneration; Sarmatian invasion. Kingdom of Atheas	Links with Pontic forest steppe. Thracian princely graves	Hybrid forms in northern Caucasus		Early Sarmat. stage
300	Seleucid Empire. Bactria and Parthia independent	256: abdication of last Chou emperor 221: unification under Ts'in dynasty 206: Han dynasty	Scythian state in the Crimea	Sarmatian influences		Transition to P'ianobor culture	Animal style. vitality and importance
200	Parthian Empire. Bactria in hands of barbarians	Struggles with Hsiung-nu				Animal motifs continue to play important part	
100	Further Saka invasions of eastern Iran and India	Conquests in Tarim basin. Silk Route	Numerous Sarmatian finds: 'Khokhlach kurgan'		Sarmatian settlement in northern Caucasus		Middle Sarma. stage; animal
0	In the east, the Kushans consolidate their power	9–22: Wang-Mang 24: 2nd Han dynasty				Renewal of Sarmatian influence (cf. Ch. XIV)	style with Mi. Asian influenc. polychromy
100	Decline of Parthians	Hsiung-nu driven off westwards					
200							Modelling

| | = Abrupt beginning of decoration in animal style | | = Fully-fledged animal style | | = Preliminary stages, degenerate forms or scattered traces of animal style |

...insk (...er VII)	High Altai (Chapter VIII)	Transbaikalia and Northern Mongolia (Chapter IX)	Inner Mongolia Ordos region (Chapter X)	Tuva (Chapter XI)	Middle Asia (Chapter XII)	Northern and Eastern Kazakhstan (Chapter XIII)	
...k culture			Groups of live-stock-breeders with Karasuk-type culture		Neither inhabitants of oases nor nomads employ animal style	Late Andronovo culture	900
s decorated ...imals; ...g animals'	Offshoots of Andronovo culture with Karasuk influences					No animal sculptures of note	
...els with ...'s head	Animals rarely depicted		Knife-handles with animal-head terminals; survival of Shang influences				800
...culture, ...ase; ...animal ...added: animals, ...f birds of —	Maiemir culture Limited number of animal motifs	Slab-grave culture with Karasuk influences Animal style decoration adopted in isolated instances	?	Uiuk culture, first phase	Isolated grave of horseman with animal sculpture	Groups of kurgans in Eastern Kazakh-stan, constructed as in Pontic area	700
	Stag motifs		?	Limited stock of animal motifs, but stag stelae appear	Graves of nomads in eastern Pamirs with animal style of Tagar I type	Chilikty; animal style fully developed and particularly conservative	600
	First large kurgans erected; Pazyryk culture		Ordos bronzes in animal style fully developed Links with Altai and Middle Asia	Uiuk culture, second phase	Animal sculptures on cauldrons and altar-tables in Semirech'e; 'Achaemenid' animal style among settled peoples	Earliest specimens of Siberian gold work (curled animal)	500
... phase of ...culture; ...ng stag ...pertoire of ...style introduced ...igrants ...iddle ...')	Pazyryk II (?)			Many tribes, each with own type of grave	Oxus treasure Animal style in Syr-Dar'ia area	Finest gold plaques with brightly-coloured inlays, belonging to tribes of different artistic traditions	400
	Pazyryk V (?)			Several variants of animal style		Late plaques; some influenced by Chinese art	300
...tric scroll	Shibe phase	Rule of Hsiung-nu	Rule of Hsiung-nu	Shurmak culture; many local groups continue to exist	Sakian finds in Pamirs and Karakorum, on route to India	Last gold objects	200
...hase of ...culture		Derestui	Abstract ornamentation appears alongside animal style			Survival of kurgans 'with moustaches'	100
...k culture	Dominant ethnic element migrates or is destroyed	Chinese imports		Employment of animal figures in ritual as in Tashtyk culture			
...l figures used ...al accessories ...mental ...res		Princely graves of Noin Ula Scenes of animals in combat			Catacomb graves of Sarmatian immigrants		0
...motifs ...d							100
							200

239

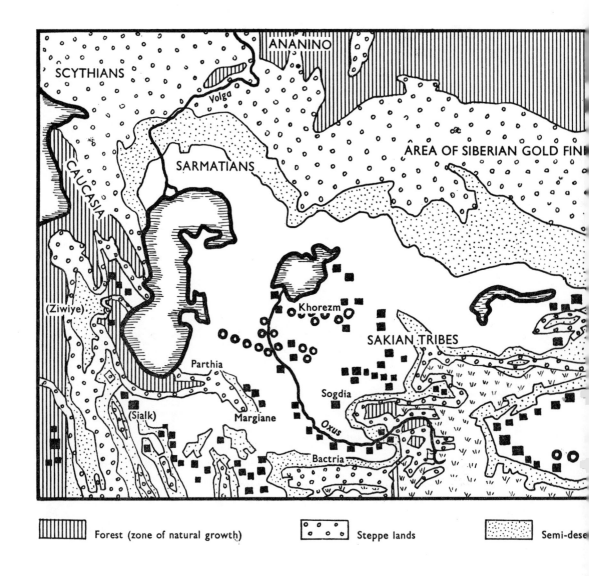

The following labels appear on the map:

SCYTHIANS

ANANINO

Volga

SARMATIANS

CAUCASIA

AREA OF SIBERIAN GOLD FIN[D]

(Ziwiye)

Khorezm

SAKIAN TRIBES

Parthia

Sogdia

(Sialk)

Margiane

Oxus

Bactria

Legend:

|||||||| Forest (zone of natural growth)

o o o Steppe lands

Semi-dese[rt]

THE ASIATIC STEPPES

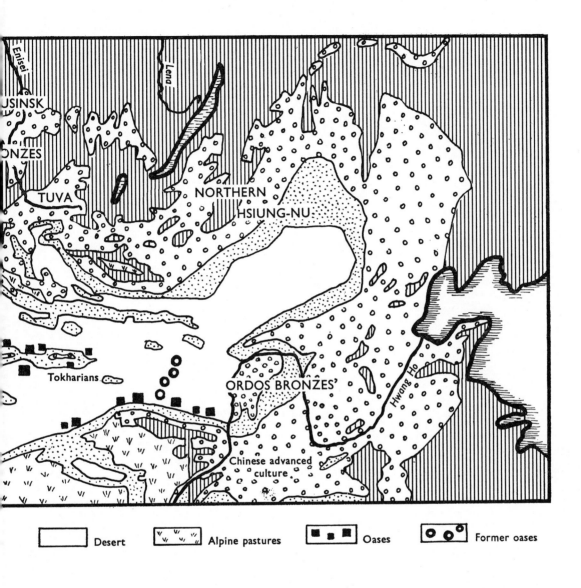

Provinces of animal style in the Asiatic Steppes are shown here in capitals. Other entries refer to non-nomadic peoples, provinces and cultures.   (After Kussmaul's map in von Wissmann, 1957)

I. THE DISCOVERY OF EARLY STEPPE ART

Basenov, T. K., Ornament Kazakhstana v arkhitekture. Alma-Ata, 1957.

Glück, H., Die Weltstellung der Türken in der Kunst, in: Wiener Beiträge, vol. 2, 1927, pp. 29ff.

Glück, H., Islamisches Kunstgewerbe, in: Geschichte des Kunstgewerbes aller Zeiten und Völker, ed. H. Th. Bossert, vol. 4, Berlin-Zürich, 1930, pp. 352–431.

Glück, H. and Diez, E., Die Kunst des Islam, 2nd ed. Propyläen-Kunstgeschichte, vol. 5, Berlin, 1925.

Ivanov, S. V., Realisticheskie osnovy iskusstva tunguso-man'zhurov, in: KSIE, no. 5, 1949, pp. 86–90.

Ivanov, S. V., Ornamentika, religioznye predstavleniia i obriady, sviazannye s amurskoi lodkoi, in: SE, 1935, nos. 4–5, pp. 62–84.

Ivanov, S. V., Kirgizskii ornament kak etnogeneticheskii istochnik, in: Trudy kirgizskoi arkheologo-etnograficheskoi ekspeditsii, no. 3, Frunze, 1959, pp. 59–73.

Lopatin, I. A., Animal style among the Tungus on the Amur, in: Anthropos, vol. 56, Fribourg, 1961, pp. 856–868.

Moschkova, W. G. (tr. by S. Kuntschik), 'Göls' auf turkmenischen Teppichen, in: Archiv für Völkerkunde, vol. 3, Vienna, 1948, pp. 24–43.

Strzygowski, J., Altai-Iran und Völkerwanderung. Leipzig, 1917.

Strzygowski, J., Asiens bildende Kunst in Stichproben: ihr Wesen und ihre Entwicklung. Augsburg, 1930.

Tokarev, S. A., Etnografiia narodov SSSR. Moscow, 1958.

Veimarn, B. V., Iskusstvo Srednei Azii. 1940.

II. PONTIC SCYTHIA

Artamonov, M. I., Obshchestvennyi stroi skifov, in: Vestnik LGU, 1947, no. 9, pp. 70ff.

Bobrinskii, A., Kurgany i sluchainye arkheologicheskie nakhodki bliz mestechka Smely. 3 vols. 1887–1901.

Borovka, G. I., Bronzovyi olen' iz Ul'skogo aula, in: IGAIMK, vol. 2, 1922.

Borovka, G. I., Kunstgewerbe der Skythen, in: Geschichte des Kunstgewerbes aller Zeiten und Völker, ed. H. Th. Bossert, vol. 1, Berlin, 1928, pp. 101–157.

Borovka, G. I., Scythian Art. London, 1928.

Brandenstein, W., Die Abstammungssagen der Skythen, in: Wiener Zeitschrift für die Kunde des Morgenlandes, vol. 52, Vienna, 1953, nos. 1 and 2, pp. 183–211.

Carter, D., The Symbol of the Beast. New York, 1957.

Elagina, N. G., O rodoplemennoi strukture skifskogo obshchestva po materialam chetvertoi knigi Gerodota, in: SE, 1963, no. 3, pp. 76–82.

Farmakovskii, B. V., Arkhaicheskii period v Rossii, in: MAR, vol. 34, 1914.

Fettich, N., Die Tierkampfszene in der Nomadenkunst, in: Recueil d'études dédiées à la mémoire de N. P. Kondakov. Seminarium Kondakovianum, Prague, 1926, pp. 81–92.

Gibellino-Krasceninnicowa, M., Gli Sciti. Rome, 1942.

Grakov, B. N., Skifi. Kiev, 1947.

Grakov, B. N., Ocherednye zadachi arkheologii v izuchenii skifosarmatskogo perioda, in: KSIIMK, no. 34, 1950, pp. 3–6.

Grakov, B. N., Skifskii Gerakl', in: KSIIMK, no. 34, 1950, pp. 7–18.

Grakov, B. N., Kamenskoe gorodishche na Dnepre, in: MIA, vol. 36, 1954.

Grakov, B. N., Skifskie pogrebeniia na Nikopol'skom kurgannom pol'e, in: MIA, vol. 115, 1962, pp. 56–113.

Grakov, B. N. and Meliukova, A. I., Ob etnicheskikh i kul'turnykh razlichiiakh v stepnykh i lesostepnykh oblastiakh Evropeiskoi chasti SSSR v skifskoe vrem'ia, in: Voprosy skifo-sarmatskoi arkheologii, Moscow, 1954, pp. 39–93.

Grakov, B. N., Pogrebal'nye sooruzheniia i ritual riadovykh obshchinnikov stepnoi Skifii, in: Arkheologicheskii sbornik, no. 6, 1964, pp. 118–127.

Hančar, F., Die Skythen als Forschungsproblem, in: Reinecke-Festschrift, Mainz, 1950, pp. 67–83.

Iatsenko, I. V., Skifiia VII-V vv. do n. e., in: Trudy GIM, vol. 36, 1959.

Iessen, A. A., K voprosu o pamiatnikakh VIII-VII vv. do n. e. na iuge Evropeiskoi chasti SSSR, in: SA, vol. 18, 1953, pp. 49–110.

Il'inskaia (=Illins'ka), V. A., Kurgan Starsha Mogili: pamiatka arkhaichnoi Skifii, in: Arkheologiia, Kiev, 1951, no. 5, pp. 196–212.

Il'inskaia, V. A., Nekotorye motivy ranneskifskogo zverinogo stilia, in: SA, 1965, no. 1, pp. 86–107.

Jettmar, K., Die Entstehung des skythischen Tierstils, in: Umschau, vol. 55, 1955, no. 7, pp. 203–5.

Jettmar, K., In den Jahren 1955 bis 1962 erschienene Werke zur frühen Nomadenkunst der asiatischen Steppen, in: Kunstgeschichtliche Anzeigen, new series, vol. 5, Graz-Cologne, 1961–2, pp. 184–197.

Jettmar, K., Ausbreitungsweg und sozialer Hintergrund des eurasiatischen Tierstils, in: MAGW, vol. 92 (Hančar-Festschrift), 1962, pp. 176–191.

Khanenko, B. N. and V. I., Drevnosti Pridneprov'ia. 1899–1900.

Korovina, A. K., K voprosu ob izuchenii Semibratnikh kurganov, in: SA, 1957, no. 2, pp. 174–187.

Lappo-Danilevskii, A. and Mal'berg, V., Drevnosti Iuzhnoi Rossii: kurgan Karagodeuashkh, in: MAR, vol. 3, 1894.

Liberov, P. D., Mastiuginskie kurgany, in: SA, 1961, no. 3, pp. 152–165.

Mantsevich, A. P., O skifskikh poiaskakh, in: SA, 1941, no. 7, pp. 19–30.

Mantsevich, A. P., Sheinye ubory skifskogo perioda, in: KSIIMK, 1948, no. 22, pp. 68–73.

Mantsevich, A. P., K voprosu o torevtike v skifskuiu epokhu, in: VDI, 1949, no. 2, pp. 196–220.

Meliukova, A. I., Skifskie kurgany Tiraspol'shchiny, in: MIA, no. 115, 1962, pp. 114–166.

Minns, E. H., Scythians and Greeks. Cambridge, 1913.

Minns, E. H., The Scythians and the Northern Nomads, in: Cambridge Ancient History, vol. 3, 1925.

Minns, E. H., The Art of the Northern Nomads, in: Proceedings of the British Academy, vol. 28, 1945, pp. 47–99.

Phillips, E. D., The Legend of Aristeas: Fact and Fancy in Early Greek Notions of East Russia, Siberia and Inner Asia, in: Artibus Asiae, vol. 18, Ascona, 1955, no. 2, pp. 161–177.

Phillips, E. D., A Further Note on Aristeas, in: Artibus Asiae, vol. 20, Ascona, 1957, nos. 2–3, pp. 159–162.

Phillips, E. D., The Argippaei of Herodotus, in: Artibus Asiae, vol. 23, Ascona, 1960, no. 2, pp. 124–128.

Phillips, E. D., New Light on the Ancient History of the Eurasian Steppe, in: American Journal of Archaeology, vol. 61, pp. 269–280.

Phillips, E. D., The Royal Hordes: Nomad Peoples of the Steppes. London, 1965.

Pogrebova, N. N., Grifon v iskusstve Severnogo Prichernomor'ia v epokhu arkhaiki, in: KSIIMK, 1948, no. 22, pp. 62–67.

Pogrebova, N. N., K voprosu o skifskom zverinom stile, in: KSIIMK, no. 34, 1950, pp. 129–141.

Potratz, J. A. H., Die Skythen und Vorderasien, in: Orientalia, vol. 28, Rome, 1959, pp. 57–73.

Potratz, J. A. H., Skythische Kunst, in: Orientalia, vol. 29, Rome, 1960, pp. 46–62.

Potratz, J. A. H., Die Skythen in Südrussland. Basle, 1963.

Pridik, E., Mel'gunovskii klad 1763 goda, in: MAR, no. 31, 1911.

Rabinovich, B., O datirovke nekotorykh skifskikh kurganov Srednego Pridneprov'ia, in: SA, vol. 1, 1936, pp. 79–102.

Rawlinson, G., History of Herodotus. 4 vols. London, 1879.

Rice, T. Talbot, The Scythians. London, 1957.

Rostovtseff (=Rostovtsev), M., Iranians and Greeks in South Russia. Oxford, 1922.

Rostovtzeff (=Rostovtsev), M., Le centre de l'Asie, la Russie, la Chine et le style animal, in: Skythika, vol. 1, Seminarium Kondakovianum, Prague, 1929.

Rostovtzeff (=Rostovtsev), M., The Animal Style in South Russia and China. Princeton, 1929.

Rostowzew (=Rostovtsev), M., Skythien und der Bosporus, vol. 1. Berlin, 1931.

Salmony, A., An Unknown Scythian Find in Novocherkassk, in: ESA, vol. 10, Helsinki, 1936, pp. 54–60.

Salmony, A., Lead Plates in Odessa, in: ESA, vol. 11, Helsinki, 1937, pp. 91–102.

Sarkisyanz, E., Russland und der Messianismus des Orients. Tübingen, 1955.

Schefold, K., Der skythische Tierstil in Südrussland, in: ESA, vol. 12, Helsinki, 1938, pp. 1–78.

Schefold, K., Die skythische Kunst in Südrussland, in: Handbuch der Archäologie, ed. W. Otto and R. Herbig, vol. 2, 1954.

Shleev, V. V., K voprosu o skifskikh naver-shiiakh, in: KSIIMK, 1950, no. 34, pp. 53–61.

Speiser, W., Vorderasiatische Kunst. Berlin, 1952.

Spitsyn, A. A., Kurgany skifov-pakharei, in: IAK, 1918, pp. 87–143.

Sulimirski, T., Scythian Antiquities in Western Asia, in: Artibus Asiae, vol. 17, Ascona, 1954, nos. 3–4, pp. 282–318.

Sulimirski, T., Scythian Notes, in: Palaeologia, vol. 4, 1955, nos. 3–4, pp. 280–284.

Tallgren, A. M., Zum Ursprungsgebiet des sog. skythischen Tierstils, in: Acta Archeologica, vol. 4, Copenhagen, 1933, pp. 258–264.

Terenozhkin, A. I., K voprosu ob etnicheskoi prinadlezhnosti lesostepnykh plemen Severnogo Prichernomor'ia v skifskoe vrem'ia, in: SA, 1955, no. 24, pp. 7–28.

Tolstoi, I. I. and Kondakov, N. P., Russkie drevnosti v pamiatnikakh iskusstva. 3 vols. St. Petersburg, 1888–1900.

Vos, M. F., Scythian Archers in Attic Black-Figure Vase Painting. Diss., Utrecht 1963. Groeningen, 1963.

Zamiatnin, S. N., Skifskii mogil'nik 'Chastye kurgany' pod Voronezhem, in: SA, 1946, no. 6, pp. 9–50.

Zgusta, L., Die Personennamen griechischer Städte der nördlichen Schwarzmeerküste. Prague, 1955.

III. SCYTHIAN FINDS IN CENTRAL EUROPE

Blavatskii, V. D., Frakiia i Severnyi Pont, in: KSIA AN SSSR, 1962, no. 89, pp. 94–96.

Böhm, J. and Jankovich, J., Skythovie na Podkarpatske Rusi Mohilové pohrebište v Kuštanovicich, in: Carpatica, vol. 1, Prague, 1936.

Csallany, G. and Parducz, M., Funde aus der Skythenzeit im Museum zu Szentes. Arch. Értesitö, 1944–5, nos. 5–6, pp. 106–7.

Fettich, N., La trouvaille Scythe de Zöldhalompuszta, in: Archaeologia Hungarica, vol. 3, Budapest, 1928.

Fettich, N., Der Goldhirsch von Tápiózentmárton, in: Archeoligai Értesitö, vol. 41, Budapest, 1927.

Fettich, N., Das Tiermotiv der Parierstange des Schwertes von Aldoboly, Siebenbürgen, in: Prähistorische Zeitschrift, vol. 19, Berlin, 1928, nos. 3–4.

Fettich, N., Bestand der skythischen Altertümer Ungarns, in: M. Rostovtsev, Skythien und der Bosporus, vol. 1, pt. 2, Berlin, 1931.

Fettich, N., Der skythische Fund von Gartschinowo, in: Archaeologia Hungarica, vol. 15, Budapest, 1934.

Furtwängler, A., Der Goldfund von Vettersfelde. 43. Winckelmanns Festprogramm. 1883.

Hampel, J., Scythische Denkmäler in Ungarn. Ethnologische Mitteilungen aus Ungarn, vol. 4. Budapest, 1895.

Jahn, M., Die Skythen in Schlesien, in: Schlesiens Vorzeit in Bild und Schrift, vol. 9, Breslau, 1928.

Meliukova, A. I., K voprosu o pamiatnikakh skifskoi kul'tury na territorii Srednei Evropy, in: SA, 1955, no. 22, pp. 239–253.

Nestor, J., Der Stand der Vorgeschichtsforschung in Rumänien. 22. Bericht der Röm.-Germ. Kommission 1932. Frankfurt-on-Main, 1933.

Párducz, M., Le cimetière Hallstattien de Szentes-Vekerzug, in: Acta Archaeologica Academiae scientiarum Hungaricae, vol. 2, Budapest, 1952, nos. 1–3, pp. 143–169.

Preidel, H., Skythen in Böhmen, in: Deutsche Heimat, vol. 4, 1928, pp. 340 ff.

Preidel, H., Der Skytheneinfall in Ostdeutschland und die skythischen Funde aus Böhmen, in: Altschlesien, vol. 5, 1934.

Reinecke, P., Die skythischen Altertümer im mittleren Europa, in: Zeitschrift für Ethnologie, vol. 28, Berlin, 1896.

Roska, M. von, Der Bestand der skythischen Altertümer Siebenbürgens, in: ESA, vol. 11, Helsinki, 1937, pp. 167–203.

Rozen-Pshevorskaia, Y., K voprosu o kel'to-skifskikh otnosheniiakh, in: SA, 1963, no. 3, pp. 67–78.

Schmidt, H., Skythischer Pferdegeschirrschmuck aus einem Silberdepot unbekannter Herkunft, in: Prähistorische Zeitschrift, vol. 18, Berlin, 1927, pp. 1 ff.

Sulimirski, T., Scytowie na zachodniem Podolu, in: Prace Lwowskiego Towarzystwa Prehistorycznego, Lwów, 1936, no. 2.

Sulimirski, T., Scythian Antiquities in Central Europe, in: Antiquaries Journal, 1945, no. 1, 2, pp. 1–11.

Sulimirski, T., Kultura lużycka a Scytowie, in: Wiadomości Archeologiezne, vol. 16, Warsaw, 1939–1948, pp. 76–100.

IV. SCYTHIAN ELEMENTS IN THE CAUCASUS

Alekseeva, E. P., Pozdnekobanskaia kul'tura

Tsentral'nogo Kavkaza, in: Uchenie zapiski LGU, seriia ist. nauk, vol. 3, Leningrad, 1949.

Artamonova-Poltavtseva, O. A., Kul'tura Severo-vostochnogo Kavkaza v skifskii period, in: SA, 1950, vol. 14, pp. 20–101.

Aslanov, G. M., Vaidov, R. M. and Ione, G. I., Drevnii Mingechaur. Baku, 1959.

Hančar, F., Einige Gürtelschliessen aus dem Kaukasus, in: ESA, vol. 6, Helsinki, 1931, pp. 146–158.

Hančar, F., Die Nadelformen des prähistorischen Kaukasusgebiets, in: ESA, vol. 7, Helsinki, 1932, pp. 113–182.

Hančar, F., Die Beile aus Koban in der Wiener Sammlung kaukasischer Altertümer, in: Wiener Prähistorische Zeitschrift, vol. 21, 1934, pp. 12–44.

Hančar, F., Zum Problem des 'kaukasischen' Tierstils, in: Wiener Beiträge, vol. 9, 1934, pp. 3–34.

Hančar, F., Kaukasus – Luristan. Züge kultureller Verwandtschaft des prähistorischen Kaukasusgebietes mit dem Alten Orient, in: ESA, vol. 9, Helsinki, 1934, pp. 47–112.

Hančar, F., Probleme des kaukasischen Tierstils, in: MAGW, vol. 65, Vienna, 1935, pp. 367–385.

Iessen, A. A., Severokavkazskie sosudy s izobrazheniem olenia, in: SGAIMK, 1931, no. 2.

Iessen, A. A., Nekotorye pamiatniki VIII – VII vv. do n. e. na Severnom Kavkaze, in: Voprosy skifo-sarmatskoi arkheologii, Moscow, 1954, pp. 112–131.

Kaziev, S. M., Arkheologicheskie raskopki v Mingechaure. Material'naia kul'tura Azerbaidzhana. Baku, 1949.

Krupnov, E. I., Drevniaia istoriia Severnogo Kavkaza. Moscow, 1960.

Kuftin, B. A., Arkheologicheskie raskopki v Trialeti. Tiflis, 1941.

Makalatiia, S. Ia., Raskopki Dvanskogo mogil'nika, in: SA, vol. 11, 1949, pp. 225–240.

Piotrovskii, B. B., Arkheologiia Zakavkaz'ia. Leningrad, 1949.

Piotrovskii, B. B. and Iessen, A. A., Mozdokskii mogil'nik. Leningrad, 1940.

Tallgren, A. M., Caucasian Monuments: the Kazbek Treasure, in: ESA, vol. 5, Helsinki, 1930, pp. 109–182.

Wesendonk, O. G., Archäologisches aus dem Kaukasus, in: Archäologischer Anzeiger, vol. 11, Berlin, 1925.

V. THE ANAN'INO CULTURE IN EASTERN RUSSIA

Eding, D. N., Idoly Gorbunovskogo torfianka, in: SA, vol. 4, 1937, pp. 133–146.

Eding, D. N., Novye nakhodki na Gorbunovskom torfianke, in: MIA, vol. 1, 1940, pp. 41–57.

Smirnov, A. P., Ocherki drevnei i srednevekovoi istorii narodov srednego Povolzh'ia i Prikam'ia, in: MIA, vol. 28, 1952.

Tallgren, A. M., Die 'altpermische' Pelzwarenperiode an der Pečora, in: SMYA, vol. 11, 1934, pp. 152–181.

Zbrueva, A. V., Ideologiia naseleniia Prikam'ia v Anan'inskuiu epokhu, in: TIE, Moscow-Leningrad, 1947, pp. 25–54.

Zbrueva, A. V., Istoriia naseleniia Prikam'ia v Anan'inskuiu epokhu, in: MIA, vol. 30, Moscow, 1952.

VI. THE EXPANSION OF THE SARMATIANS

Abramova, M. P., Sarmatskaia kul'tura II v. do n. e. – I v. n. e., in: SA, 1959, no. 1, pp. 52–71.

Abramova, M. P., Sarmatskie pogrebeniia Dona i Ukrainy, in: SA, 1961, no. 1, pp. 91–110.

Anfimov, N. V., Meoto-sarmatskii mogil'nik u stanitsy Ust'-Labinskoi, in: MIA, vol. 23, 1951, pp. 155–207.

Ebert, M., Südrussland. D. Skythisch-sarmatische Periode, in: Reallexikon der Vorgeschichte, vol. 13, Berlin, 1929, pp. 52–114.

Fettich, N., Archäologische Beiträge zur Geschichte der sarmatisch-dakischen Beziehungen, in: Acta Archaeologica, vol. 3, Budapest, 1953.

Grakov, B., Monuments de la culture scythique entre le Volga et les monts Oural, in: ESA, vol. 3, Helsinki, 1928, pp. 25–62.

Grakov, B., Deux tombeaux de l'époque scythique aux environs de la ville d'Orenbourg, in: ESA, vol. 4, Helsinki, 1929, pp. 169–182.

Grakov, B., Perezhitki matriarkhata u sarmatov, in: VDI, 1947, no. 3, pp. 100–122.

Iatsenko, I. V., Rannee sarmatskoe pogrebenie v basseine Severnogo Dontsa, in: KSIA, 1962, no. 89, pp. 42–50.

Iessen, A. A., Tak nazyvaemyi 'Maikopskii poias', in: Arkheologicheskii sbornik, vol. 2, Leningrad, 1961, pp. 163–177.

Maksimova, M. I., O date Artiukhovskogo kurgana, in: SA, 1960, no. 3, pp. 46–58.

Moshkova, M. G., Sarmatskie pamiatniki vostochnykh raionov Orenburgskoi oblasti, in: KSIA AN SSSR, no. 83, 1961, pp. 115–126.

Moshkova, M. G., Novo-Kumakskii kurgannyi mogil'nik bliz g. Orska, in: MIA, vol. 115, 1962, pp. 206–241.

Párducz, M., Denkmäler der Sarmatenzeit Ungarns. Budapest. Vol. 1, 1941; vol. 2, 1944 (1947); vol. 3, 1950.

Rau, P., Die Hügelgräber römischer Zeit an der unteren Wolga. Mitteilungen des Zentralmuseums der ASR d. Wolgadeutschen, Pokrovsk, 1927, vol. 1, no. 1.

Rau, P., Prähistorische Ausgrabungen auf der Steppenseite des deutschen Wolgagebietes im Jahre 1926. Mitteilungen des Zentralmuseums der ASR der Wolgadeutschen, Pokrovsk, 1927, vol. 2, no. 1.

Rau, P., Die Gräber der frühen Eisenzeit im unteren Wolgagebiet. Mitteilungen des Zentralmuseums der ASR der Wolgadeutschen, Pokrovsk, 1929.

Rostovtsev, M. I., Kurgannyia nakhodki Orenburgskoi oblasti epokhi ranniago i pozdniago Ellinizma, in: MAR, Petrograd, 1918, no. 37.

Rostovtsev, M. I., Sarmatskiia i indoskifskie drevnosti, in: Receuil d'études dédiées à la mémoire de N. P. Kondakov (Seminarium Kondakovianum), Prague, 1926, pp. 239–258.

Rostovtsev, M. I., Sarmatae, in: Cambridge Ancient History, vol. 11, 1936.

Rykov, P. S., Suslovskii kurgannyi mogil'nik. Saratov, 1947.

Shilov, V. P., Kalinovskii kurgannyi mogil'nik, in: MIA, vol. 60, 1959, pp. 323–523.

Sinitsyn, I. V., K materialam po sarmatskoi kul'ture na territorii nizhnego Povolzh'ia, in: SA, 1946, vol. 8, pp. 73–95.

Smirnov, K. F., O pogrebeniiakh roksolan, in: VDI, 1948, no. 1, pp. 213–214.

Smirnov, K. F., Sarmatskie pogrebeniia iuzhnogo Priural'ia, in: KSIIMK, 1948, no. 22, pp. 80–86.

Smirnov, K. F., Sarmatskie plemena Severnogo Prikaspiia, in: KSIIMK, 1950, no. 34, pp. 97–114.

Smirnov, K. F., O nekotorykh itogakh issledovaniia mogil'nikov meotskoi i sarmatskoi kul'tury Prikuban'ia i Dagestana, in: KSIIMK, 1951, no. 37, pp. 151–160.

Smirnov, K. F., Itogi i ocherednye zadachi izucheniia sarmatskikh plemen i ikh kul'tury, in: SA, 1953, no. 17, pp. 133–148.

Smirnov, K. F., Voprosy izucheniia sarmatskikh plemen i ikh kul'tury v sovetskoi arkheologii, in: Voprosy skifo-sarmatskoi arkheologii, Moscow, 1954, pp. 195–219.

Smirnov, K. F., Problema proiskhozhdeniia rannykh sarmatov, in: SA, 1957, no. 3, pp. 3–19.

Smirnov, K. F., Meotskii mogil'nik u stanitsy Pashkovskoi, in: MIA, vol. 64, 1958, pp. 272–312.

Smirnov, K. F., Vooruzhenie savromatov, in: MIA, vol. 101, 1961.

Smirnov, K. F., Savromaty: ranniaia istoriia i kul'tura sarmatov. Moscow, 1964.

Spitsyn, A. A., Falary Iuzhnoi Rossii, in: IAK, no. 29, 1909.

Tallgren, A. M., Portable Altars, in: ESA, vol. 11, Helsinki, 1937, pp. 47–68.

Viaz'mitina, M. I., Vivcheniia sarmativ na teritorii Ukrains'koi RSR, in: Archeologiia, vol. 7, Kiev, 1953.

VII. MINUSINSK BRONZES

Alekseev, V. P., Materialy po paleantropologii naseleniia Minusinskoi kotloviny vremeni tashtykskoi kul'tury, in: KSIE, 1954, no. 20, pp. 52–58.

Alekseev, V. P., Paleoantropologiia Chakassii epokhi zheleza, in: Sbornik MAE, vol. 20, 1961, pp. 238–327.

Alekseev, V. P., Paleoantropologiia Altae-Saianskogo nagor'ia epokhi neolita i bronzy, in: TIE, vol. 71, 1961, pp. 107–206.

Chlenova, N. L., Bronzovye nozhi Minusinskogo kraia i nekotorye voprosy razvitiia karasukskoi kul'tury. Leningrad, 1962.

Chlenova, N. L., Osnovnye voprosy proiskhozhdeniia tagarskoi kul'tury Iuzhnoi Sibiri, in: Voprosy istorii Sibiri i Dal'nego Vostoka: sbornik, Novosibirsk, 1961.

Chlenova, N. L., Pamiatniki perekhodnogo karasuk-tagarskogo vremeni v Minusinskom kotlovine, in: SA, 1963, no. 3, pp. 48–66.

Chlenova, N. L., Proiskhozhdenie i ranniaia istoriia plemen tagarskoi kul'tury Iuzhnoi Sibiri. Avtoreferat dissertatsii. Moscow, 1964.

Devlet, M. A., K voprosu o tagaro-tashtykskikh vzaimootnosheniiakh, in: SA, 1961, no. 4, pp. 78–83.

Fedorov, V. I., Drevnee iskusstvennoe oroshenie v raione Minusinskogo ponizheniia, in: MIA, vol. 24, 1952, pp. 137–146.

Gaul, J. H., Observations on the Bronze Age in the Yenisei Valley, Siberia, in: Papers of the Peabody Museum, vol. 20, Cambridge, Mass., 1943, pp. 149–186.

Ghirshman, R., review of: S. V. Kiselev, Histoire ancienne de la Sibérie du Sud; matériaux et recherches archéologiques en U.R.S.S., in: Artibus Asiae, vol. 14, Ascona, 1951, pts. 1–2, pp. 169–189.

Griaznov, M. P., Boiarskaia pisanitsa, in: Problemy istorii material'noi kul'tury, Leningrad, 1933, nos. 7–8, pp. 41–45.

Griaznov, M. P., Drevniaia bronza Minusinskikh stepei, in: Trudy Otdela Istorii Pervobytnoi Kul'tury, Leningrad, 1941, vol. I, pp. 237–271.

Jettmar, K., The Karasuk Culture and its South-eastern Affinities, in: BMFEA, no. 22, Stockholm, 1950, pp. 83–126.

Khlobystina, M. D., Bronzovye nozhi Minusinskogo kraia i nekotorye voprosy razvitiia karasukskoi kul'tury. Leningrad, 1962.

Kiselev, S. V., Drevniaia istoriia Iuzhnoi Sibiri. 2nd ed. Moscow, 1951.

Kyzlasov, L. P., Tashtykskaia epokha v istorii Khakassko-Minusinskoi kotloviny. Moscow, 1960.

Merhart, G. von, Bronzezeit am Jenissei. Vienna, 1926.

Merhart, G. von, Daljoko: Bilder aus sibirischen Arbeitstagen. Innsbruck, n.d.

Novgorodova, E., Nozhi karasukskogo vremeni iz Mongolii i Iuzhnoi Sibiri, in: Mongol'skii arkheologicheskii sbornik, Moscow, 1962, pp. 11–17.

Roudenko (= Rudenko), S. I., Les sépultures de l'époque des kourganes de Minoussinsk, in: L'Anthropologie, vol. 39, Paris, 1929.

Salmony, A., Origin and Age of the 'Grazing' Animal, in: Silver Jubilee Volume of the Zinbun-Kagaku-Kenkyusho, Kyoto, 1954, pp. 336–338.

Tallgren, A. M., Collection Tovostine des antiquités préhistoriques de Minoussinsk. Helsingfors, 1917.

Tallgren, A. M., Trouvailles tombales sibiriennes en 1889, in: SMYA, vol. 29, 1922.

Tallgren, A. M., review of: S. A. Teplouchov (= Teploukhov), Alte Begräbnisse im Minusinsk-Gebiet; M. P. Grjaznov (= Griaznov), Bronzezeitliche Gräber im westlichen Kasakstan, in: ESA, vol. 3, 1928, pp. 186–188.

Teploukhov, S. A., Drevnie pogrebeniia v Minusinskom krae, in: Materialy po etnografii, vol. 3, Leningrad, 1927, pt. 2.

Teploukhov, S. A., Opyt klassifikatsii drevnykh metallicheskikh kul'tur Minusinskogo kraia, in: Materialy po etnografii, vol. 4, Leningrad, 1929, pt. 2.

Teploukhov, S. A., Drevnemetallicheskie kul'tury Minusinskogo kraia, in: Priroda, 1929, no. 6, pp. 539–552.

Zalkind, N. G., Kraniologicheskie materialy iz tashtykskikh i tagarskikh pogrebenii Bol'shogo Salbykskogo kurgana. Sovetskaia Antropologiia, 1959, no. 1, pp. 57–66.

VIII. GRAVES OF THE SCYTHIAN ERA IN THE ALTAI

Alekseev, V. P., Paleoantropologiia lesnykh plemen Severnogo Altaia, in: KSIE, vol. 21, 1954, pp. 63–69.

Alekseev, V. P., Paleoantropologiia Altaia epokhi zheleza, in: Sovetskaia Antropologiia, 1958, no. 1, pp. 45–49.

Artem'ev, V. V., Butomo, S. V., Drozhzhin, V. M., Romanova, E. N., Rezul'taty opredeleniia absoliutnogo vozrasta riada arkheologicheskikh i geologicheskikh obraztsov po radiouglerodu (C14), in: SA, 1961, no. 2, pp. 3–11.

Azarpay, G., Some Classical and Near Eastern Motives in the Art of Pazyryk, in: Artibus Asiae, vol. 22, 1959, pp. 313–339.

Chernikov, S. S., Vostochnyi Kazakhstan v epokhu bronzy, in: MIA, vol. 88, 1960.

Dittrich, E., Das Motiv des Tierkampfes in der altchinesischen Kunst. Asiatische Forschungen, vol. 13, Wiesbaden, 1963.

Findeisen, H., Die 'Skythen' im Altai vor 2400 Jahren, in: Kosmos, July 1956, no. 7, pp. 306–311.

Gavrilova, A. A., Raskopki vtorogo Katandinskogo mogil'nika, in: SA, vol. 27, 1957, pp. 250–268.

Grjaznoff (= Griaznov), M., Fürstengräber im Altaigebiet, in: Wiener Prähistorische Zeitschrift, vol. 15, Vienna, 1928, pp. 120–123.

Griaznov, M. P., Raskopka kniazheskoi mogily na Altae, in: Chelovek, 1928, nos. 2–4, pp. 217–219.

Griaznov, M. P., Pazyrykskoe kniazheskoe pogrebenie na Altae, in: Priroda, 1929, no. 11, pp. 971–985.

Griaznov, M. P., Drevnie kul'tury Altaia. Novosibirsk, 1930.

Griaznov, M. P., Pazyrykskii kurgan. Moscow-Leningrad, 1937.

Griaznov, M. P., Raskopki na Altae, in: Soobshcheniia Gosud. Ermitazha, Leningrad, 1940, vol. I, pp. 17–21.

Griaznov, M. P., Pamiatniki maiemirskogo

etapa epokhi rannikh kochevnikov, in: KSIIMK, 1947, no. 18, pp. 9–17.

Griaznov, M. P., Raboty Altaiskoi ekspeditsii, in: KSIIMK, 1947, no. 21, pp. 77–78.

Griaznov, M. P., Pervyi Pazyrykskii kurgan. (Gos. Ermitazh), Leningrad, 1950.

Griaznov, M. P., Kolesnitsa rannikh kochevnikov Altaia, in: SGE, 1955, no. 7, pp. 30–32.

Griaznov, M. P., Voilok s izobrazheniem bor'by mificheskikh chudovishch iz piatogo Pazyrykskogo kurgana na Altae, in: SGE, 1956, no. 9, pp. 40–42.

Griaznov, M. P., Istoriia drevnikh plemen Verkhnei Obi po raskopkam bliz s. Bol'shaia Rechka, in: MIA, vol. 48, 1956.

Griaznov, M. P., Drevnee iskusstvo Altaia (L'art ancien de l'Altai), fotografii: A Bulgakov. Leningrad, 1958.

Griaznov, M. P. and Golomshtok, E. A., The Pazirik Burial of the Altai, in: American Journal of Archaeology, vol. 37, 1933, pt. 1, pp. 30–45.

Hančar, F., The Eurasian Animal Style and the Altai Complex: Cultural-historical Interpretation with a Consideration of the Newest Pazyryk Discoveries of 1946–1949, in: Artibus Asiae, vol. 15, Ascona, 1952, pts. 1–2, pp. 171–194.

Haskins, J. F., Sarmatian Gold collected by Peter the Great: VII. The Demidov Gift and Conclusions, in: Artibus Asiae, vol. 22, Ascona, 1959, pts. 1–2, pp. 64–78.

Jettmar, K., The Altai before the Turks, in: BMFEA, Stockholm, 1951, no. 23, pp. 135–223.

Jettmar, K., Die Pferdemasken des I. Pazyryk-Kurgans, in: Veröffentlichungen der Urgeschichtlichen Arbeitsgemeinschaft in der Anthropologischen Gesellschaft in Wien, Vienna, 1952, no. 1, pp. 63–66.

Jettmar, K., Die Fürstengräber der Skythen im Altai, in: Umschau, vol. 61, Frankfurt-on-Main, 1961, no. 12, pp. 368–371.

Jettmar, K., Zum 'Spielteppich' aus dem V. Pazyryk-Kurgan, in: Central Asiatic Journal, vol. 8, 1963, pt. 1, pp. 47–53.

Kiselev, S. V., Saiano-Altaiskaia arkheologicheskaia ekspeditsiia v 1937 g., in: VDI, 1938, no. 2, pp. 237 ff.

Kiselev, S. V., Saiano-Altaiskaia arkheologicheskaia ekspeditsiia v 1938 g., in: VDI, 1939, no. 1, pp. 252 ff.

Kyzlasov, L. P. and Smirnov, K. F., review of: S. I. Rudenko, Gornoaltaiskie nakhodki i

skifi, Leningrad-Moscow, 1952, in: SA, vol. 19, 1954, pp. 328–335.

Maenchen-Helfen, O., Crenellated Mane and Scabbard Slide, in: Central Asiatic Journal, vol. 3, 1957, pt. 2, pp. 85–138.

Meister, P. W., Ergebnisse der Grabungen im Altai 1939, in: Ostasiatische Zeitschrift, new series, vol. 18, 1942–3, pp. 62–64.

Poltoratskaia, V. N., Mogil'nik Berezovka I, in: Arkheologicheskii sbornik, Leningrad, 1961, no. 3, pp. 74–88.

Poltoratskaia, V. N., Znaki na predmetakh iz kurganov epokhi rannikh kochevnikov v gornom Altae, in: Arkheologicheskii sbornik, Leningrad, 1962, no. 5, pp. 76–90.

Radloff, W., Aus Sibirien. 2 vols. Leipzig, 1884.

Ricard, M.-Th., Quelques observations sur le costume scythique, in: Studia Antiqua Antonio Salac Septuagenario Oblata, Prague, 1955, pp. 152–155.

Roes, A., Achaemenid Influence upon Egyptian and Nomad Art, in: Artibus Asiae, vol. 15, Ascona, 1952, pts. 1–2, pp. 18–30.

Rudenko, S. I., Vtoroi Pazyrykskii kurgan. Leningrad, 1948.

Rudenko, S. I., Predvaritel'noe soobshchenie o raskopkakh v Ulagane 1947 g., in: SA, vol. 11, 1949, pp. 261–270.

Rudenko, S. I., Drevneishaia 'skifskaia' tatuirovka, in: SE, 1949, no. 3, pp. 133–143.

Rudenko, S. I., Piatyi Pazyrykskii kurgan, in: KSIIMK, vol. 37, 1951, pp. 106–116.

Rudenko, S. I., Der zweite Kurgan von Pasyryk (translated by I.-M. Görner). 2. Beiheft 'Sowjetwissenschaft', Berlin, 1951.

Rudenko, S. I., Gornoaltaiskie nakhodki i skifi. Moscow-Leningrad, 1952.

Rudenko, S. I., Bashadarskie kurgany, in: KSIIMK, 1952, no. 45, pp. 30–39.

Rudenko, S. I., Kul'tura naseleniia gornogo Altaia v skifskoe vrem'ia. Moscow, 1953.

Rudenko, S. I., K voprosu o datirovke i istoriko-kul'turnoi otsenke gornoaltaiskikh nakhodok, in: SA, vol. 27, 1957, pp. 301–306.

Roudenko (=Rudenko), S. I., The Mythological Eagle, the Gryphon, the Winged Lion and Wolf in the Art of Northern Nomads, in: Artibus Asiae, vol. 21, 1958, pt. 2.

Rudenko, S. I., Kul'tura naseleniia tsentral'nogo Altaia v skifskoe vrem'ia. Moscow-Leningrad, 1960.

Rudenko, S. I., Iskusstvo Altaia i Perednei Azii. Moscow, 1961.

Rudenko, S. I. and N. M., Iskusstvo skifov Altaia. Moscow, 1949.

Semenov, S. A., Obrabotka dereva na drevnem Altae (po materialam Pazyrykskikh kurganov), in: SA, vol. 26, 1956, pp. 204–226.

Sergeev, S. M., O reznykh kostianykh ukrasheniiakh konskoi uzdy iz 'skifskogo' kurgana na Altae, in: SA, vol. 8, 1946, pp. 289–292.

Smirnov, K. F., review of: S. I. Rudenko, Gornoaltaiskie nakhodki i skifi, Moscow-Leningrad, 1952, in: Voprosy istorii, 1953, no. 2, pp. 119–122.

Swoboda, K. M., In den Jahren 1950–1955 erschienene Werke zur Kunst Asiens vor dem Islam, in: Kunstgeschichtliche Anzeigen, new series, vol. 1, Graz-Vienna-Cologne, 1955–6, no. 3–4.

Tallgren, A. M., Archaeological Studies in Soviet Russia, in: ESA, vol. 10, Helsinki, 1936, pp. 129–170.

Tsalkin, V. I., K izucheniiu loshadei iz kurganov Altaia, in: MIA, 1952, no. 24, pp. 147–156.

Umanskii, A., Pamiatniki kul'tury Altaia. Barnaul, 1959.

Vidonova, E. S., Katandinskii khalat, in: Sbornik statei po arkheologii SSSR izd. Istoricheskogo Muzeia, Moscow, 1938, no. 8.

Vitt, O. A., Loshadi Pazyrykskikh kurganov, in: SA, vol. 16, 1952, pp. 163–205.

Wiesner, J., Zur Archäologie Sibiriens, in: Atlantis, vol. 31, Zürich, 1959, no. 1, pp. 44–50.

Zamotorin, I. M., Otnositel'naia khronologiia Pazyrykskikh kurganov, in: SA, 1959, no. 1, pp. 21–30.

Zavitukhina, M. P., Mogil'nik vremeni rannikh kochevnikov bliz g. Biiska, in: Arkheologicheskii sbornik, Leningrad, 1961, no. 3, pp. 89–108.

IX. THE HSIUNG-NU IN TRANSBAIKALIA AND NORTHERN MONGOLIA

Bernshtam, A. N., Izobrazhenie byka-iaka na bliakhakh iz Noin-Ulinskikh kurganov, in: PIDO, 1933, nos. 5–6, pp. 127–130.

Bernshtam, A. N., K voprosu o sotsial'nom stroe vostochnykh gunnov, in: PIDO, 1935, nos. 9–10, pp. 226–234.

Bernshtam, A. N., Gunnskii mogil'nik Noin-Ula i ego istoriko-arkheologicheskoe znachenie, in: Izvestiia AN SSSR: Otdelenie obshchestvennykh nauk, 1937, no. 4.

Bernshtam, A. N., Kenkol'skii mogil'nik. Arkh.

ekspeditsii Gos. Ermitazha, vol. 2, Leningrad, 1940.

Bernshtam, A. N., Iz istorii gunnov I v. do n. e., in: Sovetskoe vostokovedenie, vol. 1, Moscow-Leningrad, 1940, pp. 51–77.

Bernshtam, A. N., Ocherk istorii gunnov. Leningrad, 1951.

Borovka, G. I., Kul'turno-istoricheskoe znachenie arkheologicheskikh nakhodok ekspeditsii. Kratkie otchety ekspeditsii po issledovaniiu Severnoi Mongolii v sviazi s Mongolo-tibetskoi ekspeditsii P. K. Kozlova. AN SSSR, Leningrad, 1925.

Boroffka (=Borovka), G., Die Funde der Expedition Kozlow in der Mongolei 1924/25, in: Archaeolog. Anzeiger, 1926, pp. 341–368.

Borovka, G. I., Arkheologicheskoe obsledovanie srednego techeniia r. Toly, in: Severnaia Mongoliia, Leningrad, 1927, pp. 43–88.

Davydova, A. V., Ivolginskoe gorodishche, in: SA, vol. 25, 1956, pp. 261–300.

Davydova, A. V. and Shilov, V. P., K voprosu o zemledelii u gunnov, in: VDI, 1953, no. 2, pp. 193–201.

Dorozhsuren, Ts., Raskopki mogil khunnu v gorakh Noin-Ula na reke Khuni-gol (1954–1957 gg.), in: Mongol'skii arkheologicheskii sbornik, Moscow, 1962, pp. 36–44.

Gokhman, I. I., Materialy po antropologii drevnego naseleniia nizov'ev Selengi, in: KSIE, vol. 20, 1954, pp. 59–67.

Gokhman, I. I., Antropologicheskie materialy iz plitochnykh mogil Zabaikal'ia, in: Sbornik MAE, vol. 18, 1958, pp. 428–443.

Griaznov, M. P., Kinzhal s ozera Koto-Kël'. Izd. Nauchnogo obshchestva im. Banzarova. Verkhneudinsk, 1929.

Gumilev, L. N., Khunnu. Moscow, 1960.

Khoroshikh, P. P., Olennyi kamen' iz Zabaikal'ia, in: SA, 1962, no. 3, pp. 291–292.

Lubo-Lesnichenko, E., Simvolicheskoe znachenie ornamenta Noin-Ulinskoi tkani MR 1330, in: SGE, vol. 12, 1957, pp. 50–52.

Lubo-Lesnichenko, E., Drevnie kitaiskie shelkovye tkani i vyshivki V-go v. do n. e. – III-go v. n. e. v sobranii Gosud. Ermitazha: katalog. Leningrad, 1961.

Okladnikov, A. P., Novaia 'skifskaia' nakhodka na verkhnei Lene, in: SA, vol. 8, 1946, pp. 285–288.

Okladnikov, A. P., Arkheologicheskie issledovaniia v Buriat-Mongol'skoi ASSR, in: KSIIMK, 1949, no. 27, pp. 7–11.

Okladnikov, A. P., Novye dannye po drevneishei

istorii Vnutrennei Mongolii, in: VDI, 1951, no. 4, pp. 162–174.

Okladnikov, A. P., Arkheologicheskie issledovaniia v Buriat-Mongolii, IAN SIF, vol. 8, Moscow, 1951, no. 5, pp. 440–450.

Okladnikov, A. P., Raboty Buriat-mongol'skoi arkheologicheskoi ekspeditsii v 1947–1950 gg., in: KSIIMK, 1952, no. 45, pp. 40–47.

Okladnikov, A. P., Iakutiia do prisoedineniia k russkomu gosudarstvu, in: Istoriia Iakutskoi ASSR, Moscow-Leningrad, 1955.

Rudenko, S. I., Kul'tura khunnov i Noinulinskie kurgany. Moscow-Leningrad, 1962.

Salmony, A., The Small Finds of Noin-Ula, in: Parnassus, vol. 8, 1936, no. 2.

Ser-Odzhav, N., Arkheologicheskie issledovaniia v Mongol'skoi Narodnoi Respublike, in: Mongol'skii arkheologicheskii sbornik, Moscow, 1962, pp. 5–10.

Sosnovskii, G. P., Nizhne-Ivolinskoe gorodishche, in: PIDO, 1934, no. 7–8, pp. 150–156.

Sosnovskii, G. P., Derestuiskii mogil'nik, in: PIDO, 1935, no. 1–2, pp. 168–176.

Sosnovskii, G. P., Rannie kochevniki Zabaikal'ia, in: KSIIMK, 1940, no. 8, pp. 36–42.

Sosnovskii, G. P., Plitochnye mogily Zabaikal'ia, in: Trudy Otdela istorii pervobytnoi kul'tury Gosud. Ermitazha, vol. 1, Leningrad, 1941, pp. 273–309.

Sosnovskii, G. P., Raskopki Il'movoi padi, in: SA, vol. 8, 1946, pp. 51–67.

Sosnovskii, G. P., O poselenii gunnskoi epokhi v doline r. Chikoia (Zabaikal'e), in: KSIIMK, 1947, no. 14, pp. 35–39.

Tal'ko-Gryntsevich, Iu. L., Materialy k paleoetnologii Zabaikal'ia. Soobshcheno v obshchem sobranii Troitskosavsko-Kiakhtinskogo Otdeleniia Priamurskogo Otdela RGO 19 dekabria 1896 g. Tomsk, 1897.

Tal'ko-Gryntsevich, Iu. L., Sudzhinskoe doistoricheskoe kladbishche v Il'movoi padi. Trudy Troitskosavsko-Kiakhtinskogo Otdeleniia RGO, 1899, nos. 1–2.

Tal'ko-Gryntsevich, Iu. L., Materialy po paleoetnologii Zabaikal'ia. Trudy Troitskosavsko-Kiakhtinskogo Otdeleniia RGO, vol. 4, 1900, no. 3.

Teploukhov, S. A., Raskopki kurganov v gorakh Noin-Ula. Kratkie otchety ekspeditsii po issledovaniiu Severnoy Mongolii v sviazi s Mongolo-tibetskoi ekspeditsiei P. P. Kozlova. Moscow, 1925.

Trever, K. V., Nakhodki iz raskopok v Mongolii 1924–1925 gg., in: SGAIMK, 1931, nos. 9–10.

Trever, C. (= Trever, K. V.), Excavations in Northern Mongolia (1924–1925). Leningrad, 1932.

Umehara, S., Studies of Noin-Ula Finds in North Mongolia. The Toyo Bunko Publication Series A, no. 27. Tokyo, 1960. (In Japanese, with English summary.)

Viatkina, K. V., Arkheologicheskie pamiatniki v Mongol'skoi Narodnoi Respublike, in: SE, 1959, no. 1, pp. 93–106.

Vorob'ev, M. V., Drevniaia Koreia. Moscow, 1961.

Voskresenskii, A. A. and Tikhonov, N. P., Tekhnologicheskoe izuchenie materialov kurgannykh pogrebenii Noin-Uly, in: IGAIMK, vol. 11, 1932, nos. 7–9.

Werner, J., Ein hunnisches Lager der Han-Zeit in Transbaikalien, in: Sinica, 1939, pp. 193–196.

Werner, J., Beiträge zur Archäologie des Attila-Reiches. Abhandlungen der Bayerischen Akademie der Wissenschaften, Phil.-Hist. Klasse, new series, nos. 38A, 38B. Munich, 1956.

X. ORDOS BRONZES

Andersson, J. G., Der Weg über die Steppen, in: BMFEA, Stockholm, 1929, no. 1.

Andersson, J. G., Hunting Magic in the Animal Style, in: BMFEA, Stockholm, 1932, no. 4, pp. 221–317.

Andersson, J. G., Selected Ordos Bronzes, in: BMFEA, Stockholm, 1933, no. 5, pp. 143 ff.

Andersson, J. G., Researches into the Prehistory of the Chinese, in: BMFEA, Stockholm, 1943, no. 15.

Arne, T. J., Die Funde von L'uan-ping und Hsüan-hua, in: BMFEA, Stockholm, 1933, no. 5, pp. 155–175.

Carter, D., Four Thousand Years of China's Art. New York, 1951.

Chang, Kwang-chih, The Archaeology of Ancient China. New Haven – London, 1963.

Chêng Tê-k'un, Archaeology in China, vol. 3: Chou China. Cambridge, 1963.

Egami, N. and Mizuno, S., Inner Mongolia and the Region of the Great Wall, in: Archaeologia Orientalis, Series B, 1935, no. 1.

Griessmaier, V., Entwicklungsfragen der Ordos-Kunst, in: Artibus Asiae, vol. 7, Leipzig, 1937, nos. 1–4, pp. 122–257.

Griessmaier, V., Sammlung Baron Eduard von der Heydt, in: Wiener Beiträge, 1936.

Janse, O., Le style du Houai et ses affinités, in: Revue des arts asiatiques, vol. 8, no. 3.

Janse, O., Notes sur quelques épées anciennes trouvées en Chine, in: BMFEA, Stockholm, 1930, no. 2, pp. 67–176.

Janse, O., Tubes et boutons cruciformes trouvés en Eurasie, in: BMFEA, Stockholm, 1932, no. 4, pp. 187–209.

Jisl, L., Několik nových 'ordoských' bronzu a jejich postavní v rámci eurasijského zvěrného stylu, in: Acta Universitatis Carolinae, Philosophica et Historica, 1959, no. 3, Filipúv Sborník, Prague, 1962, pp. 195–206.

Karlgren, B., Ordos und Huai, in: BMFEA, Stockholm, 1937, no. 9.

Karlgren, B., Huai and Han, in: BMFEA, Stockholm, 1941, no. 13, pp. 1–116.

Karlgren, B., Some Weapons and Tools of the Yin Dynasty, in: BMFEA, Stockholm, 1945, no. 17, pp. 101–144.

Karlgren, B., Some Bronzes in the Museum of Far Eastern Antiquities: Postcript, in: BMFEA, Stockholm, 1949, no. 21, pp. 1–22, 22–25.

Kiselev, S. V., Mongoliia v drevnosti, in: IAN SIF, vol. 4, 1947, no. 4, pp. 355–372.

Kiselev, S. V., Neolit i bronzovyi vek Kitaia, in: SA, 1960, no. 4, pp. 244–266.

Kühn, H., Chronologie der Sino-Sibirischen Bronzen, in: Jahrbuch für prähistorische Kunst, vol. 12, 1937, pp. 162–165.

Larichev, V. E., Bronzovyi vek Severo-vostochnogo Kitaia, in: SA, 1961, no. 1, pp. 3–25.

Loehr, M., Weapons and Tools from Anyang and Siberian Analogies, in: American Journal of Archaeology, vol. 53, 1949, no. 2, pp. 126–144.

Loehr, M., The Earliest Chinese Swords and the Akinakes, in: Oriental Art, vol. 1, 1949, no. 3, pp. 132–142.

Loehr, M., Ordos Daggers and Knives. First Part: Daggers. In: Artibus Asiae, vols. 12, 14, Ascona, 1949, 1951, nos. 1–2.

Loehr, M., Ordos Daggers and Knives. Second Part: Knives, in: Artibus Asiae, vol. 14, Ascona, 1951, nos. 1–2, pp. 77–162.

Loehr, M., Zur Ur- und Vorgeschichte Chinas, in: Saeculum, vol. 3, 1952, no. 1, pp. 15–55.

Maenchen-Helfen, O., Die Träger des Tierstils im Osten, in: Wiener Beiträge, vol. 9, Vienna, 1935, pp. 61 ff.

Maenchen-Helfen, O., The Yüeh-chih Problem Re-examined, in: Journal of the American Oriental Society, vol. 65, New Haven, 1945, pp. 71–81.

Maenchen-Helfen, O., review of: F. Altheim, Attila und die Hunnen, Baden-Baden, 1951 and H. Homeyer, Attila: der Hunnenkönig von seinen Zeitgenossen dargestellt, Berlin, 1951, in: Gnomon, 1952, no. 24, pp. 500–504.

Maenchen-Helfen, O. J., The Ethnic Name Hun, in: Studia Serica B. Karlgren Dedicata, Copenhagen, 1959, pp. 223–238.

Meister, P. W., Zur Datierung einer Gruppe von Tierstilbronzen der Nach-Han-Zeit, in: Ostasiatische Zeitschrift, new series, vol. 11, 1935, no. 6, pp. 264–265.

Minns, E. H., Small Bronzes from Northern Asia, in: Antiquaries' Journal, vol. 10, London, 1930, no. 1, pp. 1–21.

Pelliot, P., Quelques réflexions sur l'art 'sibérien' et l'art chinois à propos de bronzes de la collection David-Weill. Documents, I. Paris, 1929.

Rostovtzeff (=Rostovtsev), M., Inlaid Bronzes of the Han Dynasty in the Collection of C. T. Loo. Paris-Brussels, 1927.

Salmony, A., Die alte Kunst Sibiriens und ihre Beziehungen zu China, in: Sinica, vol. 6, Frankfurt-on-Main, 1931, no. 4.

Salmony, A., Der waagrechte Stangenabschluss an der nordchinesischen Grenze und in China, in: Seminarium Kondakovianum, vol. 6, Prague, 1933, pp. 131–136.

Salmony, A., Sino-Siberian Art in the Collection of C. T. Loo. Paris, 1933.

Vasil'ev, K. V., Arkheologicheskie issledovaniia vo Vnutrennei Mongolii, in: VDI, 1959, no. 3, pp. 163–170.

Werner, J., Zur Stellung der Ordosbronzen, in: ESA, vol. 9, 1934, pp. 259–269.

XI. TUVA: AN AREA OF WITHDRAWAL

Alekseev, V. P., Ocherk paleoantropologii Tuvinskoi avtonomnoi oblasti, in: TIE, vol. 33, 1956, pp. 374–393.

Alekseev, V. P., Paleoantropologiia Altae-Saianskogo nagor'ia epokhi neolita i bronzy, in: TIE, vol. 71, 1961, pp. 107–206.

Chlenova, N. L., Mesto kul'tury Tuvy skifskogo vremeni v riadu drugikh 'skifskikh' stepnykh kul'tur Evrazii. Uchenye zapiski Tuvinskogo nauchno-issledovatel'skogo instituta iazyka, istorii i literatury, vol. 9, Kyzyl, 1961.

Chlenova, *N. L.*, Ob olennykh kamniakh Mongolii i Sibiri, in: Mongol'skii arkheologicheskii sbornik, Moscow, 1962, pp. 27–35.

Debets, *G. F.*, K paleoantropologii Tuvy, in: KSIE, vol. 10, 1950, pp. 97–111.

Grach, *A. D.*, Arkheologicheskie issledovaniia v zapadnoi Tuve, in: KSIE, vol. 33, 1955, pp. 19–33.

Grach, *A. D.*, Petroglify Tuvy, I, in: Sbornik MAE, vol. 17, 1957, pp. 385–428.

Grach, *A. D.*, Petroglify Tuvy, II, in: Sbornik MAE, vol. 18, 1958, pp. 339–384.

Kyzlasov, *L. P.*, Etapy drevnei istorii Tuvy, in: Vestnik Moskovskogo Universiteta, istoriko-filologicheskaia seriia, 1958, no. 4, pp. 71–99.

Kyzlasov, *L. P.*, Trudy Tuvinskoi kompleksnoi arkheologo-etnograficheskoi ekspeditsii Instituta etnografii AN SSSR, I. Materialy po arkheologii i etnografii zapadnoi Tuvy. Otv. red. L. P. Potapov, Moscow-Leningrad, 1960, in: SE, 1961, no. 4, pp. 225–230.

Potapov, *R. L.*, O nekotorykh naskal'nykh izobrazheniiakh zhivotnykh v gorakh Tannu-Ola i Mongun-Taigi, in: Sbornik MAE, vol. 18, 1958, pp. 385–389.

XII. THE SAKA IN MIDDLE ASIA

Ageeva, *E. I.* and *Patsevich, G. I.*, Otchet o rabotakh Iuzhno-Kazakhstanskoi arkheologicheskoi ekspeditsii 1953 g., in: TIIAE, Alma-Ata, 1956, vol. 1, pp. 33–60.

Akishev, *K. A.*, Otchet o rabote Iliiskoi arkheologicheskoi ekspeditsii 1954 g., in: TIIAE, vol. I, Alma-Ata, 1956, pt. 1, pp. 5–32.

Akishev, *K. A.*, Shestoi Besshatyrskii kurgan, in: KSIA AN SSSR, 1962, no. 91, pp. 61–65.

Akishev, *K. A. and Kushaev, G. A.*, Drevniaia kul'tura sakov i usunei doliny reki Ili. Alma-Ata, 1963.

Babanskaia, *G. G.*, Berkkarinskii mogil'nik, in: TIIAE, 1956, no. 1, pp. 189–206.

Bernshtam, *A. N.*, Berkkarinskaia priazhka, in: KSIIMK, 1947, no. 17, pp. 9–11.

Bernshtam, *A. N.*, Osnovnye etapy istorii kul'tury Semirech'ia i Tian'-shania, in: SA, vol. 11, 1949, pp. 336–384.

Bernshtam, *A. N.*, Istoriko-arkheologicheskie ocherki Tsentral'nogo Tian'-shania i Pamiro-Alaia, in: MIA, vol. 26, 1952.

Bernshtam, *A. N.*, Saki Pamira, in: VDI, 1956, no. 1, pp. 121–134.

Chernikov, *S. S.*, Zagadka zolotogo kurgana. Moscow, 1965.

Dalton, *O. M.*, The Treasure of the Oxus (with other examples of Early Oriental Metalwork). 2nd ed. British Museum, London, 1926.

Dandamaev, *M. A.*, Pokhod Dariia protiv skifskogo plemeni Tigrakhauda, in: Kratkie soobshcheniia Instituta narodov Azii, Moscow, 1963, no. 61, pp. 175–187.

Gorbunova, *N. G.*, Kul'tura Fergany v epokhu rannego zheleza, in: Arkheologicheskii sbornik, Leningrad, 1962, no. 5, pp. 91–122.

Jettmar, *K.*, Archäologische Spuren von Indogermanen in Zentralasien, in: Paideuma, vol. 5, 1952, no. 5, pp. 236–254.

Junge, *J.*, Saka-Studien. Leipzig, 1939.

Kibirov, *A. K.*, Arkheologicheskie raboty v Tsentral'nom Tian'-Shane 1953–1955 gg., in: Trudy Kirgizskoi arkheologo-etnograficheskoi ekspeditsii, vol. 2, Moscow, 1959, pp. 63–138.

Kushaev, *G. A.*, Dva tipa kurgannykh pogrebenii pravoberezh'ia reki Ili, in: TIIAE, 1956, no. 1, pp. 207–220.

Kushaev, *G. A.*, Rannekochevnicheskie kurgany v raione gorodishcha Baba-Ata, in: TIIAE, 1959, no. 7, pp. 242–247.

Kuz'mina, *E. E.*, Bronzovyi shlem iz Samarkanda, in: SA, 1958, no. 4, pp. 120–126.

Litvinskii, *B. A.*, Saki, kotorye za Sogdom, in: Trudy AN Tadzhikskoi SSR, vol. 120, 1960, pp. 91–96.

Litvinskii, *B. A.*, Dakhaninskii mogil'nik epokhi bronzy v Zapadnoi Fergane, in: KSIIMK, 1960, no. 80, pp. 47–52.

Litvinskii, *B. A.*, Archaeological Discoveries in the Eastern Pamirs and the Problem of Contacts between Central Asia, China and India in Antiquity, in: XXV International Congress of Orientalists: Papers presented by the USSR Delegation, Moscow, 1960.

Maenchen-Helfen, *O.*, A Chinese Bronze with Central Asiatic Motives, in: BMFEA, 1958, no. 30, pp. 167–175.

Maksimova, *A. G.*, Predmety epokhi rannikh kochevnikov v Tsentral'nom muzee Kazakhstana (g. Alma-Ata), in: TIIAE, vol. 1, Alma-Ata, 1956, pp. 253–261.

Maksimova, *A. G.*, Naskal'nye izobrazheniia ushchel'ia Tamgaly, in: Vestnik AN Kaz. SSR, Alma-Ata, 1958, no. 9.

Maksimova, *A. G.*, Kurgany sakskogo vremeni mogil'nika Dzhuvantove, in: KSIIMK, 1960, no. 80, pp. 60–64.

Mandel'shtam, A. M., Mogil'nik Aruk Tau v Bishkendskoi doline (Iuzhnyi Tadzhikistan), in: KSIIMK, 1959, no. 76, pp. 73–82.

Mandel'shtam, A. M., K arkheologii Karategina, in: KSIIMK, 1960, no. 80, pp. 76–79.

Martynov, G. S., Issykskaia nakhodka, in: KSIIMK, 1955, no. 59, pp. 150–156.

Masson, V. M., Pamiatniki kul'tury arkhaicheskogo Dakhistana i Iugo-zapadnoi Turkmenii, in: Trudy Iuzhno-Turkmenistanskoi arkheologicheskoi kompleksnoi ekspeditsii, vol. 7, Ashkhabad, 1956, pp. 385–457.

Masson, V. M., Drevnezemledel'cheskaia kul'tura Margiany, in: MIA, vol. 73, 1959.

Nil'sen, V. A., Kyzyl-Kyr, in: Istoriia material'noi kul'tury Uzbekistana, vol. 1, Tashkent, 1959, pp. 60–78.

Obel'chenko, O. V., Liavandakskii mogil'nik, in: Istoriia material'noi kul'tury Uzbekistana, vol. 2, Tashkent, 1961, pp. 97–176.

Pugachenkova, G. A., Grifon v antichnom i srednevekovom iskusstve Srednei Azii, in: SA, 1959, no. 2, pp. 70–84.

Schoppa, H., Die Darstellungen der Perser in der griechischen Kunst bis zum Beginn des Hellenismus. Heidelberg, 1933.

Staviskii, B. Ia., Drevneishie bronzovye izdeliia Chacha v Gosud. Ermitazhe, in: KSIIMK, 1955, no. 60, pp. 125–128.

Strelkov, A., Bol'shoi semirechenskii altar', in: Sbornik S. F. Ol'denburg, Leningrad, 1935.

Tallgren, A. M., Turkestan, Bronzezeit, in: Ebert, Reallexikon, vol. 13, 1929, pp. 485–486.

Tolstov, S. P., Les Scythes de l'Aral et le Khorezm, in: Iranica Antiqua, vol. 1, 1961, pp. 42–92.

Tolstov, S. P., Po drevnim del'tam Oksa i Iaksarta. Moscow, 1962.

Tolstov, S. P., Rezul'taty istoriko-arkheologicheskikh issledovanii 1961 g. na drevnikh ruslakh Syr-Dar'i, in: SA, 1962, no. 4, pp. 12–148.

Tolstov, S. P., Scythians of the Aral Sea Area and Khorezm, in: Trudy XXV mezhdunarodnogo kongressa vostokovedov, vol. 3, Moscow, 1963.

Tolstov, S. P., Vorob'eva, M. G. and Rapoport, Iu. A., Raboty Khorezmskoi arkheologoetnigraficheskoi ekspeditsii v 1957 g., in: Materialy Khorezmskoi ekspeditsii, Moscow, 1960, pt. 4, pp. 3–62.

Voevodskii, M. V. and Griaznov, M. P., Usun'skie mogil'niki na territorii Kirgizskoi SSR (k istorii usunei), in: VDI, 1938, no. 3, pp. 162 ff.

XIII. SIBERIAN GOLD: THE STEPPES OF NORTHERN AND EASTERN KAZAKHSTAN

Ageeva, E. I. and Maksimova, A. G., Otchet Pavlodarskoi ekspeditsii 1955 g., in: TIIAE, 1959, no. 7, pp. 32–58.

Akishev, K. A., Pamiatniki stariny Severnogo Kazakhstana, in: TIIAE, 1959, no. 7, pp. 3–31.

Chernikov, S. S., Raboty Vostochno-Kazakhstanskoi arkheologicheskoi ekspeditsii v 1956 g., in: KSIIMK, 1959, no. 73, pp. 99–106.

Chernikov, S. S., K izucheniiu drevnei istorii Vostochnogo Kazakhstana, in: KSIIMK, 1957, no. 69, pp. 12–21.

Fettich, N., Zur Chronologie der sibirischen Goldfunde der Eremitage, in: Acta Archaeologica (Academiae Scientiarum Hungaricae), vol. 2, Budapest, 1952, pp. 251–268.

Griaznov, M. P., Zolotaia bliakha s izobrazheniem bor'by zhivotnykh, in: Sokrovishcha Ermitazha, Moscow-Leningrad, 1949, pp. 71–74.

Griaznov, M. P., Pamiatniki karasukskogo etapa v Tsentral'nom Kazakhstane, in: SA, vol. 16, 1952, pp. 129–162.

Griaznov, M. P., Severnyi Kazakhstan v epokhu rannikh kochevnikov, in: KSIIMK, 1956, no. 61, pp. 8–16.

Hentze, C., Beiträge zu den Problemen des eurasischen Tierstils, in: Ostasiatische Zeitschrift, new series, vol. 6, 1930, pt. 1, pp. 150–169.

Kadyrbaev, M. K., Pamiatniki rannikh kochevnikov Tsentral'nogo Kazakhstana, in: TIIAE, Alma-Ata, 1959, no. 7, pp. 162–203.

Kyzlasov, L. P. and Margulan, A. Kh., Plitochnye ogrady mogil'nika Begazy, in: KSIIMK, vol. 32, Moscow-Leningrad, 1950, pp. 126–136.

Meister, P. W., Zur Technik der sibirischen Goldarbeiten, in: Pantheon, vol. 30, 1942, pp. 225–227.

Rudenko, S. I., Sibirskaia kollektsiia Petra I. Arkheologiia SSSR, D 3–9, Moscow-Leningrad, 1962.

Rudenko, S. I., Die Sibirische Sammlung Peters I. Archaeologie der UdSSR – Sammlung arch. Quellen. ed. D 3–9 (translated and ed. by Dr. H. Pollems), n.d.

Salmony, A., Sarmatian Gold Collected by Peter the Great. I: Introduction; II: The

Group with All-over Cloisonné, in: Gazette des Beaux Arts, series VI, vol. 31, New York, 1947, pt. 1, pp. 5–14.

Salmony, A., Sarmatian Gold Collected by Peter the Great, III: The Early Group with Winged Circle Sockets, in: Gazette des Beaux Arts, series VI, vol. 33, New York – Paris, 1948, pt. 1, pp. 321–326.

Salmony, A., Sarmatian Gold Collected by Peter the Great, IV: The Early Sarmatian Group with Embossed Relief, in: Gazette des Beaux Arts, series VI, vol. 35, New York – Paris, 1949, pt. 1, pp. 5–10.

Salmony, A., Sarmatian Gold Collected by Peter the Great, V: The Middle Sarmatian Group; Embossed Relief and Isolated Inlay Cells, in: Gazette des Beaux Arts, series VI, vol. 40, New York – Paris, 1952, pt. 2, pp. 85–92.

Spitsyn, A., K voprosu o khronologii zolotykh sibirskikh bliakh s izobrazheniem zhivotnykh, in: Zapiski Russk. Arkh. Obshchestva, vol. 12, St. Petersburg, 1901.

Spitsyn, A., Sibirskaia kollektsiia Kunstkamery, in: Zapiski Otdela russkoi i slavianskoi arkheologii Imp. Russk. Arkh. Obshchestva, vol. 8, 1906, pt. 1, pp. 227ff.

Tallgren, A. M., Portable Altars, in: ESA, vol. 11, 1937, pp. 47–68.

XIV. THE AFTERMATH

Appelgren-Kivalo, H., Die Grundzüge des permisch-skythischen Ornamentstiles, in: SMYA, vol. 26, 1912, pt. 1.

Appelgren-Kivalo, H., Vogelkopf und Hirsch als Ornamentmotive in der Vorzeit Sibiriens, in: Finnisch-Ugrische Forschungen, vol. 12, 1912, pp. 294ff.

Chernetsov, V. N., review of: S. I. Rudenko, Kul'tura naseleniia Gornogo Altaia v skifskoe vremia, Moscow-Leningrad, 1953, in: SE, 1954, no. 2, pp. 183–187.

Chernetsov, V. N., Nizhnee Priob'e v I-m tysiacheletii nashei ery, in: MIA, vol. 58, 1957, pp. 136–245.

Fettich, N., Das Kunstgewerbe der Avarenzeit in Ungarn, in: Archaeologia Hungarica, vol. 1, Budapest, 1926.

Fettich, N., Bronzeguss und Nomadenkunst (mit einem Anhang von L. Bartucz), in: Skythika, Prague, 1929, no. 2.

Fettich, N., Der Schildbuckel von Harpály, in: Acta Archaeologica, vol. 1, Copenhagen, 1930, pp. 221–263.

Fettich, N., Archäologische Studien zur Geschichte der späthunnischen Metallkunst, in: Archaeologia Hungarica, vol. 31, Budapest, 1951.

Gorodtsov, V. A., Podcheremskii klad, in: SA, vol. 2, 1937, pp. 113–150.

Laufer, B., The Decorative Art of the Amur Tribes, in: Memoirs of the American Museum of Natural History, vol. 7, 1902.

Mavrodinov, N., Le trésor protobulgare de Nagyszentmiklós.

Roerich, I. N., The Animal Style among the Nomad Tribes of Northern Tibet. Seminarium Kondakovianum, Prague, 1930.

Rudenko, S. I. and *Glukhov, A. N.,* Mogil'nik Kudyrge na Altae, in: Materialy po etnografii, vol. 3, Leningrad, 1927, pt. 2, pp. 37–52.

Salin, B., Die altgermanische Thierornamentik. Stockholm, 1904.

Schuster, C., A Survival of the Eurasiatic Animal Style in Modern Alaskan Eskimo Art. Tax: Indian tribes of Aboriginal America, vol. 3. Proceedings of the 29th Congress of Americanists, Chicago, 1952.

Shmidt, A. V., K voprosu o proiskhozhdenii Permskogo zverinogo stilia, in: Sbornik MAE, vol. 6, Leningrad, 1927, pp. 125–164.

Shmidt (=Schmidt), A. V., Kachka. Beiträge zur Erforschung der Kulturen Ostrusslands in der Zeit der Völkerwanderung (III. – V. Jh.), in: ESA, vol. 1, Helsinki, 1927, pp. 18–50.

Shmidt, A. V., Einige Motive der prähistorischen Kunst Transuraliens, in: Artibus Asiae, vol. 3, 1928–9, pp. 224 ff.

Shmidt, A. V., O klade iz Podcherema, in: SGAIMK, nos. 11–12, 1931, pp. 51–55.

Smirnov, A. P., Mogil'niki p'ianoborskoi kul'tury, in: KSIIMK, 1949, no. 25, pp. 22–32.

Smirnov, A. P., Ocherki drevnei i srednevekovoi istorii narodov srednego Povolzh'ia i Prikam'ia, in: MIA, vol. 28, Moscow, 1952.

Spitsyn, A. A., Drevnosti Kamskoi Chudi po kollektsii Teploukhovykh, in: MAR, St. Petersburg, 1902, no. 26.

Spitsyn, A. A., Shamanskiia izobrazheniia, in: Zapiski Otd. russk. i slavyansk. arkh. Imp. Russk. Arkh. Obshchestva, vol. 8, St. Petersburg, 1906, no. 1, pp. 29–145.

Tallgren, A. M., Collection Zaoussailov, 2 vols. Helsingfors, 1916–1918.

Tallgren, A. M., Permian Studies. The Genealogy of the Permian Idols, in: ESA, vol. 3, 1928, pp. 63–92.

Tallgren, A. M., Zur westsibirischen Gruppe der 'schamanistischen' Figuren. Seminarium Kondakovianum, vol. 4, Prague, 1931.

Toll, N., Bronze Plaque from the Collection of Count E. Zichy, in: ESA, vol. 9, Helsinki, 1934, pp. 270–276.

XV. THE RISE OF THE MOUNTED WARRIORS AND THE BIRTH OF ANIMAL STYLE

Abaev, V. I., Osetinskii iazyk i fol'klor, vol. 1. Moscow-Leningrad, 1949.

Alföldi, A., Die geistigen Grundlagen des hochasiatischen Tierstiles, in: Forschungen und Fortschritte, 7th year, Berlin, 1931, no. 20, pp. 278–279.

Alföldi, A., Die theriomorphe Weltbetrachtung in den hochasiatischen Kulturen, in: Archäologischer Anzeiger, 1931, pts. 1–2 (Sitzungsbericht), pp. 394–418.

Alföldi, A., Königsweihe und Männerbund bei den Achämeniden, in: Schweizer Archiv für Volkskunde, vol. 47, 1951, pp. 11–16.

Amandry, P., Un motif 'scythe' en Iran et en Grèce, in: Journal of Near Eastern Studies, vol. XXIV, 1965, no. 3.

Anderson, I. K., Ancient Greek Horsemanship. Berkeley – Los Angeles, 1961.

Barnett, R. D., The Treasure of Ziwiye, in: Iraq, vol. 18, 1956, pp. 111–116.

Barnett, R. D., Median Art, in: Iranica Antiqua, 1962, no. 2, pp. 77–95.

Bleichsteiner, R., Zum eurasiatischen Tierstil, in: Berichte des Asien-Arbeitskreises, no. 2, 1939, pp. 9–64.

Bleichsteiner, R., Zeremonielle Trinksitten und Raumordnung bei turko-mongolischen Nomaden, in: Archiv für Völkerkunde, vols. 6–7, Vienna, 1952, pp. 181–208.

Calmeyer, P., Altiranische Bronzen der Sammlung Bröckelschen. Berlin, 1964.

Chernikov, S. S., O termine 'rannie kochevniki', in: KSIIMK, 1960, no. 80, pp. 17–21.

Chlenova, N. L., Skifskii olen', in: MIA, vol. 115, 1962, pp. 167–205.

Christian, M. V., Vorderasiatische Vorläufer des eurasiatischen Tierstils, in: Wiener Beiträge, vol. 11, 1937.

Dewall, M. von, Der Gräberverband von Wukuan-ts'un/Anyang, in: Oriens Extremus, 7th year, 1960, no. 2, pp. 129–151.

Dewall, M. von, Pferd und Wagen im Frühen

China. Saarbrücker Beiträge zur Altertumskunde, vol. 1, Bonn, 1964.

D'iakonov, I. M., Istoriia Midii. Moscow-Leningrad, 1956.

Eding, D. N., Reznaia skul'ptura Urala, in: Trudy GIM, vol. 10, Moscow, 1940.

Eliade, M., Les Daces et les loups, in: Numen, vol. 6, 1959, no. 1, pp. 15–31.

Gallus, S. and Horváth, T., Un peuple cavalier préscythique en Hongrie, 2 vols. Dissertationes Pannonicae, ser. II, 9. Budapest, 1939.

Ghirshman, R., Fouilles de Sialk près de Kashan, 1933, 1934, 1937, II. Musée du Louvre, Département des antiquités orientales, série archéologique, vol. 5, Paris, 1939.

Ghirshman, R., Recherches préhistoriques en Afghanistan: Fouilles de Nad-i-Ali dans le Seistan afghan, in: Revue des Arts Asiatiques, vol. 13, Paris, 1939, no. 1, pp. 10–22.

Ghirshman, R., Notes iraniennes, IV: Le trésor de Sakkez, les origines de l'art mède et les bronzes du Luristan, in: Artibus Asiae, vol. 13, Ascona, 1950, pt. 3, pp. 181–206.

Ghirshman, R., Masjid-i-Solaiman, résidence des premiers Achéménides, in: Syria, vol. 27, Paris, 1950, no. 3–4, pp. 205–220.

Ghirshman, R., Village perse-achéménide, in: Mémoires de la Mission Archéologique en Iran, vol. 36 (Mission de Susiane), Paris, 1954.

Ghirshman, R., Iran: from the Earliest Times to the Islamic Conquest. Penguin Books, Harmondsworth, 1954.

Ghirshman, R., Notes iraniennes, VII: A propos de Persépolis, in: Artibus Asiae, vol. 20, Ascona, 1957, no. 4, pp. 265–278.

Ghirshman, R., Perse: Proto-iraniens, Mèdes, Achéménides. Paris, 1963.

Ghirshman, R., Invasions des nomades sur le Plateau Iranien aux premiers siècles du Ier millénaire avant J.-C., in: Dark Ages and Nomads c. 1000 B.C., Istanbul, 1964, pp. 3–8.

Gimbutas, M., Borodino, Seima and their Contemporaries, in: Proceedings of the Prehistoric Society for 1956, vol. 22, no. 9.

Gimbutas, M., The Treasure of Michalkov, in: Archaeology, vol. 12, 1959, pt. 2, pp. 84–87.

Godard, A., Le trésor de Ziwiyè, in: Académie des Inscriptions et des Belles-Lettres, Comptes rendus, Paris, 1949, pp. 168–172.

Godard, A., Le trésor de Ziwiyè (Kurdistan). Publications du Service archéologique de l'Iran. Haarlem, 1950.

Godard, A., A propos du trésor de Ziwiyè, in: Artibus Asiae, vol. 14, Ascona, 1951, no. 3, pp. 240–245.

Godard, A., L'art de Iran. Paris, 1962.

Gorodtsov, V. A., K voprosu o kimmeriiskoi kul'ture, in: Trudy sektsii arkheologii RANION, vol. 2, 1928, pp. 54–59.

Griaznov, M. P., Nekotorye voprosy istorii slozheniia i razvitiia rannikh kochevykh obshchestv Kazakhstana i Iuzhnoi Sibiri, in: KSIE, vol. 24, 1955, pp. 19–29.

Griaznov, M. P., Etapy razvitiia khoziaistva skotovodcheskikh plemen Kazakhstana i Iuzhnoi Sibiri v epokhu bronzy, in: KSIE, vol. 26, 1957, pp. 21–28.

Griaznov, M. P., Drevneishie pamiatniki geroicheskoi epokhi narodov Iuzhnoi Sibiri, in: Arkheologicheskii sbornik (Gos. Ermitazh), 1961, no. 3, pp. 7–31.

Hančar, F., Ross und Reiter im urgeschichtlichen Kaukasus, in: IPEK, year 1935, Berlin-Leipzig, 1936, pp. 49–65.

Hančar, F., Urgeschichtliche Erkenntnisse zum eurasiatischen Viehzüchternomadentum, in: Palaeologia, vol. 4, Osaka, 1955, pts. 3–4, pp. 264–273.

Hančar, F., Die Kunst der Nomaden. Kleine Weltkunstgeschichte. Stuttgart, 1955.

Hančar, F., Das Pferd in prähistorischer und früher historischer Zeit, in: Wiener Beiträge, vol. 11, Vienna-Munich, 1955.

Harmatta, J., The Dissolution of the Hun Empire, part I: Acta Archaeologica ASH, vol. 2, Budapest, 1952, pp. 277–306.

Heine-Geldern, R., Das Tocharerproblem und die Pontische Wanderung, in: Saeculum, 1951, no. 2, pp. 225–255.

Jettmar, K., Entstehung des Reiterkriegertums, in: Handbuch der Weltgeschichte, ed. A. Randa, vol. 1, Olten, 1953, cols. 341–348.

Jettmar, K., Zur Wanderungsgeschichte der Iranier, in: Die Wiener Schule der Völkerkunde, Festschrift zum 25-jährigen Bestand, Vienna, 1956, pp. 327–348.

Jettmar, K., Urgeschichte Innerasiens (Asiatischer Steppengürtel und Sibirien), in: Abriss der Weltgeschichte – Abriss der Vorgeschichte, Munich, 1957, pp. 150–161.

Jettmar, K., review of F. Hančar, Das Pferd in prähistorischer und früher historischer Zeit, in: Central Asiatic Journal, vol. 3, The Hague – Wiesbaden, 1957, no. 2, pp. 155–160.

Kantor, H. I., Oriental Institute Museum Notes, no 11: a Fragment of a Gold Appliqué from Ziviye and Some Remarks on the Artistic Traditions of Armenia and Iran during the Early First Millennium B.C., in: Journal of Near Eastern Studies, vol. 19, 1960, no. 1, pp. 1–14.

Kiselev, S. V., Arkheologicheskaia poiezdka v Mongoliiu, in: KSIIMK, 1947, no. 21, pp. 35–38.

Kiselev, S. V., Neolit i bronzovyi vek Kitaia, in: SA, 1960, no. 4, pp. 244–266.

König, F. W., Der falsche Bardija. Dareios der Grosse und die Lügenkönige, in: Klotho, Vienna, 1938, no. 4.

König, F. W., Die Götterwelt Armeniens zur Zeit der Chalder-Dynastie (9.–7. Jh. v. Chr.), in: Archiv für Völkerkunde, vol. 8, Vienna, 1954, pp. 21–65.

Komarova, M. N., Otnositel'naia khronologiia pamiatnikov andronovskoi kul'tury, in: Arkheologicheskii sbornik, Leningrad, 1962, no. 5, pp. 50–75.

Kossack, G., Pferdegeschirr aus Gräbern der älteren Hallstattzeit Bayerns. Jahrbuch des Römisch-germanischen Zentralmuseums Mainz, vol. 1, 1953/54.

Kothe, H., Die Herkunft der kimmerischen Reiter, in: Klio, vol. 41, 1963, pp. 5–37.

Krupnov, E. I., Pervye itogi izucheniia Vostochnogo Predkavkaza, in: SA, 1957, no. 2, pp. 154–173.

Krupnov, E. I., Kimmeriitsy na Severnom Kavkaze, in: MIA, vol. 68, 1958, pp. 176–195.

Kussmaul, F., Frühe Nomadenkulturen in Innerasien, in: Tribus, Stuttgart, 1952–1953, pp. 305–360.

Kuz'mina, E. E., O iuzhnykh predelakh rasprostraneniia stepnykh kul'tur epokhi bronzy v Srednei Azii, in: Pamiatniki kamennogo i bronzovogo vekov Evrazii, Moscow, 1964, pp. 141–159.

Larichev, V. E., Bronzovyi vek Severo-vostochnogo Kitaia, in: SA, 1961, no. 1, pp. 3–25.

Laufer, B., The Bird-Chariot in China and Europa, in: Boas Anniversary Volume, New York, 1906, pp. 410 ff.

Loehr, M., The Stag Image in Scythia and the Far East, in: Archives of the Chinese Art Society of America, vol. 9, 1955.

Maenchen-Helfen, O., Obituary of Sir Ellis Hovell Minns, 1874–1953, in: Man, vol. 13, London, 1953, article 264.

Mozsolics, A., Die Herkunft der ältesten Hirschgeweihtrensen, in: Acta Archaeologica ASH, vol. 12, Budapest, 1960, pp. 125–135.

Nagel, W., review of K. Jettmar, Die frühen Steppenvölker: Der eurasiatische Tierstil – Entstehung und sozialer Hintergrund. Kunst der Welt, Baden-Baden, 1964, in: Berliner Jahrbuch für Vor- und Frühgeschichte, vol. 5, Berlin, 1965, pp. 269–272.

Nestor, J., Zu den Pferdegeschirrbronzen aus Stillfried a.d. March, N.Ö., in: Wiener Prähistorische Zeitschrift, vol. 21, 1934, pp. 108–130.

Okladnikov, A. P., Neolit i bronzovyi vek Pribaikal'ia. Istoriko-arkheologicheskie issledovanie, I – II, in: MIA, vol. 18, 1950.

Okladnikov, A. P., Neolit i bronzovyi vek Pribaikal'ia, III (Glazkovskoe vrem'ia), in: MIA, vol. 43, 1955.

Okladnikov, A. P., Peshchera Dzhebel: pamiatnik drevnei kul'tury prikaspiiskikh plemen Turkmenii, in: Trudy Iuzhno-Turkmenistanskoi arkheologicheskoi kompleksnoi ekspeditsii, vol. 7, Ashkhabad, 1956, pp. 11–219.

Okladnikov, A. P., Issledovaniia pamiatnikov kamennogo veka Tadzhikistana, in: MIA, vol. 66, 1958, pp. 11–71.

Piotrovskii, B. B., Karmir-blur, I: Arkheologicheskie raskopki v Armenii, vol. 1. Erevan, 1950.

Piotrovskii, B. B., Skifi i drevnii Vostok, in: SA, vol. 19, 1954, pp. 141–158.

Piotrovskii, B. B., Iskusstvo Urartu VIII – VI vv. do n. e. Leningrad, 1962.

Porada, E., Nomads and Luristan Bronzes: Methods proposed for a Classification of the Bronzes, in: Dark Ages and Nomads c. 1000 B.C., Istanbul, 1964, pp. 9–31.

Porada, E., Ancient Iran: The Art of Pre-Islamic Times. With the collaboration of R. H. Dyson and contributions by C. K. Wilkinson. (ART OF THE WORLD.) London, 1965.

Salmony, A., An Ivory Carving from Malta (Siberia) and its Significance, in: Artibus Asiae, vol. 11, Ascona, 1948, no. 4, pp. 285–288.

Shchepinskii, A. A., Pogrebenie nachala zheleznogo veka u Simferopolia, in: KSIA, Kiev, 1962, no. 12, pp. 57–65.

Schmidt, E. F., The Treasury of Persepolis and Other Discoveries in the Homeland of the Achaemenians. Oriental Institute Communications, no. 21. Chicago, 1939.

Smirnov, K. F., O pogrebeniiakh s koniami i truposozhzheniiakh epokhi bronzy v Nizhnem Povolzh'e, in: SA, vol. 27, 1957, pp. 209–221.

Smirnov, K. F., Arkheologicheskie dannye o drevnikh vsadnikakh Povolzhsko-Ural'skikh stepei, in: SA, 1961, no. 1, pp. 46–72.

Struve, V. V., Pokhod Dariia na sakov-massagetov, in: IAN SIF, 1946, no. 3, pp. 231–250.

Sulimirski, T., Les anciens archeurs à cheval, in: Revue Internationale de l'Histoire Militaire, no. 3, Paris, 1952, no. 12, pp. 447–461.

Sulimirski, T., The Cimmerian Problem, in: Univ. of London, Inst. of Archaeology, Bulletin no. 2, 1959 (1960), pp. 45–64.

Tallgren, A. M., La pontide préscythique après l'introduction des métaux, in: ESA, vol. 2, Helsinki, 1926.

Tchlenova, T. (=Chlenova N. L.), L'art animalier de l'époque scythique en Sibérie et en Pontide. VI Congrès International de sciences préhistoriques et protohistoriques. Les rapports et les informations des archéologues de l'URSS, Moscow, 1962.

Tchlenova, N. L. (=Chlenova), Le cerf scythe, in: Artibus Asiae, vol. 26, Ascona, 1963, pp. 27–71.

Terenozhkin, A. I., Srednee Podneprov'e v nachale zheleznogo veka, in: SA, 1957, no. 2, pp. 47–63.

Terenozhkin, A. I., Bronzovyi psalii s gorodishcha Kiuzeli-gyra v Khorezme, in: KSIE, vol. 30, 1958, pp. 34–39.

Terenozhkin, A. I., Predskifskii period na Dneprovskom Pravoberezh'e. Kiev, 1961.

Terenozhkin, A. I., Osnovy khronologii predskifskogo perioda, in: SA, 1965, no. 1, pp. 63–85.

Tolstov, S. P., Raboty Khorezmskoi arkheologo-etnograficheskoi ekspeditsii AN SSSR v 1949-1953 gg., in: Trudy Khorezmskoi arkheologo-etnograficheskoi ekspeditsii, vol. 2, Moscow, 1958, pp. 7–258.

Vanden Berghe, L., La nécropole de Khūrvin. Istanbul, 1964.

Viaz'mitina, M. I., Rannie pamiatniki skifskogo zverinogo stilia, in: SA, 1963, no. 2, pp. 158–170.

Widengren, G., Stand und Aufgaben der iranischen Religionsgeschichte, in: Numen, 1954, no. 1, pp. 16–83 and 1955, no. 2, pp. 47–134.

Widengren, G., Some Remarks on Riding Costume and Articles of Dress among

Iranian Peoples in Antiquity, in: Arctica, Studia Ethnografica Upsaliensia, vol. 11, Uppsala, 1956, pp. 228–276.
Wiesner, J., Eurasische Kunst in Steppenraum und Waldgebiet, in: Illustrierte Welt-Kunstgeschichte, ed. E. Th. Rimli/K. Fischer, Zürich, etc., 1959.
Wikander, S., Der Arische Männerbund. Lund, 1938.

Wissmann, H. von, Ursprungsherde und Ausbreitungswege von Pflanzen- und Tierzucht und ihre Abhängigkeit von der Klimageschichte, in: Erdkunde, Archiv für wissenschaftliche Geographie, vol. 11, Bonn, 1957, no. 2, pp. 81–94, no. 3, pp. 175–193.
Zadneprovskii, Iu. A., Drevnezemledel'cheskaia kul'tura Fergany, in: MIA, vol. 118, 1962.

ABBREVIATIONS

BMFEA	Bulletin of the Museum of Far Eastern Antiquities, Stockholm
ESA	Eurasia Septentrionalis Antiqua, Helsinki
GIM	Gosudarstvennyi istoricheskii muzei, Moscow
IAK	Izvestiia Arkheologicheskoi Komissii, Moscow
IAN SIF	Izvestiia Akademii Nauk SSSR, seriia istorii i filosofii, Moscow
IGAIMK	Izvestiia Gosudarstvennoi Akademii istorii material'noi kul'tury, Leningrad
IPEK	Jahrbuch für prähistorische und ethnographische Kunst, Berlin
KSIA	Kratkie soobshcheniia Instituta arkheologii, Kiev
KSIA AN SSSR	(continues KSIIMK) Kratkie soobshcheniia Instituta arkheologii Akademii Nauk SSSR, Moscow-Leningrad
KSIE	Kratkie soobshcheniia Instituta etnografii, Moscow
KSIIMK	Kratkie soobshcheniia Instituta istorii material'noi kul'tury, Moscow
LGU	Leningradskii gosudarstvennyi universitat
MAE	Muzei antropologii i etnografii Akademii Nauk SSSR, Moscow-Leningrad
MAGW	Mitteilungen der Anthropologischen Gesellschaft, Vienna
MAR	Materialy po arkheologii Rossii, St. Petersburg/Petrograd
MIA	Materialy i issledovaniia po arkheologii SSSR, Moscow
PIDO	Problemy istorii dokapitalisticheskikh obshchestv, Moscow
RANION	Rossiiskaia assotsiatsiia nauchno-issledovatel'skikh institutov obshchestvennykh nauk, Moscow
RGO	Russkoe geograficheskoe obshchestvo, St. Petersburg/Leningrad – Moscow
SA	Sovetskaia arkheologiia, Moscow
SE	Sovetskaia etnografiia, Moscow
SGAIMK	Soobshcheniia Gosudarstvennoi Akademii istorii material'noi kul'tury, Leningrad
SGE	Soobshcheniia Gosudarstvennogo Ermitazha, Leningrad
SMYA	Suomen Muinaismuistoyhkistyksen Aikakauskirya, Helsinki
TIE	Trudy Instituta etnografii Akademii Nauk SSSR, new series, Moscow
TIIAE	Trudy Instituta istorii, arkheologii i etnografii Akademii Nauk Kazakhskoi SSR, Alma-Ata
Umschau	Die Umschau in Wissenschaft und Technik, Frankfurt-on-Main
VDI	Vestnik drevnei istorii, Moscow
Wiener Beiträge	Wiener Beiträge zur Kunst- und Kulturgeschichte, Vienna

INDEX

The numerals in italics refer to the plates and figures.

Date Due

MAR 3 1969			

Demco 38-297